Oregon's
Wilderness Areas

THE COMPLETE GUIDE

TEXT AND PHOTOGRAPHY BY
GEORGE WUERTHNER

WESTCLIFFE PUBLISHERS

.com

This book is dedicated to Oregon's
hardworking wildlands supporters,
from the tree sitters in the old-growth,
to those who labor with the suits in
Washington, D.C. Without their hard
work, I would not be writing a
book on Oregon wilderness.

Wenaha River, Wenaha-Tucannon Wilderness

4

Table of Contents

Cascades Range *(continued)*

Blue Mountains 190

Basin and Range 250

*Not federally designated wilderness but included as a critical wildlands area

ISBN: 1-56579-434-6

TEXT AND PHOTOGRAPHY: George Wuerthner, © 2002. All rights reserved.

MAP ILLUSTRATIONS: Rebecca Finkel, © 2002. All rights reserved.

EDITOR: Martha Ripley Gray

DESIGN AND PRODUCTION: Rebecca Finkel, F + P Graphic Design, Inc.; Fort Collins, CO

PRODUCTION MANAGER: Craig Keyzer

PUBLISHED BY: Westcliffe Publishers, Inc.
P.O. Box 1261
Englewood, Colorado 80150
www.westcliffepublishers.com

PRINTED IN CHINA BY: H & Y Printing, Ltd.

LIBRARY OF CONGRESS CATALOGING-IN-PUBLICATION DATA:

Wuerthner, George.
Oregon's wilderness areas : the complete guide / text and
photography by George Wuerthner.
p. cm.
Includes bibliographical references and index.
ISBN 1-56579-434-6
1. Wilderness areas—Oregon—Guidebooks.
2. Natural History—Oregon—Guidebooks. 3. Trails—
Oregon—Guidebooks. 4. Hiking—Oregon—Guidebooks.
5. Oregon—Guidebooks. I. Title.

QH76.5.O7 W84 2003
508.795—dc21

2002028895

*For more information about other fine books and calendars from
Westcliffe Publishers, please contact your local bookstore, call us at
1-800-523-3692, write for our free color catalog, or visit us on the
Web at www.westcliffepublishers.com.*

PLEASE NOTE:
Risk is always a factor in backcountry and high-mountain travel. Many
of the activities described in this book can be dangerous, especially when
weather is adverse or unpredictable, and when unforeseen events or
conditions create a hazardous situation. The author has done his best to
provide the reader with accurate information about backcountry travel, as
well as to point out some of its potential hazards. It is the responsibility of
the users of this guide to learn the necessary skills for safe backcountry
travel, and to exercise caution in potentially hazardous areas, especially on
avalanche-prone terrain. The author and publisher disclaim any liability for
injury or other damage caused by backcountry traveling or performing
any other activity described in this book.

COVER:
*View of Mount Jefferson
from Russell Lake, Mount
Jefferson Wilderness*

OPPOSITE:
*Whitebark pine snag atop
Mount McLoughlin,
Sky Lakes Wilderness*

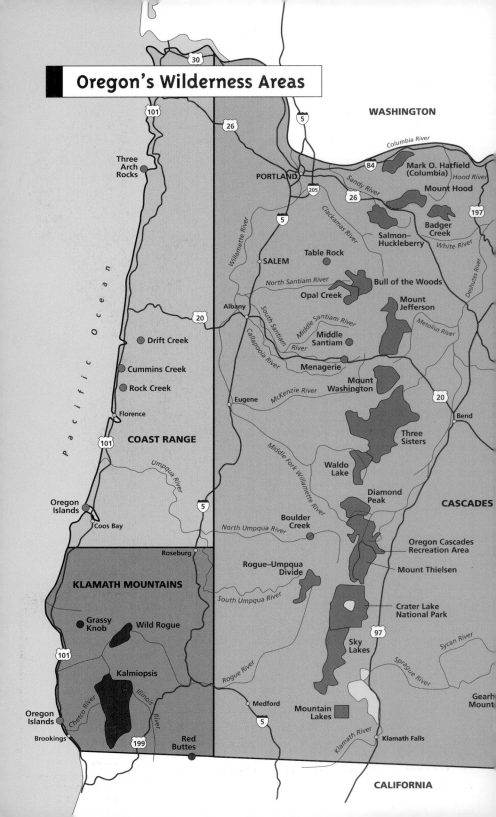

Oregon's Wilderness Areas

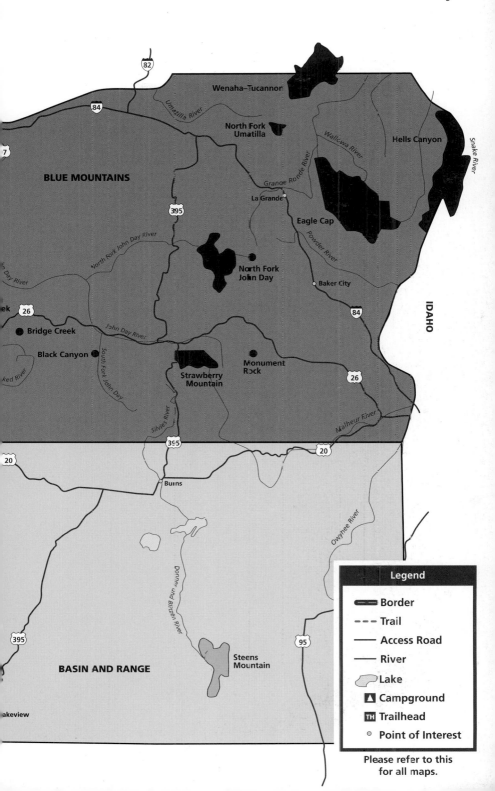

About Oregon

THE TENTH LARGEST STATE, Oregon is a rectangle roughly the same size as Colorado, running 368 miles east to west and 276 miles north to south. Elevations range from sea level up to 11,245 feet on Mount Hood. The Columbia River forms much of the northern border of the state, separating it from Washington and emptying west into the Pacific Ocean. An arbitrary line at the 42nd parallel forms the southern boundary with California. Along much of the eastern border, the Snake River—the major tributary of the Columbia—cuts the boundary between Oregon and Idaho.

The state is usually divided into ten physiographic provinces, each with distinctive climate, geology, and plant communities: Coast Range, Klamath Mountains, Western Interior Valleys, Western Slope Cascades, Eastern Slope Cascades, Columbia Basin, High Lava Plains, Blue Mountains, Basin and Range, and Owyhee Uplands. At this time, however, federally designated wilderness exists in only five of the ten regions. Many of the state's wilderness areas lie in the magnificent western Cascades; in some cases, a single wilderness like the Three Sisters can straddle two provinces—in that case, the western and eastern slopes of the Cascades.

Despite the huge amount of land that has been developed, manipulated, and otherwise exploited for timber, livestock, mining, and other commercial enterprises, Oregon still has significant amounts of unprotected wildlands. Depending upon how it is used, "wilderness" can have several meanings. With a proper name, "wilderness" is capitalized in references to congressionally designated wilderness areas, for example, Three Sisters Wilderness. "Wilderness" can also mean, however, undeveloped landscapes that have no formal legislative protection but have wildlands—that is, lack of human manipulation—characteristics. Formal designation as a "Big W" wilderness requires an act of Congress under the guidelines set forth in the 1964 Wilderness Act, created to provide permanent protection for federal wildlands.

Currently 40 areas, encompassing 3.5 percent of the state's land, are protected within the National Wilderness System. The latest addition to this system in Oregon came with the designation of the 175,000-acre Steens Mountain Wilderness in 2000. But much work remains to be done. Only 7.5 percent of Oregon's forestlands are permanently protected by Congress as wilderness. Though most of the more productive public and private forested landscape has already been given over to timber production, some 5 million acres of public forestlands are still roadless and eligible for wilderness designation. In addition, another 6 million acres of roadless BLM desert lands in southeastern Oregon await some kind of federal wilderness designation.

Autumn snowfall, Mount Jefferson Wilderness

What This Book Covers

THIS IS NOT YOUR TYPICAL TRAIL GUIDEBOOK, detailing every nuance of the hike, including where to stop for a lunch break, take a photo, or place your tent. Rather this is a guide to the remarkable diversity of Oregon's wild places, with enough information on how to enjoy them to allow you to sample them as you might taste the rich variety of food at a buffet dinner. For each wilderness you'll find "vital statistics" including size, location, elevation, directions, and land-management contact; a description of major attributes and physical features; weather; species habitats; historical notes; and hikes and/or other recreation in the area. The activity descriptions will help you select one that interests you but will not guide you across every stream crossing or up each steep ascent. It is not that of kind of a guidebook.

This book includes all 40 federally designated wilderness areas in Oregon. I also included descriptions of Crater Lake National Park and the Oregon Cascades Recreation Area, since both are critical ecological links and essentially are managed as wilderness by their respective agencies. I have grouped the wilderness areas by region: Coast Range, Klamath Mountains, Cascade Range, Blue Mountains, and Basin and Range. Each chapter has an opening introduction to the region and a locator map that gives the general outline of the wilderness and shows featured trails.

Because of space, I have not included detailed descriptions of the numerous proposed wilderness areas now under consideration. I do, however, discuss briefly some of the larger roadless areas of particular significance that adjoin existing wilderness areas. Please refer to Appendix B, p. 266, for an annotated list of conservation organizations, and to Appendix C, p. 267, for general information about the Oregon Wild Campaign wildlands proposal, to learn more about Oregon wilderness proponents and their goals.

Arch Rock viewpoint from Samuel H. Boardman State Park, southern Oregon coast. Offshore rocks constitute the Oregon Islands Wilderness.

Climate, Population Distribution, and Land Use

THE PACIFIC OCEAN is the single most dominant influence on the state's climate, bringing wet weather in winter and mild temperatures to the western part of the state. Though the Cascades dramatically affect Oregon's overall climatic regime, creating a wet western third and dry eastern two-thirds, the proximity of the ocean means Oregon's climate is on the whole less severe than that of other parts of the country at the same latitude, such as Burlington, Vermont. Even eastern Oregon, which tends to experience cold winters by Oregon standards, nevertheless is considerably milder in winter than, say, Wyoming, South Dakota, or Iowa—all at the same latitude. Extremes in temperature do occur, but they are not the norm. Although temperatures above 100 degrees have been recorded in Eugene and Portland, summer temperatures there are typically below 90 degrees. By the same token, in winter both Eugene and Portland have experienced lows down to 0 degrees, but again this is not the usual pattern. Even eastern Oregon, where lows to minus 50 have been recorded, does not regularly get a temperature below zero.

These climatic generalizations are greatly influenced by the local topography of Oregon's ten physiographic provinces. Mountains compose the land all along the wet Pacific Coast: The Coast Range runs parallel to the coast from the Columbia River south to Coos Bay. South of this point lies the Klamath Mountains region, sometimes known as the Siskiyous. The Klamath Mountains stretch eastward to the Upper Rogue Valley near Medford and Ashland, where they join the Cascades.

Three broad valleys separate these coastal ranges from the Cascades: the Willamette, Umpqua, and Rogue Valleys—each progressively smaller, warmer, and drier as you approach the California border. The Cascades are the dominant physiographic feature in the state. The range runs the entire north-south length of Oregon and includes all the famous high peaks in the state, including Mount Hood, Mount Jefferson, and the Three Sisters. Indeed, the range is broken only by the celebrated gorge of the Columbia River—and north of it the Cascades continue into Washington. The Columbia Basin ecoregion, sometimes known as the Umatilla Plateau, lies along the Columbia River.

In northeastern Oregon, "the Blue Mountains" is a collective term used to describe the Ochoco, Strawberry, Elkhorn, Wallowa, and other smaller sub-ranges. The Basin and Range takes in southeastern Oregon and includes Steens Mountain, Hart Mountain, and other fault-scarp ranges in this arid region. The Owyhee Uplands lie at the junction of Idaho, Nevada, and Oregon and are drained by the Owyhee River. The High Lava Plains is a catchall phrase for the region directly east of Bend, taking in the Crooked River and parts of the John Day River Basin.

Despite all the attention given to growth in recent years, only 1 percent of the state is urbanized or used for residential and industrial purposes. Indeed, most of the state is unpopulated, if not officially designated wilderness. As anyone who has done any traveling around the state can attest, human population is not evenly distributed. Nearly the entire state's population lives west of the Cascades, with more than 70 percent residing in the 100-mile Willamette Valley with Portland, Salem, and Eugene/Springfield the largest urban centers. Yet, even in the Willamette Valley, farmland

and not urban centers dominates the landscape. This is in part due to Oregon's historic statewide land-use laws, which require every community to designate urban growth boundaries. It's remarkable how you can leave a major urban area like Eugene and quickly find yourself in a rural landscape.

This sense of space is even more pronounced when you go east of the Cascades. Here is a region with almost no people at all. The few population centers, such as Bend-Redmond, Klamath Falls, La Grande, Pendleton, and Ontario, are swallowed up in the vastness of the landscape. Several eastern Oregon counties have less than one person per square mile, a population density matching that of Alaska. But east of the Cascades isn't the only lightly populated region. Most of the Cascade Range has no residents at all. And the southwest corner that includes the Klamath Mountains region is only lightly populated. In fact, taken as a whole, a good portion of Oregon is uninhabited.

Hiker above French Pete drainage, Three Sisters Wilderness

Why Establish Wilderness Areas?

Economic Justifications

Many good arguments exist for wildlands protection. There is the obvious recreational value. People find excellent opportunities for hiking, camping, canoeing, fishing, hunting, and nature study in protected wildlands. In addition, wilderness provides high-quality habitat for many species whose ecological requirements are not met in managed landscapes. This includes preserving habitat for salmon, spotted owl, and other species that are currently in decline. Another value of wilderness is what some call "ecological services." For instance, these wildlands help preserve clean sources of water that is used for domestic and industrial water needs. Many Oregon cities, including Portland, Ashland, Salmon, and Baker City, all rely on protected landscapes for all or part of their drinking water supply.

Wilderness is also an economic engine. Though recreation jobs are created by protecting wildlands, these are a relatively small contribution to the overall economic value of wildlands protection. More important, many businesses and individuals choose to inhabit areas with protected wildlands because they enhance the quality of life. This is particularly the case when outdoor opportunities are combined with cultural attributes.

A study on the economic value of wildlands protection was prepared in August 2000 by Southwick Associates for the Oregon Natural Resources Council and the World Wildlife Fund (see www.onrc.org/info/econstudy for the complete summary findings). The study found that extractive industries such as logging, livestock grazing, and mining are in decline as a source of employment, representing some 5 percent of the state's economy. On the other hand, tourism-related sectors, including everything from outdoor recreation to entrepreneurial start-ups, continue to rise as a state income source. Further, both retirees and new businesses are settling in Oregon in increasing numbers. This data suggest that the best way to stimulate your economy and improve the overall employment opportunities in your community is not by attracting a new mine or lumber mill but by trying to create a large wilderness area or national park.

Still, the biggest economic impact of wilderness preservation results from what economists call "opportunity cost," or the cost of passing up one investment in favor of another—in Oregon's case, what we'd have to pay to get the same things we get "for free" by protecting natural sources. By protecting watersheds, cities spend less on water treatment to obtain their water supply. By keeping intact plant communities, whether in old-growth forests or on ungrazed rangeland, we reduce the intensity, frequency, and cost of floods. If genetic resources found in our plants and animals allow us to develop a new medicine to fight disease or if we find a resistant strain of a tree that is not vulnerable to some blight or insect, this opportunity is preserved in wilderness. If we did not have those genetic materials, we would either have to spend far more to develop such resources or do without. In either case, we suffer accordingly.

Biological Justifications

While it's important to understand that wildlands protection does not harm economies—indeed, it boosts them—an even more important reason for creating many large wilderness areas is to protect our natural heritage and biodiversity. The

Hiker and old-growth near French Pete Creek, Three Sisters Wilderness

growing science of conservation biology has some basic guiding principles. The first is that preservation of biodiversity—the diversity of all life at multiple scales—is worthwhile. These include the genetic, individual, population, and landscape scales. Protection of biodiversity is critical at the landscape scale, as its important ecological processes—predation, wildfires, floods, insect outbreaks, and other events—are the engines of evolution. All of these are selective factors that influence evolutionary history and interaction at the population, individual, and genetic scales.

Conservation biology research has shown that protection of large natural landscapes is one of the best ways to ensure that a sufficient amount of habitat is available for native species and ecological processes to operate. We do not yet and probably never will have the knowledge to "manage" ecosystems to preserve biodiversity.

In addition to protecting large natural areas, we need to make sure they are in close relationship to others. Clustering protected areas can be crucial. If, say, a population of spotted owls declines in one area to the point of local extinction because of random events like disease or multiple nest failures, the habitat can potentially be recolonized from adjacent protected areas—so long as they are not too far away. This "rescue effect" is an important biological phenomenon. Besides providing for closeness, we need to maintain suitable corridors for species to move across the landscape. These corridors need to be large enough to sustain not only migrating individuals but, for many species, breeding individuals—if not breeding populations.

These principles illuminate the growing biodiversity crisis in Oregon and the country, as we continue to destroy more and more of our natural landscapes and replace them with "domesticated" landscapes that are intensively managed for human commercial industries. A strong counterbalance to this trend can be the protection of all our remaining unmanaged landscapes and the restoration of some degraded habitats or processes. Examples include re-creating the Klamath Basin wetlands, restoring wolves to Oregon, or permitting wildfires to burn across the landscape where no homes or lives are threatened.

What Does Wilderness Designation Do?

The passage of the Wilderness Act institutionalized an idea—that maintaining some of our natural landscape in an undeveloped condition has a value to humanity equal to using that landscape for consumptive purposes. The act seeks to preserve for posterity an "enduring resource" of wilderness on those federal lands that are essentially "untrammeled" or undeveloped. As defined by the act, these are lands that "generally appear to have been affected primarily by the forces of nature, with the imprint of man's work substantially unnoticeable." Thus lands that are heavily logged, mined, and roaded usually do not qualify for wilderness. However, intrusions such as dams, fencing for livestock, and cabins for administration or recreational users can be found in designated wilderness—even previously developed mining or logging areas that have largely reverted to a more wild condition.

Besides natural appearance, other qualities that an area must possess to be designated as wilderness include some opportunities for solitude and unconfined recreation and a minimum size of 5,000 acres (exceptions are made for smaller areas that may be adjacent to larger wildlands complexes). Wilderness areas may also preserve features that are of historical, geological, or ecological significance.

In order to maintain these qualities, activities like timber harvest, road building, mining, motorized vehicle use, and even some modern recreational activities like mountain biking are not permitted. However, a few existing commercial activities are allowed, such as livestock grazing and outfitting. Unless otherwise prohibited by other agency mandates, recreational uses like hunting, fishing, cross-country skiing, canoeing, hiking, and camping are recognized as legitimate wilderness uses. But the most important "use" of wilderness is protection of watersheds, biological diversity, ecological processes, and scenic qualities.

It's important to note that Congress does not "create" wilderness, any more than a weather bureau creates a sunny day. All Congress can do is recognize the existing qualities of the landscape, and decide to maintain those landscape features in an undeveloped state. Wilderness designation is thus a generous act, giving future generations the opportunity to know something of Oregon's natural landscape and make decisions about its future.

Wilderness in Oregon

MANY OF THE ENVIRONMENTAL BATTLES to protect Oregon's wildlands have influenced the movement well beyond its borders. Though Oregon was for decades one of the biggest timber producers in the nation, it was also, perhaps in response, one of the centers for the national wilderness movement. In looking back, we can appreciate what we have saved and learn from our mistakes. Generally speaking, those organizations that capitulated and sought to make compromises with politicians and commercial interests usually lost far more than they gained. Those who held strong may not have achieved as much as they would have liked, but they often got more than anyone would have predicted.

James Monteith of the Oregon Natural Resources Council exemplifies this truth. Monteith met with Congressman Al Ullman over the Hells Canyon issue. The congressman told him, "Don't you know the rules of the game? I have to move your line." Monteith later told me the take-home message he got from the encounter was never to compromise your goals. It was, he came to understand, the role of politicians to compromise on whatever is advocated, so hold fast and let them do the compromising. It is to far-seeking citizens like Monteith that we owe many of our finer wildlands.

Between the passage of the Wilderness Act in 1964 and 1980, some 14 wilderness areas were created in Oregon, but public pressure to designate additional wilderness acres continued, and citizens began working for additional wilderness designation outside of agency recommendation. In 1984, 21 statewide wilderness bills, establishing more than 8 million acres of new wilderness areas, passed the U.S. Congress. In Oregon, this effort culminated in the Oregon Wilderness Act of 1984, which established 23 new wilderness areas in the state.

A couple of famous battles may illustrate the Oregon conservation legacy. As early as 1951, groups of citizens based in Eugene were trying to garner greater protection for the Three Sisters area and French Pete Creek, the latter one of the last major, low-elevation drainages in the Willamette National Forest. The Forest Service had argued that the area west of Horse Creek, including the forested French Pete drainage, did not have wilderness qualities and "nothing of especially outstanding scenic quality." The proposal to drop protection for this area was supported by the timber industry.

In 1954, the Forest Service announced its decision to delete 50,000 acres in the Horse Creek area from the Three Sisters Primitive Area. In response to this challenge, a new group, the Friends of the Three Sisters (FOTS), was organized in Eugene. In June 1956, Senator Hubert Humphrey introduced a bill, supported by FOTS and by Oregon senators Morse and Neuberger, that was only the first of many versions of what would eventually become the 1964 Wilderness Act. But opposition in Congress was strong, and passage of the bill would take eight years.

After the decisive Republican presidential election in 1957, the Forest Service was emboldened to release its final recommendations for the Horse Creek area, calling for removal of 53,000 acres from the Three Sisters Primitive Area, including lands west of Horse Creek and the headwaters of the French Pete drainage. As a bone to conservationists, the Forest Service asked for recommendations for natural areas that could

View of Mount Washington from Big Lake in autumn, Mount Washington Wilderness

be designated within the 53,000-acre exclusion zone. After several years of study, the FOTS submitted their report asking for protection of 13,600 acres.

In 1960, the Forest Service released its final plan. It reduced the acreage for protected natural areas from the 13,600 acres proposed by the FOTS to 2,725 acres—and added new roads for French Pete Creek and several other drainages. The same year, the Oregon Cascades Conservation Council was organized and became the second statewide organization (after the Montana Wilderness Association) created to promote wilderness protection. In 1962, the Eugene Group of the Sierra Club was established and became the first local group in the Pacific Northwest chapter to bring a national presence to local Oregon wilderness issues.

The 1964 Wilderness Act established the Three Sisters Wilderness, but the controversial area west of Horse Creek was not part of it. In 1968, the Forest Service announced plans to road and log the French Pete drainage. A group of Eugene citizens then formed the Save French Pete Committee. By 1974, legislation was introduced in both the Senate and the House calling for wilderness protection of the French Pete area.

Meanwhile, a national effort to protect wilderness throughout the West culminated in the Endangered American Wilderness Act of 1978, protecting 285,000 Oregon acres in two new areas, plus additions to three others. Among other provisions, the act gave wilderness protection to the French Pete drainage. Twenty-four years after the area had been proposed for logging by the Forest Service, citizen involvement and initiative finally returned wilderness protection to the original 53,000 acres that Bob Marshall had added to the old Three Sisters Primitive Area in 1938. Today, French Pete remains among the finest lower-elevation, unlogged drainages left in the Cascades.

Yet despite these promising results, many other deserving areas were left on the chopping block, soon to be roaded and logged. At the same time that the French Pete battle was being played out, national organizations like the Wilderness Society and the Sierra Club established field offices in the Northwest. The Oregon Wilderness Coalition, now the Oregon Natural Resources Council (ONRC), was formed in 1974. (In the late 1990s, a new Oregon Wilderness Coalition was created to advance the Oregon Wild Campaign). In 1977, OWC organizer James Monteith began to advocate a lawsuit as the only way to get a just review and consideration of the Roadless Area wilderness values, as required by Congress. Monteith wanted to take the Forest Service to court.

National groups like the Sierra Club were wary of a lawsuit, believing that it would cause a backlash and that Monteith was both politically naïve and too aggressive in his advocacy. By 1978, some members of the OWC board with close ties to the Sierra Club tried to fire Monteith. In a close vote they lost, and Monteith remained at the helm, but the conflict colored later relationships. Disagreement over political strategy became an issue dividing wildlands advocates in Oregon and elsewhere.

The Forest Service's second Roadless Area Review Evaluation (RARE II) in 1978 again failed to properly conduct an inventory as required by Congress, concluding that only 370,000 acres in Oregon had wilderness values. It was obvious that the agency excluded from consideration any lands that had commercial timber or other economic values. This was in direct opposition to Congress's explicit directions to identify lands only according to wildlands values—no matter what the economic values may be.

I think any reasonable assessment of how well the Forest Service has protected the public interest on the non-wilderness lands under its management since 1982 would have to agree that the so-called wilderness extremists were right. The only real alternative that has shown consistently to protect public values including wildlife habitat, old-growth forests, water quality, scenic quality, natural ecological processes, biodiversity, and wildlands values is wilderness designation. If unprotected, sooner or later the agency attempts to develop it on behalf of commercial interests.

Oregon legislators continued to propose Oregon wilderness bills, while the newly named Oregon Natural Resources Council continued to lobby for additional wilderness. Despite numerous proposals, Congress passed no Oregon wilderness bill in 1983. After this failure, ONRC concluded it was time to force the issue. Roadless areas were being whittled away by logging roads, and without wilderness protection many fine areas would be lost and soon. ONRC decided to file a RARE II lawsuit, as had been done in California after RARE I, to provide interim protection to all roadless lands until Congress passed a wilderness bill. ONRC believed the suit would make the timber industry press the Oregon's delegation to craft some kind of wilderness bill and get it passed.

The boldness of ONRC was the opposite of the situation in most conservation battles, where national organizations like the Sierra Club typically propose more extensive protection than local groups under greater pressure to conform and compromise.

Opal Creek, Opal Creek Wilderness

After lengthy political maneuverings, a watered-down Oregon Wilderness bill passed Congress in 1984, covering 828,803 acres by creating 23 new wilderness areas and enlarging five existing ones.

Some argue that while this bill ultimately protected some of Oregon's finer wildlands, it also set up the state for future conflict over issues concerning spotted owl, marbled murrelet, bull trout, salmon, and other endangered species that continued to be threatened by the failure of the Forest Service and Oregon's congressional delegation to protect the ecosystems upon which these species depend.

By the mid-1980s and early 1990s, once again the timber industry—with favorable federal policies from the Reagan and Bush administrations and help from former Oregon Senator Hatfield and other Western timber-industry supporters—were driving the timber harvest in Oregon's forests to record levels. The growing web of logging roads prompted the ONRC to play another card by filing what is now known as the spotted-owl lawsuit.

Against the advice of the national environmental organizations, ONRC filed a lawsuit in federal court to have the owl listed under the Endangered Species Act and to designate critical habitat to save the owl. ONRC won in court. Until the owl's critical habitat could be delineated, no loss of old-growth could occur. The spotted-owl lawsuit brought much of the timber harvest in western Oregon to a grinding halt. In stepped Senator Hatfield, ever friend of the timber industry, to attach one of several "riders" to appropriation bills that basically nullified the court's findings. The logging continued.

After the election of President Bill Clinton, some changes were finally implemented to improve the future of Oregon wildlands. The first was the designation of critical spotted-owl habitat, which protected some old-growth from logging. The listing of other species under the Endangered Species Act helped to strengthen the environmentalists' assertion that present rates of timber harvest were neither sustainable nor ecologically benign.

The final legacy of the Clinton years was the Roadless Initiative, promoted by Forest Service Chief Mike Dombeck. The Roadless Initiative provided protection for more than 58 million acres of roadless Forest Service lands in the United States. While the initiative did not have the same protective values as designated wilderness, it did provide some breathing room for future congressional action.

The second Bush administration, however, immediately sought to dismantle the initiative. At the time of this writing, the administration has not yet succeeded, but in the long run, the only secure protection for these roadless lands will be afforded by their congressional designation as wilderness.

Threats to Oregon's Wildlands

Logging

Few untrammeled landscapes remain in Oregon; in one way or another, most of the state has been domesticated, that is, managed and manipulated for human ends. Commercial forests cover roughly 42 percent of the landscape, and little of that commercial timber base hasn't been roaded and logged. Clear-cuts have removed all trees on over 2.3 million acres. Indeed, there are 190,000 miles of logging roads in the state. That's enough roads to circle the globe nearly eight times! Only major urban centers have a road density that matches or exceeds that found in western Oregon's mountains, with their spaghetti network of logging roads. Even a place as densely settled as New Jersey has fewer roads per square mile than the Coast Range of Oregon!

Roads impact the landscape in many ways. They are a major source of sedimentation in streams and a factor in the decline of many salmon and steelhead runs. Roads also serve as a vector for disease and weed invasion. For instance, Port Orford cedar, an endemic only found in southwestern Oregon and adjacent parts of California, is being decimated by a root-rot fungus introduced into watersheds in the mud cast off from logging trucks and other vehicles. Roads also provide access for hunters and even poachers, affecting the distribution of wildlife and population structure.

Besides the proliferation of roads, logging on the massive scale that has occurred in western Oregon has had other negative effects, since it has changed the natural age and size structure of forest stands. Prior to logging, much of Oregon's forests were old-growth, with large-diameter trees the norm. Now many stands are younger—yet those now largely absent, large-diameter trees are critical to various ecological processes. There is no such thing as a wasted tree. In fact, some ecologists argue that a large dead tree—the snags providing important wildlife habitat, hiding cover for land and water species, stability to stream channels, and even nursery habitat for marine organisms—is more valuable to the ecosystem than a live one.

Livestock Production

Domestic livestock dominates eastern Oregon. And the effects of livestock east of the Cascades have been every bit as far-reaching and ubiquitous as the effects of logging west of the Cascades. Cows have grazed, trod, and trashed most of the native grassland-shrub of eastern Oregon. Even more disastrous for native wildlife has been the impact upon riparian zones—those fragile, narrow watercourses used by 75 to 80 percent of all wildlife in this arid region. Domestic livestock breeds now raised for beef production evolved in moist woodlands in Eurasia and gravitate to areas that most resemble their former habitat—those wet, shrubby woodlands found along streams and springs. Livestock have left few riparian areas intact and in proper functioning condition.

The effects of livestock production on riparian-dependent species are exacerbated by the use of the scarce water in this region for irrigation. Agriculture uses nearly all of the water consumed in Oregon, and the majority of it is used to grow water-thirsty crops, like alfalfa, ultimately fed to livestock. This has had disastrous consequences for everything from salmon to waterfowl.

By consuming the more desirable grass species, the animals create a competitive advantage for weedy species in the race for nutrients and space. Livestock are also a major factor in the spread of exotic weeds, the seeds of which are borne on their hides or in their feces. Further, the trampled earth in the animals' wake is favorable to seed germination. Livestock consume forage that would otherwise support native species, literally taking the food out of the mouth of other creatures from insects to large mammals. Species like elk and antelope avoid areas actively being grazed by domestic livestock and are thus displaced, often to less desirable habitat.

By consuming fine fuels, livestock have even altered fire regimes. The reduction in fires, combined with the competitive advantage given trees by consumption of grasses, has given rise to the invasion of tree species like ponderosa pine and juniper. The dense thickets of these species are a greater potential fuel hazard than were the grasses they replaced, increasing fire-suppression costs for everyone.

Farming

The third most extensive use of the landscape is for farming. Some 8.5 percent of Oregon lands are cultivated. Although some may sing the praises of the bucolic agricultural landscape, farming has probably had the greatest impact of any activity on Oregon's native communities, because of the effects of replacing the native vegetation with one or two exotics. While all but the most intensively urbanized city landscape may retain some native vegetation and wildlife habitat, fields of wheat, grass seed, or hay are nothing more than monocultures of exotic plants that provide almost no food or shelter for native wildlife. With farming comes greater soil erosion, water pollution, and the introduction of genetically modified seeds, pesticide use, and other factors that negatively affect native biodiversity. With the exception of some wildlife refuges like the Klamath Marshes and other wildlife refuges including those in the Willamette Valley, farming doesn't usually occur on public lands.

Fire Suppression

Besides extractive uses, other threats to Oregon's wildlands and biodiversity exist. Fire suppression has probably affected more lands in the state than any other single management activity. Our efforts to eliminate fire from the landscape is no different and even more ecologically disastrous than our efforts to remove large predators like wolves from the landscape. Fires are a natural event and a major ecological process that shapes evolution on all of Oregon's landscapes.

Analysis of charcoal found in lakes and ponds reveals thousands of years of fire history. A review of this legacy shows that periodic large blazes are the norm for all forest ecosystems that burn at all. Even the wet, old-growth rain forests of the Coast Range and western slope of the Cascades burned occasionally every 200 to 500 years. In the drier landscapes east of the Cascades, including the ponderosa pine and grassland ecosystems, fires were far more frequent, burning on an average of every 5 to 50 years, depending on the habitat type.

Fires help to reset the ecological balance and rejuvenate the landscape, providing new opportunities for growth. The heat and even the smoke from fires help to cleanse a forest or grassland of detrimental disease. Furthermore, most fires burn in a mosaic pattern; even in the hottest and biggest blazes, not all trees are consumed. This natural mosaic provides recolonization sources for plant seeds, wildlife, and fungi. Plant and animal communities are well adapted to fires. It is the greatest ignorance to suggest that a forest was "destroyed" by a fire. In fact, what most plant communities need more than anything is to burn.

Fire suppression has almost certainly altered the fire regime of lower-elevation forest stands, but it may not have deviated the range of viability that much. Many higher-elevation or west-side timber stands had fires at 100- to 500-year intervals. Fire suppression hasn't altered these stands significantly, although if fire suppression continues unabated, ill effects may result. Many stands, even of ponderosa pine, have often gone as long as 50 years or more without a blaze. Now thick with new young trees, the stands need to burn.

Old-growth ponderosa pine forest, Three Sisters Wilderness

Exotics

Another long-term threat to Oregon's native biodiversity is the prevalence of weeds and other exotics. Whether they are introduced fish that compete with native fish, plants deemed "weeds" that invade and compete with more desirable species, or imported diseases that threaten wildlife and plants, exotics are a growing menace. Exotics also homogenize our landscapes, as species relatively common worldwide tend to outcompete and replace locally adapted species, creating a biological impoverishment.

Exotics are favored by the kind of disturbed habitat created by many of the land uses mentioned earlier, including farming, livestock grazing, logging, and urbanization. Exotics are also favored by declining ecosystem health. The best long-term solution is to reduce activities that favor exotics and to restore natural ecosystem processes and landscapes. In the fight against exotics, protection of wilderness and wildlands is a critical tool.

The Future Is Not Completely Bleak

Despite all of this development, all is not lost, in part because so much of Oregon is public land. Some 57 percent of the state is controlled by federal, state, county, or local government. Only 43 percent of the land base is in private hands. The abundance of public lands forms the nucleus for the existing protected wilderness in the state, and provides outstanding opportunities for wilderness restoration.

Exploring the Wilderness

Low-Impact Camping and Travel

People using Oregon Wilderness Areas—or any public lands, for that matter—should practice low-impact use techniques. Treat these public lands better than you would treat your own property. Treat them with respect for those who will follow, and those unborn.

1. Whenever possible, walk on preexisting trails and roads. Where there are no trails—a common condition in much of the Oregon desert—hikers should concentrate travel on sites, such as in desert washes and on rocky ridges, where cryptogamic crusts aren't common. If in a group, walk in a single file as much as possible to avoid disturbing soils more than necessary.

2. When driving, use preexisting roads and established access routes. Avoid establishing new tracks or routes.

3. When camping, use preexisting campsites or choose sites that already have either bare soil or rock.

4. If you must have a campfire or have brought wood from other regions, limit use to existing fire rings. Build fires in sandy washes where future floods will remove all traces of previous fires.

5. Remove all trash. Remember that aluminum doesn't burn, so pack it out. When leaving a campsite, pick up all your trash, and even the trash left by others. Leave your site in better condition than you found it.

6. Bury all human waste in the ground 6 to 8 inches deep, at least 200 feet from water sources.

Maps

Often the most difficult thing about exploring an Oregon wilderness area is finding the trailhead. Although I have tried to keep the directions to wilderness areas simple and accurate, you won't find the name of every road you will pass en route to the trailheads—there are just too many roads scattered across the Oregon public lands to make such descriptions practical. Also realize that new roads are continuously being made, and thus directions may be out of date even before this book is printed. Further, any severe winter storm can wash out a road, turning a formerly passable route into a riverbed, so always be mindful of weather conditions and alternate routes. Finally, the maps provided in this guidebook can only give a general outline of the designated wilderness and the location of selected trailheads.

If you expect to find your way to a trailhead that isn't located on a major highway, you had better invest in good maps. There is probably no perfect map. As the juggernaut of new logging roads continues almost unabated, any map you purchase will be out of date even before you get it. Still, you can usually figure out where you should be if you employ a number of different maps at the same time. Of course, if the way to the trailhead is complicated, it's not a bad idea to call ahead to the appropriate public lands agency for explicit directions (see Appendix A, p. 264).

You'll encounter two kinds of maps. By the use of lines to show elevation intervals, topographic maps give the general configuration of the landscape. They indicate how steep or flat the land is and locate all major land features. Once you learn how to read them, they are almost like looking at a photograph. By contrast, a planimetric map, like your typical highway map, shows political boundaries such as county lines, highways, and major features, on a much smaller scale. I found that both kinds of maps are necessary for negotiating Oregon wilderness areas. You need one map to find the trailhead and another map to find your way on the trails once you're in the wilderness. But the map that gets you to the trailhead is essential.

The first map you should get is an Oregon state highway map. Provided free from the state of Oregon, this map can be obtained at gas stations, visitor centers, and shops, or by contacting the Oregon Department of Transportation at 503-986-3200 or 888-275-6368. It shows all the major highways and the major U.S. Forest Service wilderness areas. Use the highway map to get you close to the wilderness area.

The next map to consider purchasing is the appropriate Forest Service (FS) or Bureau of Land Management (BLM) map. Each national forest and each major BLM division has its own set of maps. These maps show all the major roads, and most of the trails and trailheads. I find that if I am only going to have one map of an area, I want to have the appropriate FS or BLM map. Road numbers on FS maps usually correspond to the numbers you'll encounter on signs. Paying attention to the road signs is often critical to finding your way in the maze of logging roads.

Besides maps that cover an entire national forest or BLM district, many of the national forest offices have produced maps of specific wilderness areas. You can, for instance, buy a map of the Eagle Cap Wilderness, Mount Hood Wilderness, and Salmon-Huckleberry Wilderness, among others. These are often excellent. Other fine cartographers for Oregon wilderness areas include IMUS Geographics (Box 161, Eugene, OR 97440) and Geo-Graphics (970 NW Muirfield Court, Beaverton, OR 97006).

Also useful are the DeLorme and Benchmark Maps topographic atlases. DeLorme's *Oregon Atlas and Gazetteer* shows most of the roads and many of the trails. Benchmark Maps' *Oregon Road and Recreation Atlas* also shows roads, trails, and recreation information. While I use both maps frequently, be forewarned that finding your way among logging roads can be difficult given the respective scales of these atlases. You often need to have an FS or a BLM map to comprehend the road network.

For the most detailed information, the U.S. Geological Survey produces topographical maps in a variety of standard scales, notably the 1:24,000 quadrangle. A "quad" map shows nearly every road, lake, stream, and cultural feature of a given 7.5-minute section. These maps are excellent for use within designated wilderness areas, since the features don't change much, but they are often severely outdated when it comes to Oregon's 190,000 miles of logging roads. Get an index to all the USGS maps of Oregon by contacting USGS Map Sales, Box 25286, Denver Federal Center, Building 810, Denver, CO 80225, or by calling 303-202-4700 or 800-435-7627.

A number of computerized mapping sources also exist. Maptech's CDR products allow you to read, analyze, manipulate, and print out USGS maps of major sections of Oregon. DeLorme's Topo USA lets you create and print out maps of any U.S. area you plan to visit. As with the caution about the USGS maps, these maps can vary in completeness. Still, when combined with an FS or a BLM map, computer-generated maps can be very handy to have.

Safety Matters

Plan Your Trip

Tell a responsible person, preferably a relative or close friend, your general location and planned itinerary. If you are injured or hurt, you will be truly on your own. When you leave your vehicle, place a note inside (obviously not in the windshield for potential thieves to read) that tells your proposed hiking route and how long you plan to be gone, and date it.

Take a compass and map with you. For better or worse, most Oregon wilderness areas are not more than a day's hike from a major road—provided you walk in the right direction. But there may be a maze of down logs, deep streams, and steep canyons between you and the road. Often the best advice should you become disoriented is to simply stay put along a major trail and hope that someone will eventually find you.

Water and Heat

Water is the single limiting factor for all life. Most of Oregon's wildlands are well watered. Exceptions are those arid areas of southeastern Oregon. Every agency will advise that you never drink directly from a stream without first treating the water with a chemical disinfectant or using a filter. Many different filters are available, and most are reliable.

Dehydration can be a problem almost anywhere if you don't consume enough water, but it's particularly acute in low-elevation areas of Oregon during the summer. If dehydration continues beyond a 10 percent water loss of bodily fluids, most people suffer from heat exhaustion. They collapse and a sweat breaks out. Sweating helps to reduce internal body heat that would otherwise kill them, thus reducing the danger. Sometimes, however, people don't sweat, and the more serious condition of heatstroke ensues. In this case, the body's automatic sweating mechanism fails, and internal heat builds rapidly, often to the lethal point if immediate medical aid is not received.

Summer dehydration is a serious matter not to be taken lightly when traveling in hot regions. These include not just the obvious dry desert locations of southeastern Oregon; temperatures even in Hells Canyon or Rogue Canyon can easily exceed 100 degrees on a hot summer day. It is advisable to remember that "only mad dogs and Englishmen go out in the midday sun." Follow the habits of desert-dwelling animals, which are largely active in early morning and evening when temperatures are lower and humidity is higher. Limit your activity to those time periods. During the hottest part of the day, stay in the shade—with a cool drink—if possible.

Keep your head and body covered as much for protection from sunburn as from the sun's heating effects. Wear a hat with a wide brim and light, loose-fitting cotton clothing. As much as it may seem illogical to maintain a clothing cover in hot weather, loose clothing can reduce evaporation rates by reducing water losses to wind. Of course, this only works if temperatures are not extreme, since sweating is necessary to keep heat loads below lethal levels.

The other extreme is hypothermia. If your body core temperature dips too low, you can suffer disorientation or even death. You can easily die from hypothermia at temperatures well above freezing, particularly if you are wet and it's windy. To protect against these problems, wear clothes like polar fleece that does not absorb moisture, and always have rain gear with you. A hat can help immensely to keep internal body heat inside. If someone is suffering from hypothermia, get the person out of the wet clothes and into a warm, dry environment or sleeping bag as soon as possible.

Other Essentials

Even if you are going for a short day hike, it's important to carry a few other items besides water. Be sure to carry sunscreen and a hat. In addition, it is not a bad idea to have a flashlight with extra batteries, a first-aid kit, a knife, and extra clothes and matches in case you are caught out at night.

Waldo Lake near Waldo Lake Wilderness

How to Use This Guide

FOR EACH WILDERNESS AREA, you'll find a map that shows boundaries, trailheads and major trail routes, roads adjoining the area, and, sometimes, proposed additions. Please note that I have not included specific information about restrictions and rules that may apply to any particular wilderness. Some wilderness areas require permits for entry. Some restrict the number of people in a group. Some have special regulations about campfires, campsite selection, and other factors. Since these restrictions change frequently, I have not included them in the book. But all visitors are urged to contact the appropriate managing agency prior to your first trip to find out what special restrictions or rules may apply. Contact information for the respective agencies is listed in Appendix A, p. 264.

At the beginning of each wilderness description, you'll also find vital information:

Location: I give some orientation of the area in relation to the nearest major town.

Size (in acres): This reflects currently designated acreage only, not proposed additions.

Elevation Range: Knowing the lowest and highest elevations in a wildland is useful for trip planning, since very low elevations are generally accessible year-round, while very high elevations have only a short period in which foot travel is possible.

Major Flora: The major vegetation types you can expect to see are briefly listed.

Administration: You can contact the agency responsible for the management of a particular unit for additional information, maps, and specific regulations.

Best Season: This gives my estimate of the best times to visit the particular area. For most of the forested wildlands, the summer months of June–September are the best times for access. For some of the lower-elevation areas, spring and fall will be the favored times to visit.

Getting There: This section provides directions to the edge of a given wilderness. For some of the larger areas, there can be multiple access points, so I have chosen the most popular.

I then describe the wilderness area's characteristic and special attributes, history, geology, seasonal conditions, and notable species.

FOLLOWING THE AREA DESCRIPTION are recommended day hikes and backpack trips. Most are day hikes, but some are overnight backpacks and shuttle hikes. Preceding the description and directions to each hike, you'll find:

One-way Length: This gives the one-way mileage to the destination or recommended turnaround point. (For loop trips, the total distance is given as "Trail Length.") If you are walking to a specific turnaround point, and then back along the same route, you will need to double the distance.

Elevation Range: This identifies the lowest and highest points on a particular hike, not the total elevation gain or loss. It's possible that you may climb and drop and climb again many times on a particular hike. On some hikes into canyons, be aware that the highest elevation is often the starting point, not the destination.

Difficulty: Based upon many factors, this rating is inevitably a subjective estimate of the hike. The length of the hike, the terrain, and the overall elevation gain or loss all factor into the difficulty values. In general, small children can do hikes rated "Easy." "Moderate" hikes usually involve more than a few miles distance and/or considerable elevation gain. "Strenuous" hikes are either long hikes that require more than average stamina, or hikes with other factors (such as multiple, bridgeless stream crossings) that increase the time and effort needed to complete the hike.

Directions to the trailhead are included in the hike description. Both highway and large-scale maps will aid you in your navigation. It is also important to recognize that once you are off the paved highway, your travel time will be considerably lengthened. Ten miles of driving on a curvy and rutted dirt road can take an hour. So plan accordingly, and give yourself plenty of time to reach a trailhead.

Some wilderness areas also offer skiing, rafting or kayaking. These activities are shown under the heading "Other Recreational Opportunities" (after recommended hikes or backpack trips).

ABBREVIATIONS AND MAP SYMBOLS USED throughout this book are as follows:

Abbreviations:

4WD	Four-wheel drive
BLM	Bureau of Land Management
CR	County Road
FR	Forest Service Road
FS	U.S. Forest Service
FWS	U.S. Fish and Wildlife Service
NF	National Forest
NPS	National Park Service
NWR	National Wildlife Refuge
OR	Oregon; Oregon state highway (preceding number)
ORV	Off-road vehicle
RD	Ranger District (U.S. Forest Service)
US	Federal highway (preceding number)

Map Symbols:

▬ ▬	Border
- - -	Trail
——	Access Road
——	River
⬭	Lake
▲	Campground
TH	Trailhead
◦	Point of Interest

Coast Range

The Coast Range stretches generally north-south along the margin of the Pacific Ocean, from the mouth of the Columbia River to Coos Bay. The densely populated Willamette Valley defines the range's eastern slope. At 4,097 feet, Mary's Peak is the highest point in the range. The geological features of the area were formed when an ancient, offshore volcanic island chain crashed onto the western edge of the North American continent as a result of plate tectonics. These ancient volcanoes were then overlain by sediments eroded from the adjacent continent. Continued collision of plates uplifted and crumpled these rocks, exposing them to erosion by the abundant rainfall that characterizes the coast.

It is by far the wettest region in Oregon—averaging from 80 to 120 inches or more annually at higher elevations. Fortunately for outdoor enthusiasts, this precipitation is not evenly distributed. Most of the rain comes in the winter months, and summers are comparatively dry. Temperatures are mild year-round, with nearly frost-free winters at lower elevations and cool temperatures in summer. Fog is common along the shore in summer.

The moist conditions favor forest growth, and the region is naturally the most heavily timbered in Oregon. Not surprisingly, it is also one of the most heavily logged. The dominant species include Sitka spruce, Douglas fir, western hemlock, western red cedar, and silver fir. Red alder is common along streams and in logged areas.

The heavy precipitation has spawned many rivers and streams but few lakes. A handful of rivers actually cut through the range, including the Columbia, Siuslaw, Nehalem, and Umpqua. Many still sustain relict salmon and steelhead runs.

Unlike other heavily timbered parts of the state, most of the better tree-growing land passed into private ownership through a variety of federal land giveaways and the use of both legal and fraudulent means. Today about two-thirds of the land base is in private ownership—one of the largest percentages of any major ecoregion in the state.

The public ownership includes the Siuslaw National Forest, which comprises approximately 10 percent of the land base. The BLM controls another 13 percent through its "O" and "C" lands (given to a railroad by the government to finance construction of rails, which were never built). The Fish and Wildlife Service (FWS) manages a number of small offshore

Deciduous forest in the Rock Creek Wilderness

islands as part of the Oregon Islands National Wildlife Refuge (NWR) and Three Arch Rocks NWR, both also designated wilderness areas. The small Nestucca Bay NWR, not a designated wilderness, lies at the mouth of the namesake bay. In addition, the FWS controls lands along the lower Columbia River within the Lewis and Clark National Wildlife Refuge, which encompasses 38,000 acres of islands, bars, marshes, and open water. Finally, the state of Oregon owns substantial holdings, including dozens of state parks, 500,000 acres comprising the Tillamook and Clatsop State Forests, and 97,000 acres in the Elliott State Forest.

Of all the ecoregions in the state, the Coast Range has the second greatest species diversity, with some 396 species regularly found here. It is particularly rich in freshwater fish. A number of rare amphibian species have been recorded here, including Cope's giant salamander, tailed frog, and Pacific giant salamander. Offshore islands, many of them part of the Oregon Islands Wilderness, are important nesting sites for many seabirds, including common murres and Leach's storm-petrels. Another seabird, the marbled murrelet, also resides here but nests inland in coastal old-growth forests. Murrelet nests have been discovered as much as 25 miles from the ocean. Another bird of these old-growth forests is the spotted owl, whose numbers continue to decline as the older forests they depend upon continue to fall before the saw. A special mammal species here is the mountain beaver, which reaches its greatest abundance in Oregon's coastal rainforests.

Because so much of the Coast Range consists of privately owned timberlands and exceptional timber-producing country, little of the region has escaped the chainsaws and roading associated with logging. There are only five designated wildernesses in the Coast Range ecoregion: Drift Creek, Rock Creek, Cummins Creek, Oregon Islands, and Three Arch Rocks—the last two offshore and closed to public access. Several other large (by Coast Range standards) areas of potential wilderness do exist. They include roadless lands in the Mount Hebo area, Wassen Creek, and the Oregon Dunes National Recreation Area. Perhaps more than in other regions, "rewilding," or the restoration of the landscape, will play a significant role in the future of the Coast Range ecoregion. Some conservationists are advocating that the state-owned Tillamook State Forest be redesignated a wilderness state park. At nearly 400,000 acres, it could easily be the largest wildlands restoration site in Oregon's Coast Range.

Cummins Creek Wilderness

Old-growth forest along Cummins Creek,
Cummins Creek Wilderness

OVERHUNG WITH MOSSY BIGLEAF MAPLE and bordered by giant Sitka spruce, Cummins Creek and Bob Creek represent two of the few undisturbed coastal drainages protected by wilderness designation. Both are V-shaped, water-eroded valleys with steep slopes. Located just south of Cape Perpetua, Cummins Creek Wilderness protects relict stands of old-growth coastal rain forest (though there are some revegetated clear-cuts in the area). The highest peaks that surround the creek basins include 2,470-foot Cummins Peak. The wilderness was designated in 1984 by the Oregon Wilderness Act. Like the nearby Rock Creek Wilderness, the boundaries of this wilderness are largely defined by roads, with FR 5694 on Ten Mile Ridge forming the southern border and FR 55 on Cape Ridge marking the northern border.

LOCATION: 4 miles south of Yachats; 22 miles north of Florence

SIZE: 9,300 acres

ELEVATION RANGE: Sea level to 2,400 feet

MAJOR FLORA: Sitka spruce, western hemlock, Douglas fir

ADMINISTRATION: Siuslaw NF, 541-750-7000

BEST SEASON: Year-round

GETTING THERE: From Florence, drive US 101 north 22 miles to Neptune State Park; or from Yachats, drive south 4 miles on US 101 to the same state park. The wilderness lies east of the highway and park.

The coastal weather is dominated by winter rainfall, with annual precipitation exceeding 100 inches. Freezing temperatures are extremely rare, so snowfall is uncommon, though the highest peaks will occasionally be dusted by snow. Summers tend to be cool and dry, though summer fog is common. Spring and fall are probably the best times to visit the area, since fog is less common and dry conditions often prevail.

The vegetation reflects the annual winter drenching. Sitka spruce, Douglas fir, and western hemlock reach immense sizes here under the influence of abundant moisture and mild temperatures. Understory plants include moss-draped bigleaf maple, red alder, sword fern, salmonberry, red current, and other species.

Wildlife includes larger mammals like Roosevelt elk, black-tailed deer, mountain lion, and black bear. Spotted owl and marbled murrelets are also found here. Salmon, steelhead, and cutthroat trout are reportedly in the streams. Only two official trails exist in the Cummins Creek Wilderness. One follows Cummins Ridge, while the other is a reclaimed road along Cummins Creek itself at the northern border of the wilderness.

DAY HIKE: CUMMINS RIDGE
One-way Length: 6.2 miles
Elevation Range: 1,000 to 1,800 feet
Difficulty: Moderate

Cummins Ridge is a watershed divide in this small wilderness. The first part of the trail was once an old logging road, now reverting back into a trail. The trail offers occasional views, but mostly you are walking in a tunnel of trees, so you can really just decide how far you wish to go and then turn around to go back to your vehicle. About halfway along the route, you reach a cairn that marks the end of the old road and the beginning of the trail extension. This makes a good turnaround point for those with less energy or time. If you are inclined, continue another 2.5 miles along the ridge along a newly constructed extension to the trail's end at FR 5694-515. An attractive alternative option is to do a car shuttle and hike downhill from FR 5694-515 to the lower trailhead near US 101.

From Florence, drive 22 miles north on US 101. Just under 2 miles south of Cape Perpetua, turn right at the Cummins Ridge Trailhead sign and onto FR 1051. Take FR 1051 eastward about 2.5 miles to the road's end. You can also reach the trailhead via US 101 south from Yachats, driving 4 miles to a left turn onto FR 1051.

Cummins Creek

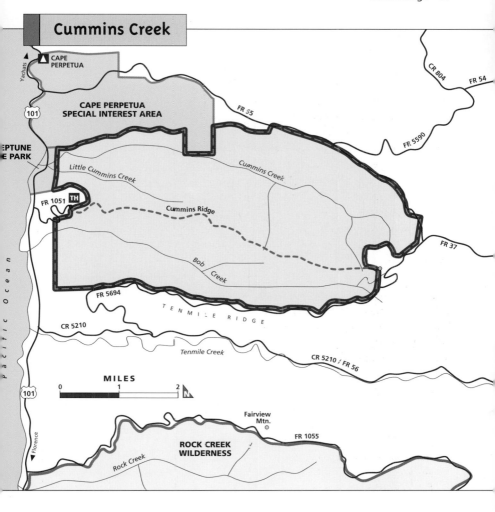

Cape Perpetua

Yachats

CR 804

FR 54

CAPE PERPETUA
SPECIAL INTEREST AREA

FR 55

FR 5590

101

NEPTUNE
E PARK

Little Cummins Creek

Cummins Creek

FR 1051 TH

Cummins Ridge

Pacific Ocean

Bob Creek

FR 37

FR 5694

T E N M I L E   R I D G E

CR 5210

Tenmile Creek

CR 5210 / FR 56

MILES

0   1   2   N

101

Florence

Fairview
Mtn.

ROCK CREEK
WILDERNESS

FR 1055

Rock Creek

2 | Drift Creek Wilderness

Heavily forested Drift Creek, Drift Creek Wilderness

SINCE FIRST HIKING THE WILDERNESS some 18 years ago, I have had a love affair with the Drift Creek Wilderness. I've returned over and over to hike among forest giants and to sit by the stream contemplating the bubbling water and scanning the flow for salmon and trout while enjoying the quiet solitude of these grand forests. There are few patches of the Coast Range that have escaped the chainsaw. Drift Creek is a gorgeous exception.

The wilderness and adjacent roadless area comprise the largest patch of old-growth forest left in the Coast Range. Here you can appreciate what has been lost but also celebrate what we are fortunate to still have. Giant Sitka spruce and western hemlock, some more than 7 feet in diameter, cloak the

LOCATION: 12 miles east of Waldport
SIZE: 5,798 acres
ELEVATION RANGE: 80 to 2,100 feet
MAJOR FLORA: Old-growth Douglas fir, western hemlock, Sitka spruce
ADMINISTRATION: Siuslaw NF, Waldport RD, 541-563-3211
BEST SEASON: May to October
GETTING THERE: From Waldport, drive east on OR 34 for about 7 miles. After crossing the Alsea River, turn left onto FR 3446, also known as Risley Creek Road. Go about 4 miles on FR 3446 to FR 346. Take a left onto FR 346 and go less than a mile to the Harris Ranch Trailhead.

hillsides, while bigleaf maple and vine maple in the understory diffuse the sunlight into a quiet green. Moss, ferns, salmonberry, thimbleberry, huckleberry, and other understory plants make this a natural emerald garden without sharp edges.

The centerpiece of the 5,798-acre Drift Creek Wilderness, Drift Creek has cut a deep canyon through the dense old-growth forests of the Coast Range. The stream seems modest in summer, but with more than 120 inches of precipitation falling in winter on the drainage, heavy flows are normal. Because of low elevation and the close proximity of the ocean, Drift Creek enjoys infrequent and fleeting snow. Fog occurs frequently in summer, even when it's sunny inland.

The Coast Range is composed of ancient volcanic islands that were swept up against the North American plate; volcanic breccias and pillow lavas make up most of the range. Sand and mud deposited over these flows later became sandstones and siltstones that were uplifted to create the Coast Range in this area.

Wildlife includes black bear, mountain lion, black-tailed deer, and Roosevelt elk, plus many smaller species like mountain beaver, bobcat, and snowshoe hare. Perhaps the most important aspect regarding the wildlife values of Drift Creek is the outstanding spotted-owl habitat. The largest concentration of spotted owls in the Coast Range reside here, as do several bald eagles. This area is thought to be the home of one of the few bald eagle pairs, which actually nest on Siuslaw National Forest land. In fall, Drift Creek comes alive with spawning Chinook and coho salmon as well as steelhead and cutthroat trout. Most of the runs occur in the fall, but there is a spring run of Chinook as well. The stream is not stocked with hatchery fish and is one of the few wild fisheries left in the Coast Range.

Surrounding the wilderness is the much larger Drift Creek Roadless Area. These 11,500 acres are among the last of the wild, untouched old-growth forest in the Coast Range. Addition of this land to the existing wilderness could create an 18,000-acre wilderness that would help maintain the purity of the Drift Creek watershed.

Three trails enter the wilderness: Harris Ranch, Horse Creek, and the northern reach of Horse Creek. The Harris Ranch Trail meets the Horse Creek Trail at Drift Creek. It's possible to hike from one trailhead to another with a shuttle, but you'll have to ford the bridgeless Drift Creek. In summer, the stream is usually no more than knee deep, but in the high water of winter or spring, fording would be out of the question. A number of small meadows and other flat forested areas near the stream afford potential campsites for those who choose to spend a night or two along the stream.

DAY HIKE: HARRIS RANCH TRAIL
One-way Length: 2.3 miles
Elevation Range: 140 to 1,320 feet
      Difficulty: Moderate (steep trail)

The Harris Ranch Trail first travels on a closed road following a ridge. The trail enters the wilderness, then descends down a ridge before switchbacking down a side slope to Drift Creek, opposite from where the Horse Creek Trail terminates. It passes through beautiful old-growth timber and lush forests. The trail ends in small meadows—relics of the old Harris Family homestead—near the creek, with good campsites under large western red cedar.

From Waldport, drive east on OR 34 for 6.9 miles. After crossing the Alsea River, watch for FR 3446, also known as Risley Creek Road, immediately on your left after the bridge. Go 4.1 miles on FR 3446 and then left onto FR 346 for 0.8 mile to the Harris Ranch Trailhead.

DAY HIKE: HORSE CREEK TRAIL
One-way Length: 3.4 miles
Elevation Range: 140 to 1,600 feet
      Difficulty: Moderate

Settlers on horseback used this trail to travel from the coast to Toledo for supplies. The Horse Creek Trail provides access to the north side of the wilderness and passes through the largest old-growth trees. The first mile or so of the trail is nearly level, before switchbacking down to the stream.

From Waldport, take US 101 north 7 miles. Turn right onto Beaver Creek Road and drive a mile to a fork. Go left and cross the Forest Service boundary. After driving less than 3 miles, you come to a junction. Turn right onto FR 51 (North Elkhorn Road), drive slightly less than 6 miles to the junction with FR 50, and turn left. Travel 1.5 miles to FR 5087, turn right, and continue 3.5 miles to the Horse Creek Trailhead.

OTHER RECREATIONAL OPPORTUNITIES

Kayakers have occasionally run Drift Creek, beginning on its upper reaches near Meadow Creek off FR 31. The run downstream has mostly Class II rapids with at least one Class III drop. Logs completely blocking the river are a hazard.

Drift Creek

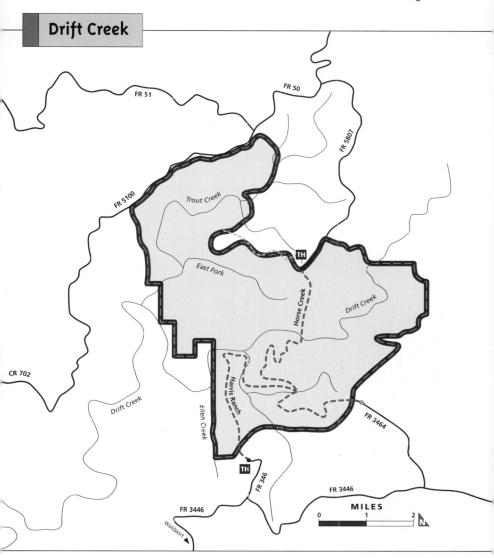

FR 51

FR 50

FR 5807

FR 5100

Trout Creek

East Fork

TH

Horse Creek

Drift Creek

CR 702

Drift Creek

Harris Ranch

Ellen Creek

FR 3464

TH

FR 346

FR 3446

FR 3446

Waldport

MILES

0   1   2

N

3 Oregon Islands Wilderness

Offshore rocks, seen here near Brookings, are part of the Oregon Islands Wilderness

LOCATION: Offshore along the Oregon Coast
SIZE: 575 acres
ELEVATION RANGE: Sea level to100 feet
MAJOR FLORA: Coastal grassland
ADMINISTRATION: U.S. FWS, 541-867-4550; Coos Bay BLM, 541-756-0100
BEST SEASON: Year-round
GETTING THERE: This wilderness is not open to the public.

HAVEN'T HEARD OF THE OREGON ISLANDS WILDERNESS BEFORE? It's not surprising. Though Congress designated the Oregon Island Wilderness in 1970, all of the islands are closed to public entry. But you can look at the wilderness from many places along the Oregon coast. The wilderness stretches from Tillamook to the California border and includes some 1,477 rocks and islets totaling 575 acres. This tiny amount of land provides nesting habitat for 1.1 million seabirds. This includes murres, tufted puffins, auklets, and murrelets. Other birds found here are grebes, loons, and seagulls. Seals and sea lions use the islands as well for breeding and haul-out sites. Approximately 64 percent of the area of these islands were designated wilderness. All of the islands are under the management of the Fish and Wildlife Service with the exception of a few islands managed by the Coos Bay BLM.

Lion Rock from Yaquina Head near Newport, part of the Oregon Islands Wilderness

4 Rock Creek Wilderness

Old-growth Sitka spruce forest, Rock Creek Wilderness

LOCATION: 17 miles south of Waldport; 15 miles north of Florence

SIZE: 7,486 acres

ELEVATION RANGE: 20 to 2,300 feet

MAJOR FLORA: Sitka spruce, western hemlock, Douglas fir, bigleaf maple

ADMINISTRATION: Siuslaw NF, 541-750-7000

BEST SEASON: Year-round

GETTING THERE: From Waldport, take US 101 south 17 miles to the Rock Creek campground. From Florence, drive US 101 north approximately 15 miles to Rock Creek Campground. The trailhead lies at the east end of the campground.

FROM A BIOLOGICAL PERSPECTIVE, Rock Creek Wilderness is significant for protecting one of the rarest major ecosystems in Oregon—virgin coastal rain forest. The wilderness simply protects a patch of rain forest and a beautiful creek. So much of the Coast Range has been logged that only a few pocket of undisturbed forest remain, and the Rock Creek drainage is one of them. Though the lower portion was once part of a homestead, the drainage overall is nearly pristine. Indeed, no official trails penetrate the dense forest. The easiest access is to wade up the creek, scrambling over and around the many large, downed logs. Magnificent trees up to 9 feet in diameter grow along the clear stream. The area was protected in 1984 as part of the Oregon Wilderness Act.

The wilderness lies just south of Cape Perpetua. The northern border of the wilderness, FR 1055 climbs up a ridge toward 2,306-foot Fairview Peak. Rock Creek Campground lies at the mouth of Rock Creek and makes a good launching point for hikes into the wilderness.

The Oregon Coast Range is part of a larger complex of coastal mountains that extends from Washington's Grays Harbor south to Coos Bay, Oregon. The crest of the range averages 1,500 feet, but the highest peaks exceed 4,000 feet. Because of the great amount of rainfall, the range has experienced significant erosion on its western slope, where drainages are longer than those on the eastern slope.

As with all of the coastal mountains, annual precipitation is heavy, exceeding 100 inches a year. Expect winters to be very wet, with infrequent snow. Summers tend to be cool but clear. Fog is common and often extends up the Rock Creek Valley. The best time of year to visit the wilderness is probably May or September, when fog is less common and rain is unlikely.

The rainfall supports a very lush, dense forest of Sitka spruce, Douglas fir, and western hemlock. Understory species include bigleaf maple, vine maple, and red alder. Salmonberry, salal, red current, oxalis, and sword fern are common. Wildlife includes Roosevelt elk, black-tailed deer, black bear, mountain beaver, marbled murrelet, and spotted owl. The endangered silverspot butterfly is found in this wilderness and in only two other locations on the Oregon coast. Salmon, steelhead, and cutthroat trout are all reported to live and spawn in the stream.

DAY HIKE: ROCK CREEK
One-way Length: 0.7 mile
Elevation Range: 20 to 200 feet
Difficulty: Easy

The Rock Creek Wilderness does not have any formal trails, but an old road that once led to a now-abandoned homestead serves as the primary access into the area. The trail takes you past lush forests to several small, open meadows. From Rock Creek Campground, hike upstream along the north bank of the creek, following the old road. After only 0.3 mile, the trail forks. The upper fork leads 200 yards to a small meadow. The lower, right-hand fork also leads to a meadow beside Rock Creek. If you continue upstream another 0.3 mile, you will come to the old homestead site, with a few old apple trees and debris from the homestead era. You can continue to work your way upstream, following elk and fisherman trails, but to go very far beyond this point requires patience and a willingness to wade the stream. Obviously, the stream is much easier to wade in late summer than in winter, when flooding occurs. You could also bushwhack down into the wilderness from FR 1055, but be sure you know what you're getting into before you try this.

From Waldport, take US 101 south past Cape Perpetua to Rock Creek Campground. Begin hiking from the eastern end of the campground.

Rock Creek

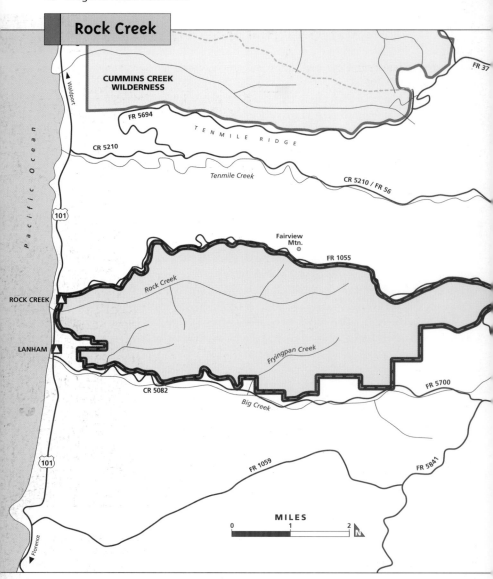

CUMMINS CREEK WILDERNESS

FR 37

Waldport

FR 5694

TENMILE RIDGE

CR 5210

Tenmile Creek

CR 5210 / FR 56

Pacific Ocean

101

Fairview Mtn.

FR 1055

Rock Creek

ROCK CREEK

LANHAM

Fryingpan Creek

CR 5082

FR 5700

Big Creek

101

FR 1059

FR 5841

MILES

0   1   2   N

Florence

Three Arch Rocks Wilderness | 5

Coast by Cape Meares and Three Arch Rocks NWR

THE WINDSWEPT, RAIN-PELTED Three Arch Rocks Wilderness was designated by Congress in 1970. This tiny wilderness consists of offshore islands several miles south of Cape Meares on the Oregon Coast. Three Arch Rocks was the first national wildlife refuge created west of the Mississippi River and later also designated a wilderness area. The rocky islands are nesting habitat for seabirds. During the nesting season as many as 200,000 common murres, 2,000 to 4,000 tufted puffins, plus dozens of petrels, pelagic cormorants, Brandt's cormorants, and other birds also visit the islands for breeding and nesting. In addition to birds, sea lions and harbor seals inhabit the islands, which are closed to public access.

LOCATION: 2 miles south of Cape Meares

SIZE: 15 acres

ELEVATION RANGE: Sea level to 100 feet

MAJOR FLORA: Coastal grassland

ADMINISTRATION: U.S. Fish and Wildlife Service, 541-867-4550

BEST SEASON: Year-round

GETTING THERE: This wilderness is not open to the public.

Klamath Mountains

Blending into the southern Cascades east of Ashland, the Klamath Mountains ecoregion is considered one of the most biologically diverse places in the United States. Here, species from California mingle with others more common in Oregon and farther north. There is also a high concentration of endemic species. This southwestern Oregon ecoregion, sometimes also called the Siskiyou Mountains (which is really a sub-range of the Klamaths), encompasses all the mountainous uplands south of Coos Bay and extends into northern California, where it includes such well-known peaks as the Trinity Alps and Marble Mountains. If you exclude the urban centers like Medford and Grants Pass, which rightfully fall into slightly different ecoregions, the area is very lightly populated, having less than 1 percent of the state's population.

The mountains differ from the Coast Mountains in that they are higher, rockier, and drier. They also have a variety of special soils and plant communities such as the serpentine bands found in the Kalmiopsis Wilderness. The highest peak in the Oregon portion of the Klamath Mountains is 7,533-foot Mount Ashland, just outside of the city of the same name. Rivers that drain or pass through the Klamath Mountains include the Rogue, Applegate, Chetco, Illinois, and North Fork of the Smith.

Geologically the Klamath Mountains are thought to be a part of southern California that drifted northward and attached onto Oregon by plate tectonics. Terranes made up of acres of unrelated islands accreted onto one another, creating a mishmash of rocks. Melded together were parts of Earth's mantle, old volcanoes, granites, ancient sea-floor sediments, and a jumble of other rocks that scraped off during the docking of the Klamath block terrane onto the North American continent. These rocks joined North America about 100 million years ago. Erosion by rivers like the Rogue have cut through these varied rocks, creating deep canyons. Alpine glaciers formed at the highest elevations during the last Ice Age, creating U-shaped valleys and glacial cirques, often occupied by lakes today.

Climatic conditions vary considerably. Ashland lies in the rain shadow of the mountains, so its annual precipitation is less than 18 inches, while some of the ocean-facing mountains may receive more than 100 inches of precipitation. Snow is common in the higher mountains. While snowpacks don't last into the summer as in the Cascades, there is still more spring snowmelt and prolonged runoff than in the Coast Range. The valleys in this part of Oregon tend to be notably warmer than those farther north in the Willamette Valley.

Serpentinite outcrop on Vulcan Peak, Kalmiopsis Wilderness

Along the coast grow forests of Sitka spruce, western hemlock, and Douglas fir. Even a small band of redwood just reaches into Oregon in this region. At higher elevations you find white fir, mountain hemlock, Shasta red fir, sugar pine, Jeffrey pine, ponderosa pine, and Port Orford cedar. California laurel (what some call myrtlewood), chinquapin, Pacific madrone, and a variety of oaks form extensive understory forests beneath tall pines. Serpentine barrens are common, dominated by grasslands and chaparral with a thin overstory of Jeffrey pine.

This ecoregion has the highest number of vertebrate species in Oregon, with more than 400 recorded here. The area also has a greater variety of amphibians, reptiles, and birds than any other part of the state and boasts some of the best salmon and steelhead runs left in Oregon. Of amphibians, the black and Siskiyou Mountain salamanders are restricted to this region, while the California slender and Del Norte salamanders reach their northern limits here. Some California birds, like blue-gray gnatcatchers, black phoebe, and Allen's hummingbird, also occur here. Other species like the osprey and the acorn woodpecker, found elsewhere in Oregon, reach their greatest abundance here. Of mammal species you find such regional endemics as the Siskiyou chipmunk.

The Klamath Mountains are a rich treasure chest of biological diversity, and every last acre of land in this area deserves protection or even restoration.

6 Grassy Knob Wilderness

Humbug Mountain from Grassy Knob Wilderness

LOCATION: 4 miles north of Port Orford

SIZE: 17,200 acres

ELEVATION RANGE: Nearly sea level to 2,342 feet

MAJOR FLORA: Douglas fir–western hemlock, Port Orford cedar, Pacific madrone

ADMINISTRATION: Siskiyou NF, Powers RD, 541-439-3011

BEST SEASON: Year-round

GETTING THERE: From Port Orford, go 4 miles north, turn right on Grassy Knob Road, and continue generally eastward for 8 miles to the trailhead on FR 5105.

DESPITE ITS NAME, Grassy Knob Wilderness is heavily forested. But a small, rocky outcrop at the summit of a former lookout site—2,342-foot Grassy Knob—does afford a relatively unobstructed view of the Pacific Ocean and surrounding forested mountains. The wilderness lies in the steep Klamath Mountains amid dense vegetation. The Elk Wild and Scenic River forms its southern boundary, and Dry Creek, a tributary of the Sixes River, forms its northern boundary. Both the Elk and Sixes Rivers are major steelhead and salmon streams. Some claim that the Elk River is the most productive salmon stream of its size outside of Alaska. Wild native cutthroat trout also dwell in these waters. The area receives more than 100 inches of precipitation annually; nevertheless, clear days prevail during most of the summer. Fog occasionally drifts in from the coast, but usually you are far enough inland or (in the case of Grassy Knob's summit) high enough to escape the fog zone.

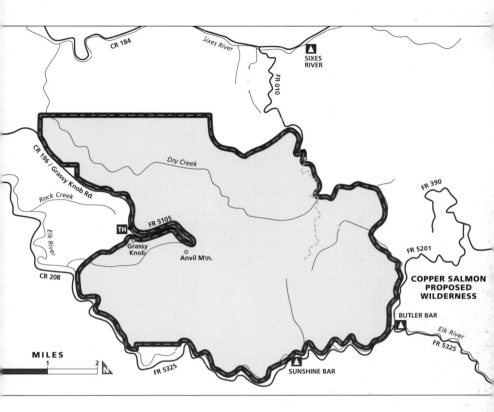

Douglas fir–western hemlock forests canopy Oregon myrtle, Pacific madrone, and rhododendron. The region's diverse vegetation also includes the Port Orford cedar, a species in decline because of an introduced, exotic root-rot disease. Wildlife includes deer, mountain lion, and black bear, plus salmon and steelhead.

On a historical note, Grassy Knob was the site of a Japanese military attack during World War II. Launched from a submarine, a fighter pilot tried to start a forest fire by dropping an incendiary bomb in the Dry Creek drainage. However, the bomb failed to ignite, and the plane made a clean getaway by flying back to sea, landing on a pontoon, and escaping before U.S. forces could respond.

Given wilderness designation by the 1984 Oregon Wilderness Act, Grassy Knob was a controversial point in the negotiations, as many logging advocates opposed designating any forested wildlands. Senator Mark Hatfield, a powerful voice in the fate of Oregon's wilderness legislation, sided with logging interests. Some environmental groups were even willing to toss in Grassy Knob as a "bargaining chip" to get wilderness designation elsewhere. Ironically it was an outrageous act of vandalism that led to the inclusion of Grassy Knob in the 1984 bill. A Forest Service official opposed to Grassy Knob's inclusion drove a bulldozer up through its heart, in an effort to disqualify the area from wilderness protection by "roading" it. But this deed so angered congressional leaders that they promptly designated the area as wilderness—complete with the road. Now barricaded and largely overgrown, the road today serves as the major hiking trail into the wilderness.

The Grassy Knob Wilderness is included in the conservationists' proposal for a million-acre Siskiyou Wild Rivers National Monument that would protect much of southwestern Oregon's prime wild salmon streams. The North Fork of the Elk River flows from the Copper Mountain Roadless Area immediately east of the present wilderness.

DAY HIKE: GRASSY KNOB
One-way Length: 0.5 mile
Elevation Range: 2,190 to 2,342 feet
Difficulty: Easy

A former Forest Service lookout site now somewhat obscured by vegetation, Grassy Knob still provides a fine panorama of the Pacific Coast. From the trailhead, walk beyond the road barricade and up the easy grade on the old road. After a walk of 0.5 mile, turn and go up a trail to the old lookout site. From this vantage point you can see Humbug Mountain, Cape Blanco, and Rocky Peak. If you wish to walk farther, the old road continues for another half mile to a turnaround point.

From Port Orford, take US 101 north for 4 miles. Turn east on Grassy Knob Road and drive about 8 miles to the trailhead on FR 5105.

OTHER RECREATIONAL OPPORTUNITIES

The jade-green waters of the Elk River run along the southern border of the wilderness. Some 15 miles or so of the river is run by kayakers. A road follows the river for most of this length, allowing you to scout before a run. The Elk is a pool-drop river that flows through canyons and gorges with Class V rapids in the uppermost segment—followed by nearly continuous Class III and IV water. Sweepers are the biggest hazard.

Kalmiopsis Wilderness 7

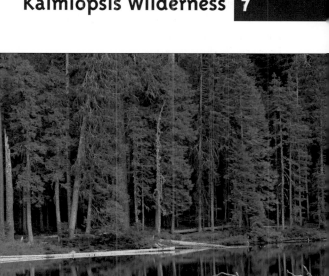

Babyfoot Lake, Kalmiopsis Wilderness

IF I WERE FORCED to designate my favorite wildlands in Oregon, the Kalmiopsis would easily rank up among the top two or three. There is just no other part of the state that possesses such lovely rivers, rugged mountains, steep canyons, and magically rich floral biodiversity. Oregon's third largest official wilderness area, 180,000-acre Kalmiopsis Wilderness provides plenty of room for exploration. The wilderness is named for a unique shrub, the *Kalmiopsis leachiana*, a relict of the pre–Ice Age era and one of the oldest members of the heath *(Ericaceae)* family, which includes huckleberry and azalea. Every season has its attractions, but my favorite time of year to visit is in May, when the flowering dogwood, kalmiopsis, and other shrubs are all in bloom. Kalmiopsis shrubs begin to flower in April at low elevations along the Illinois River and in May and June

LOCATION: West of Cave Junction and east of Brookings

SIZE: 180,000 acres

ELEVATION RANGE: 400 to 5,098 feet

MAJOR FLORA: Chaparral, Brewer's spruce, sugar pine, ponderosa pine, Jeffrey pine, Douglas fir, tan oak, Pacific madrone, Shasta red fir, knob-cone pine, kalmiopsis

ADMINISTRATION: Siskiyou NF: Gold Beach RD, 541-247-3600; Illinois Valley RD, 541-592-4000; Chetco RD, 541-469-2196

BEST SEASON: April to November

GETTING THERE: Numerous trailheads are accessible from Cave Junction, Brookings, or Crescent City, California.

near the peaks. Look for them on Vulcan Peak, along the Johnson Butte Trail near Dry Butte, and along the Upper Chetco River between Slide Creek and Taggart's Bar.

The Kalmiopsis Wilderness is surrounded by hundreds of thousands of acres of unprotected roadless land. The North and South Kalmiopsis Roadless Areas—with a combined acreage of nearly 200,000 acres—are among the largest unprotected, forested landscapes in Oregon. These expansive roadless units are often contiguous or separated by a single road corridor between the Kalmiopsis and Wild Rogue Wilderness Areas and form what is often referred to as the Kalmiopsis Wildlands—a mix of congressionally protected wilderness and unprotected roadless areas.

The Kalmiopsis is a rugged jumble of steep mountains, long ridges, and deep river canyons with some of the most complex geology in Oregon. One of the more unique rock strata found in the Kalmiopsis is the reddish-brown igneous rock called peridotite. Serpentinite is a common metamorphosed form and appears as a glossy rock of greenish color. Each different rock type represents a different slice of the Earth's crust, known as a terrane, which fused onto the North American continent.

The Kalmiopsis and surrounding wildlands are composed of at least eight discrete terranes. Some of the rocks in the Kalmiopsis Wildlands were once part of the sea-floor basin, as well as mantle rock from even deeper in the Earth's crust. These rocks, known as ophiolites, are now exposed at the surface in the Klamath Mountains region, including within the Kalmiopsis Wildlands. For instance, the Josephine ophiolite was originally a slab of ocean floor that lay between a volcanic archipelago and a continental plate. Over time these rocks were transported northward by plate tectonics, accreted onto the North American continent, and eventually uplifted.

These deep ocean rocks are rich in magnesium, iron, serpentine, nickel, and chromium. Indeed, a controversial issue surrounding the Kalmiopsis is proposals to mine both nickel and chromium, particularly on Rough and Ready Creek in the South Kalmiopsis Roadless Area. These same mineralized rocks produce unusual growing conditions for plants, and the same Rough and Ready Creek is considered to have the highest botanical biodiversity of the 1,400 watersheds in Oregon. Although generally low in elevation, some of the highest peaks above 4,000 feet in the Kalmiopsis supported Ice Age glaciers.

Magnificent old-growth forests contrast with serpentine prairies and open Jeffrey pine savannas to provide for an ever-changing landscape. If any part of Oregon feels and looks like California, this is it. Common forest species include Douglas fir, Shasta red fir, Jeffrey pine, tan oak, canyon live oak, Pacific madrone, ponderosa pine, sugar pine, incense cedar, knobcone pine, bigleaf maple, and the regional endemic Port Orford cedar. Brewer's spruce, a beautiful tree limited to northern California and southwestern Oregon, thrives at higher elevations. Chaparral is more profuse here than elsewhere in the state. Indeed, plant communities here have more in common with California's flora than that of the rest of Oregon. And this diversity of plant life includes regional endemics found no place else, not least the kalmiopsis shrub itself.

Wildlife is equally as rich, with more vertebrate species recorded here than in any other subregion of Oregon. Species more common here than elsewhere in Oregon include Hutton's vireo and the acorn woodpecker. The Siskiyou chipmunk is an endemic known only from the Klamath Mountains. Another unusual species here is the black-tailed jackrabbit—a species better known in the sagebrush country of eastern Oregon. Other wildlife here are black bear, black-tailed deer, mountain lion, bobcat, gray fox, and ringtail. Because of its extensive roadless character, the Kalmiopsis would be one of the best places for wolf restoration in Oregon.

Rivers are among the most attractive attributes of the Kalmiopsis Wilderness. The Chetco, Illinois, and North Fork of the Smith are all amazingly clear streams that have carved deep canyons through the heart of these mountains. All are National Wild and Scenic Rivers. Their jade-green waters are known for both their scenic beauty and for being some of the best remaining salmon habitat left in the state of Oregon.

Precipitation ranges from 60 to 140 inches annually, with the vast majority of it in winter. Indeed, except for fog, summers are typically clear and often very hot. Because of the overall low elevation, snowpack does not linger into summer. Instead, rivers flood in spring and then shrink dramatically, revealing rock-ribbed canyons.

What is now the Kalmiopsis Wilderness was so remote and rugged that few Europeans ventured into the area until the 1848 California Gold Rush spurred a search for gold throughout the West. Miners on Josephine Creek, a tributary of the Illinois River, discovered gold in 1850. Soon other prospectors were flooding into the state. New strikes followed at Jacksonville, Applegate River, Kerbyville, Briggs Creek, Gold Beach, Port Orford, Pistol River, and elsewhere in southwestern Oregon. The Kalmiopsis was never a big gold producer, but it held enough mineral wealth to entice miners, then and now.

The Forest Service first gave the Kalmiopsis Wilderness protection in 1946, when some 76,900 acres were set aside. The Kalmiopsis was later one of the original designated wildernesses given congressional protection under the 1964 Wilderness Act. The wilderness area was expanded as part of the Endangered American Wilderness Act of 1978 to its current 180,000-acre size.

Conservationists have unveiled a plan to protect the Greater Kalmiopsis Wilderness as part of the proposed 1-million-acre Siskiyou Wild Rivers National Monument. A jewel of fog-shrouded forests and rare plant communities, the proposed monument comprises the largest complex of wilderness and roadless lands left along the Pacific Coast. It is also perhaps the least visited of Oregon's larger wildlands. If designated, the monument would contain 863,400 acres of lands within the Siskiyou National Forest and another 184,800 acres of BLM lands. Within this acreage are five National Wild and Scenic Rivers, plus nine Wild and Scenic candidate rivers, which would protect the most valuable wild salmon and steelhead habitat in the lower 48 states.

Two important additions to the Kalmiopsis Wilderness, contained in the Oregon Natural Resources Council's Oregon Wild proposal, are the 20,603-acre Rough and Ready Creek and the 6,234-acre Rancherie Creek Roadless Areas. Rough and Ready Creek contains more than 300 plant species and is home to the largest concentration of rare and endangered plants in Oregon. The pristine Rough and Ready Creek is a major tributary of the Illinois River best known for its nickel deposits, eagerly sought by some mining companies. Rancherie Creek contains half of Pearsoll Peak, the highest summit in the Kalmiopsis Wilderness. Seventeen species of conifers have been counted in one small basin below the peak, including Brewer's spruce.

The unusual mix of rocks in the Kalmiopsis makes it a magical place, with an incredible diversity of plant communities. The rivers and streams flowing through the area are noted for their exceptional water clarity. Some consider this part of Oregon one of the major centers for biodiversity in the North America. Such a reputation is well deserved.

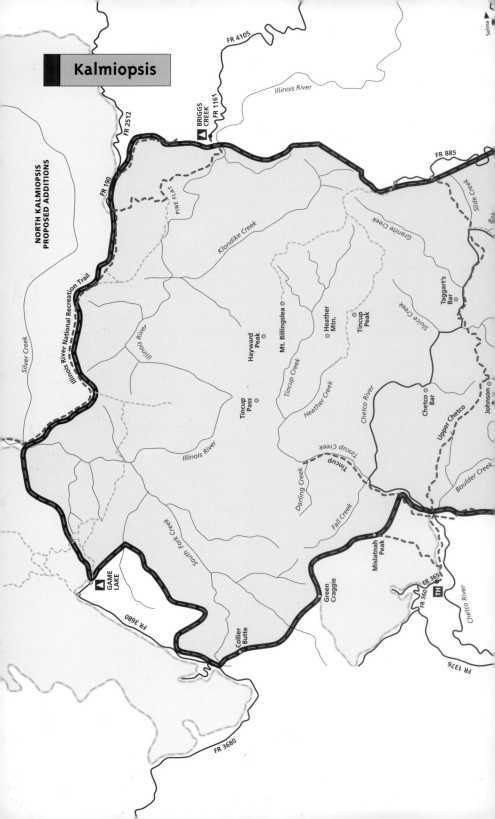

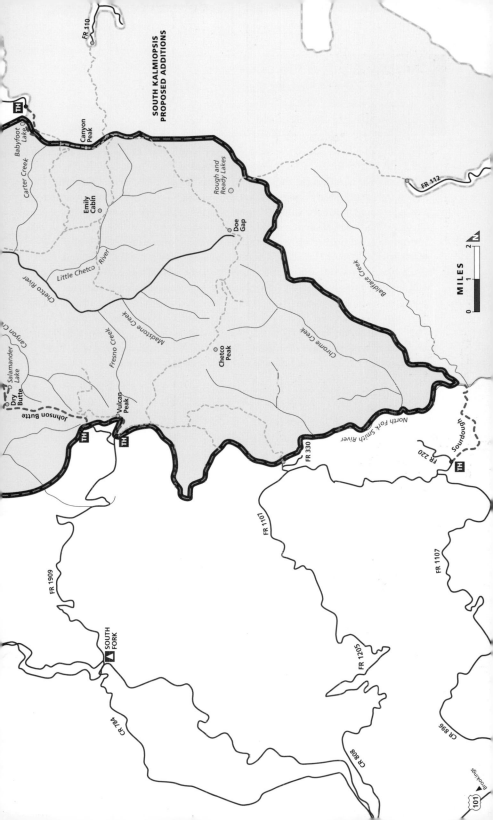

SOUTH KALMIOPSIS
PROPOSED ADDITIONS

FR 110

TH

Carter Creek

Babyfoot Lake

Canyon Peak

Little Chetco River

Chetco River

Canyon C...

Salamander Lake

Dry Butte

Johnson Butte

Emily Cabin

Rough and Ready Lakes

Doe Gap

Madstone Creek

Fresno Creek

Vulcan Peak

Chetco Peak

Chrome Creek

Baldface Creek

FR 112

North Fork Smith River

Sourdough

FR 330

FR 220

TH

TH

TH

FR 1101

FR 1909

SOUTH FORK

CR 784

FR 1205

FR 1107

CR 896

CR 808

101

Brookings

MILES

0   1   2

DAY HIKE: SOURDOUGH TRAIL #1114
One-way Length: 3.8 miles
Elevation Range: 1,000 to 2,500 feet
Difficulty: Strenuous

This trail provides access to the remote, lovely North Fork of the Smith, a National Wild and Scenic River. It lies completely outside of the current boundaries of the wilderness but is within the proposed South Kalmiopsis wilderness additions. The Sourdough Trail is fairly steep as it descends to the North Fork of the Smith River, passing through a variety of forest types including some open peridotite plant communities. The rare Darlingtonia (fly-catcher) plant can be seen along the way as well. Spring is a good time to view serpentinite-associated plant species. A historical gravesite of miner Al Hinzicker is about a half mile down the trail. The trail ends at the North Fork at Sourdough Camp, a large, fir-shaded meadow that is full of wildflowers in the spring. Just upstream from Sourdough Camp is Baldface Creek, a proposed Wild and Scenic River. A very poor road that is barely negotiable reaches the camp. The trail also accesses the Lemingsworth Gulch Research Natural Area.

Sourdough Trail is 26 miles, by road, east of Brookings. From US 101, head south, then eastward on County Road 896 (Winchuck Road) to FR 1107. Bear right on FR 1107 and follow it to FR 220 and the trailhead.

DAY HIKE: VULCAN PEAK TRAIL #1120
One-way Length: 1.5 miles
Elevation Range: 3,900 to 4,655 feet
Difficulty: Easy

Named for the Roman god of fire, red Vulcan Peak is an old fire lookout site on the southwest edge of the Kalmiopsis Wilderness. The summit provides an extraordinary view of the wilderness and lands west all the way to the Pacific Ocean. The first part of the trail follows an old road through shrubby chaparral and pines. It climbs up to the ridge and then turns east toward the peak, offering ever better views.

Vulcan Peak Trail is 30 miles, by road, northeast of Brookings. From US 101, take County Road 784 (North Bank) past Alfred Loeb State Park to FR 1376. Follow FR 1376 to the South Fork Campground. Turn right onto FR 1909 and follow it to spur FR 261 and the trailhead.

DAY HIKE: MISLATNAH PEAK
One-way Length: 4.2 miles
Elevation Range: 600 to 3,124 feet
Difficulty: Moderate

The views from the former lookout site on Mislatnah Peak into the heart of the Kalmiopsis Wilderness and the Big Craggies Botanical Area make this a good hike to consider on a clear day. You begin by hiking down to the Chetco River. Then, less than a mile from the trailhead, the trail begins to climb up a slope to a ridge that eventually leads to the peak. Take in the views at Mislatnah Prairie about a mile up the trail from the Tincup Creek Trail. After the first mile of hard climbing, the last two miles moderate as the trail follows the ridgeline to the summit. Just a half mile before the summit is Jack's Camp, a potential, if small, campsite adjacent to an azalea-lined stream. The last bit of climbing to the top of the mountain is more open and offers some views.

Mislatnah Peak splits off from the Tincup Trail. To reach the Tincup Trailhead, go 30 miles, by road, northeast of Brookings. From US 101, take County Road 784 east along the north bank of the Chetco River past Alfred A. Loeb State Park. Beyond the South Fork Campground, bear left onto FR 1376. Continue on FR 1376 to a right onto FR 360, then south to the end of FR 365.

DAY HIKE: JOHNSON BUTTE TRAIL #1110
One-way Length: 6.3 miles
Elevation Range: 3,300 to 3,800 feet
Difficulty: Strenuous

The trail to Johnson Butte offers outstanding vistas of the heart of the Kalmiopsis Wilderness and the chance to see *Kalmiopsis leachiana* on Dry Butte. The nearly 12.6 miles round-trip would make it a very long day hike, except that the trail does not climb or descend much, generally following ridges at a moderate grade. The trail first heads 1.6 miles north toward Dry Butte along an old bulldozer road, now slowly reverting back to a trail. A foot trail continues on another 1.4 miles to Dry Butte with its fields of kalmiopsis that bloom in late spring. This makes a good turnaround point for the less ambitious hiker. The trail then heads east through an old burn now colonized by knobcone pine, passing between Salamander and Valen Lakes. At about 4 miles, a side trail leads down to Salamander Lake. Both lakes are small and have no fish but are full of frogs, salamanders, and other life. If you are planning to camp, you'll find few good camping areas near the lakes. Instead, bring water from the lakes and camp on the ridge. At 5.1 miles, you reach a side trail leading right (east) toward a spring 0.25 mile off the main route. The trail ends at the junction with Upper Chetco Trail #1102 on the east flank of Johnson Butte. A longer overnight hike is possible if you plan on staying near Salamander Lake or Windy Camp near Johnson Butte.

The Johnson Butte Trail is 32 miles, by road, northeast of Brookings. From US 101, drive east on County Road 784 along the north bank of the Chetco River to FR 1376. Just beyond the South Fork Campground, bear right onto FR 1909 and follow it to its end and the trailhead.

DAY HIKE: TINCUP TRAIL #1117
One-way Length: 9.7 miles
Elevation Range: 500 to 1,200 feet
Difficulty: Moderate

The Tincup Trail crosses rolling hills as it parallels first the Scenic, then the Wild portion of the Chetco Wild and Scenic River, which flows out of the remote mountains of southern Oregon. You'll also find access to both the river and tributaries for fishing and swimming. The trail begins by dropping about 500 feet in elevation as it descends through Douglas fir, Oregon myrtle (also known as California bay), tan oak, and Pacific madrone. It passes through Mislatnah Camp, a flat campsite. The trail continues 2.7 miles upstream along a slope toward Boulder Creek Camp where there is again access to water and campsites. The trail continues upstream to Darling Creek, the turnaround point.

The Tincup Trail is 30 miles, by road, northeast of Brookings. From US 101, take County Road 784 east along the north bank of the Chetco River to FR 1376. Follow FR 1376 to a right onto FR 360, then go south onto FR 365 to the end of the road.

DAY HIKE: BABYFOOT LAKE TRAIL #1126
One-way Length: 1.3 miles
Elevation Range: 3,800 to 4,000 feet
Difficulty: Easy

This trail leads downhill through beautiful old-growth forest to glacially carved Babyfoot Lake. The lake supports small Eastern brook trout. The trail also provides access to the Babyfoot Lake Botanical Area where there are almost solid stands of Brewer's spruce. The drooping branches of this tree are distinctive. A few overused campsites exist at the lake, but this is a better day hike than a backpack trip. Enjoy nice views of the Babyfoot Creek drainage from a rocky outcrop just before reaching the lake.

From Selma, drive south about 4 miles on US 199 to a right onto County Road 5240. Go past Eight Dollar Mountain and cross the Illinois River bridge, where the road becomes FR 4201. Follow FR 4201 as it climbs up a ridge and around Fiddler Mountain toward Onion Camp. Go left on spur Road 4201-1040 to the trailhead parking.

OVERNIGHT SHUTTLE HIKE: ILLINOIS RIVER NATIONAL RECREATION TRAIL #1161
One-way Length: 27 miles
Elevation Range: 200 to 3,747 feet
Difficulty: Strenuous

The Illinois River Trail is probably the most used trail in the wilderness, but most people do not go beyond Pine Flat, some 3 miles from the Briggs Creek Trailhead. Despite its name, the trail is seldom directly next to the river; instead, you're treated to frequent views of the river winding through the canyons. Beyond Pine Flat, the trail even pulls away from the river to climb 3,000 feet over Bald Mountain, with flowery meadows and expansive views. Stands of Port Orford cedar line the tributary streams; patches of Kalmiopsis line the route. Water and campsites are abundant.

A long shuttle that could take most of a day is required for those intent on hiking the entire length end to end, so perhaps it is just as easy to simply walk from one trailhead to the other and then back again—it might only lengthen the trip by one day. Among the trail's highlights are York Creek, a Forest Service botanical site; Pine Flat, a fine campsite adjacent to the river; Indigo Creek, a wonderful jade-green tributary of the Illinois; and Buzzard's Roost, a scenic outcrop above a wild canyon of the Illinois and a proposed dam site back in the 1960s. From meadow-studded Bald Mountain, a former lookout site, you can see a great view of the trailless Silver Creek drainage; one of the wildest drainages left in the Kalmiopsis country, Silver Creek was the epicenter of the 96,000-acre Silver Creek fire and is a proposed addition to the Kalmiopsis Wilderness and proposed Wild and Scenic River. These highlights still don't do justice to the trail.

From Selma, take the Illinois River Road (FR 4103 and FR 4105) west approximately 15 miles to the end at Briggs Creek Campground and the trailhead. From Gold Beach, drive east 27 miles on FR 33 to Agness, then south on FR 450 to the Oak Flat Trailhead.

OTHER RECREATIONAL OPPORTUNITIES

The Illinois River begins in the Siskiyou Mountains near the California border and runs 79 miles to the Rogue River near Agness. The designated Wild and Scenic Illinois runs for 50.4 miles of this length, a crystal-clear stream that provides one of the premier wilderness whitewater trips in the Pacific Northwest. The river level fluctuates widely. Rapid snowmelt and winter rains swell the river in spring, while in summer the river shrinks to a nearly unrunnable stage.

The Wild section of the Illinois River runs for 32 miles through forests and steep canyons, from the put-in at Miami Bar to the take-out at Lower Oak Flat. Most people take two to four days to run the river. The Illinois is a pool-drop river, with most of the 150 rapids created by landslides. At least 11 rapids are rated as Class IV, with one Class V, the Green Wall, located at Mile 18 about halfway down the usual run. It is one of the most inaccessible rivers in the lower 48 states, and help can be difficult to obtain. The Illinois River should only be run by highly skilled and experienced boaters!

Water levels on the Illinois can rise as much as 10 feet overnight due to rain or melting snow. Be prepared to stay an extra day or two if necessary to wait out high flows. Typically, low flows requiring technical boating skills are below 1,000 cubic feet per second (cfs); ideal boating levels are between 1,500 and 2,500 cfs. Since the dominant boating season is early spring, when storms from the Pacific are common, you should be prepared for wet weather and rapidly changing water conditions. Also, most camps are located 20 to 40 feet above the water level, often on less-than-spacious sites.

Thirteen trailheads provide access to the wilderness. The most popular reaches the Illinois Valley via US 199 from Selma, while roads leading in from Brookings and Gold Beach provide access from the coast. Bear in mind that there are no bridges over rivers, so crossing streams like the Chetco River can be problematic in spring when waters are high.

Rafters on the Illinois River near Pine Flat

8 Red Buttes Wilderness

Granite outcrop in the Red Buttes Wilderness

LOCATION: California-Oregon border southwest of Ashland

SIZE: 20,323 acres

ELEVATION RANGE:
2,800 to 6,740 feet

MAJOR FLORA: Chaparral, Pacific madrone, canyon live oak, sugar pine, Douglas fir, knobcone pine, Shasta red fir, mountain hemlock, incense cedar

ADMINISTRATION: Siskiyou NF, Rogue River NF, and Klamath NF: Applegate RD, 541-899-3800

BEST SEASON: May to October

GETTING THERE: From the town of Jacksonville near Medford, take OR 238 southwest to Ruch, then follow County Road 859 (Applegate Road) south for 15 miles past Applegate Reservoir. Where you go from here depends upon the trails you wish to access. See individual trail directions for details.

SOME 13 MILES LONG and 6 miles wide, the Red Buttes Wilderness protects one of the more scenic portions of the Siskiyou Mountains along the Oregon-California border. Some folks with more than a little imagination have called these Siskiyou peaks the "Applegate Alps," but this comparison must have been made by someone who had never seen the real Alps. The Siskiyous are nevertheless beautiful mountains, boasting lush forests, small meadows, and fantastic vistas in the rocky, subalpine high country. The majority of the wilderness lies in California, but most of the access is from Oregon (some 16,150 acres in California, 3,750 acres in Oregon).

The wilderness lies at the headwaters of the Applegate River, on the watershed divide between the Rogue River and the Klamath River drainages. Drainages in the wilderness include the Middle Fork of the Applegate River, Butte Fork of the Applegate, and Sucker Creek, which drains into the Illinois River. The peaks were glaciated during the last Ice Age; U-shaped valleys, cirque lakes, and other effects of glaciation are still evident.

The Red Buttes Wilderness is part of the Siskiyou Mountain portion of the Klamath Mountains Geologic Province. The area is characterized by steep ridges and mountains and is dominated by Red Butte (6,739 feet) and Kangaroo Mountain (6,694 feet), the highest peaks in the area. The majority of the wilderness rocks are part of the Applegate Terrane, formed between 400 and 180 million years ago and the oldest rocks in the Klamath Mountains in Oregon. Large outcrops of granite occur in this region, including the Grayback Mountain and Mount Ashland plutons, with a minor amount of granite presence in the Red Buttes Wilderness as well. The Red Buttes are red peridotite, or rocks that were once part of the Earth's mantle.

Most of the area's annual precipitation, about 40 inches, comes as snow in winter. Summers tend to be cloudless—endless days of blue sky. Temperatures can become quite warm—into the low 90s or even into the 100s on very hot summer days. Autumn is delightful, with warm, sunny days and cool nights. It is probably the best time of year to visit.

Old-growth forests dominate the Red Buttes Wilderness. At lower elevations, you can find delightful old-growth stands of Jeffrey pine, ponderosa pine, canyon live oak, Pacific madrone, Shasta red fir, mountain hemlock, chinquapin, and tan oak. Look also for several rare species like Brewer's spruce, Sadler oak, and Baker cypress. The Butte Fork Canyon contains the most extensive stands of old-growth in the wilderness.

Wildlife includes black bear, black-tailed deer, ringtail, mountain lion, and coyote. Goshawks and a variety of owls, including the spotted owl, are found here. The area once supported grizzly bear and wolf populations and could easily support wolves again. According to one recent study, southwestern Oregon (along with adjacent parts of California) could support as many as 440 wolves. Big Butte Creek contains native populations of cutthroat trout. Because of the Applegate Reservoir, no steelhead or salmon exist in the wilderness.

The human history of Red Buttes is short. Like much of southwestern Oregon, it was explored by miners, but no major discoveries were unearthed here except for some chromite deposits on Red Butte and on Kangaroo Mountain. Other settlers grazed livestock, hunted, trapped, and subsistence farmed, but on the whole the area was largely passed over by those intent on resource exploitation.

Designated a wilderness in 1984, Red Buttes was originally conceived of as a more than 42,000-acre wilderness, but the acreage was reduced to a mere 25,000 acres when the Oregon Wilderness Act was introduced into Congress, then reduced further by Senator Mark Hatfield to its current size in the final bill. The loss of these roadless lands from the original conservationist proposal has resulted in logging and roading of much of that original acreage. (This is just one example of the many ways that Hatfield helped to destroy Oregon's wildlands, yet a wilderness was eventually named after him, an action that still galls environmentalists.)

A major proposed addition to the Red Buttes Wilderness is known as the Siskiyou Crest Wilderness. It surrounds the Red Buttes Wilderness and runs eastward toward the Cascades. The proposed Siskiyou Crest Wilderness contains large tracts of old-growth forests, high-elevation meadows, and spectacular peaks—and includes the drinking water supply for several cities.

The Siskiyou Crest is a critical east/west migratory link between the Coast Range and the Cascades. Across this link lie (east to west) the Cascade-Siskiyou National Monument (Soda Mountain), McDonald Peak, Condrey Mountain, and Kangaroo Inventoried Roadless Areas, as well as Red Buttes and proposed Siskiyou Crest Wilderness Areas. Interspersed between these are about two dozen uninventoried roadless areas of more than 1,000 acres. The Oregon Natural Resources Council Oregon Wild Campaign inventory counts in all more than 180,000 acres of roadless Forest Service and BLM lands here that form a tenuous web of high-quality habitat in this critical wildlife area.

In most cases, these large roadless areas are separated from each other by a single dirt road, although Interstate 5 separates the Cascades-Siskiyou National Monument from the rest of the Siskiyou Crest. Roadless units that make up the Siskiyou Crest Wilderness include the 68,000-acre Kangaroo, 20,000-acre Condrey Mountain, 12,000-acre McDonald Peak, 8,100-acre Little Grayback, and several smaller areas. Any one of these could qualify as wilderness by themselves. Despite the extensive logging that has riddled this area with roads and clear-cuts, an outstanding opportunity still exists to create a biologically significant wildlands complex in the Siskiyou Crest by linkage of the existing roadless areas, by a few judicious road closures, and their designation as official wilderness.

The 68,000-acre Kangaroo Roadless Area is named for Kangaroo Mountain, which lies along the southeastern corner of Red Buttes Wilderness. This proposed addition lies mostly in California and includes the upper Thompson Creek drainage, the Devil's Peak area directly south of the Red Buttes, and the Horse Creek, Cook, and Green drainages to the east of the wilderness. Home to nearly 30 conifer tree species and dozens of endemic plant and animal species, the Siskiyou Crest is one of the jewels of Oregon. The Pacific Crest Trail traverses a large portion of this area, offering outstanding vistas.

The 20,000-acre Condrey Mountain Roadless Area lies south of the Oregon border in California and includes the headwaters of Dutch Creek, a tributary of Elliot Creek. The highest point is 6,995-foot Scraggy Mountain. The PCT trail traverses this area from Ward Fork Gap to Cook and Green Pass. There are dozens of springs on or near Condrey Mountain.

The 9,500-acre McDonald Peak Roadless Area is the farthest east of the roadless areas along the Siskiyou Crest. It lies about 3 miles west of Ashland and includes the headwaters of Ashland Creek. Elevation ranges from 3,280 to 7,280 feet. The roadless area includes both Wagner Butte and McDonald Peak. It consists primarily of virgin old-growth forests, contains rare high-elevation meadows, and has never been grazed. Mount Ashland, the highest peak in the Siskiyous at 7,533 feet, overlooks the roadless area.

The Siskiyou Crest is noted for its biological diversity. McDonald Peak alone possesses three candidate botanical areas; one includes the Mount Ashland lupine, found only on a 45-acre plot on the Siskiyou Crest and considered one of the rarest plants in Oregon. Henderson's horkelia is also found here in its greatest abundance. Both have been petitioned for listing under the Endangered Species Act. Engelmann spruce, rare this far south, is also found in this roadless area. All three are threatened by the proposed expansion of the Mount Ashland Ski Area.

The highest concentration of recreational use occurs at Tannen Lakes and Azalea/Lonesome Lakes in the Upper Butte Fork drainage.

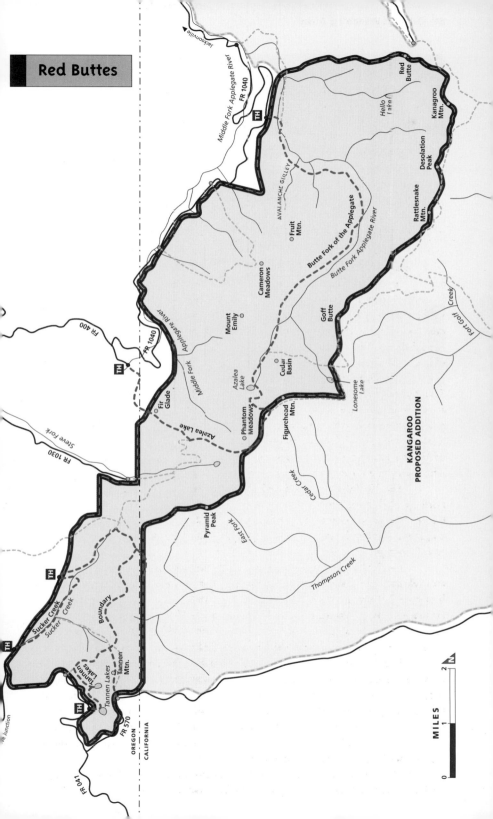

Red Buttes

Red Butte

Kanagroo Mtn.

Hello Lake

Desolation Peak

Rattlesnake Mtn.

FR 1040

Middle Fork Applegate River

Jacksonville

AVALANCHE GULLEY

Fruit Mtn.

Butte Fork of the Applegate

Butte Fork Applegate River

Goff Butte

Cameron Meadows

Mount Emily

Cedar Basin

Fort Goff Creek

FR 400

FR 1040

Applegate River

Middle Fork

Azalea Lake

Phantom Meadows

Lonesome Lake

Azalea Lake

Fir Glade

Figurehead Mtn.

KANGAROO PROPOSED ADDITION

Steve Fork

FR 1030

Pyramid Peak

Cedar Creek

East Fork

Thompson Creek

Sucker Creek

Sucker Creek

Boundary

Tannen Lakes

Tannen Mtn.

Tannen Lakes

FR 570

OREGON
CALIFORNIA

FR 041

Junction

MILES

0   1   2

N

DAY HIKE: SUCKER CREEK TRAIL #1237
One-way Length: 2.5 miles
Elevation Range: 3,800 to 5,200 feet
    Difficulty: Easy

This short hike follows a forested drainage upstream to Sucker Creek Shelter at Sucker Gap. Several trails take off from this main trail; a good 5.5-mile loop can be made by hiking the Sucker Creek Trail to Fehley Gulch Trail, which climbs about a mile up the side of Tannen Mountain and then links with Trail #1207, which leads back about 2 miles to intersect again with the Sucker Creek Trail near the trailhead.

From Cave Junction, take OR 46 east toward Oregon Caves National Monument. Just a few miles beyond Grayback Campground, turn right onto FR 4612, then turn onto FR 098 to the trailhead. This trail is also accessible from Trail #1237A at the end of Sucker Creek Road.

DAY HIKE: TANNEN LAKES
One-way Length: 1 mile
Elevation Range: 5,000 to 5,300 feet
    Difficulty: Easy

The drive to this lake offers superb mountain scenery and views south into the proposed Kangaroo Mountain additions to the Red Buttes Wilderness. The hike to the Tannen Lakes is equally as pretty. The two high, glacially carved lakes rest below Tannen Mountain. The first lake is only 0.4 mile from the trailhead, so this is a hike even small children can do. You'll pass rhododendron, Sadler oak, and wildflowers. Sadler oak is a regional endemic and found only in the mountains of southwestern Oregon and northwestern California. There is a campsite at the first lake, but dense vegetation around the lake discourages further exploration. Tie Trail #1243A makes a loop back to FR 041. A loop opportunity exists by combining this trail with the west end of Boundary Trail #1207, FR 570, and FR 041. There are some spectacular views from Trail #1207 along the south side of Tannen Mountain.

From Cave Junction, drive south on US 199 past Rough and Ready Creek about 5 miles to O'Brien. Turn left onto County Road 5560 and go east to CR 5828 and eventually FR 48. At the highest point of the road, just after crossing into California, turn left onto FR 4812. Follow this road east to FR 041 and the trailhead.

OVERNIGHT BACKPACK: AZALEA LAKE
One-way Length: 6 miles
Elevation Range: 5,000 to 6,000 feet
    Difficulty: Moderate

At 20 acres, Azalea Lake is the largest lake in the Red Buttes Wilderness. The hike there takes you through flowery meadows with beargrass, lupine, and of course azalea, along the Siskiyou Crest. You'll also encounter several rare tree species, including

Brewer's spruce and knobcone pine, as well as lodgepole pine, not usually found west of the Cascades. The first few miles pass smaller meadows and larger Fir Glade. From Fir Glade, the trail traverses the edge of the upper Middle Fork of the Applegate drainage for 2.7 miles to a rocky pass. Another mile with only modest elevation gain takes you over a second pass at 6,000 feet. The trail then switchbacks down to the lake surrounded by Brewer's spruce, lodgepole pine, and mountain hemlock. Note the camping restrictions at the lake. If you can arrange a shuttle, continue down Butte Fork of the Applegate River to its trailhead on FR 1040, providing a wonderful traverse of the wilderness from the high peaks to the old-growth forests of lower Butte Fork.

From Jacksonville, drive OR 238 west to Applegate. Turn left onto Thompson Creek Road (County Road 10). Go 12 miles south to the road's summit, then turn left onto County Road 777 toward Applegate Reservoir. Go 4 miles to Steve's Fork Road (FR 1030), turn right, and go 5 miles to the junction with FR 400. Turn left and drive another 5 miles. Drop over a watershed divide and turn right onto the first road after the summit, continuing 1 mile to the trailhead.

OVERNIGHT BACKPACK: BUTTE FORK OF THE APPLEGATE
One-way Length: 9 miles (to Azalea Lake)
Elevation Range: 3,200 to 5,600 feet
Difficulty: Moderate

The Butte Fork Trail takes you through the last major unlogged and unroaded drainage of the Applegate River. It features some of the best old-growth forest in the Red Buttes Wilderness, including massive Douglas fir and sugar pines. In spring, Pacific dogwood blooms add much color to the forest all the while as the trail follows the lovely, chattering Butte Fork upstream. There are few campsites along this trail until you reach Azalea Lake. The Shoofly Trail winds down some switchbacks to the creek to connect with the Butte Fork Trail, which then continues upstream at a gradual climb. Often the trail is up on the slope away from the stream, but you will pass many small tributaries, so water is no problem. There are occasional glimpses through the trees of the surrounding snowy peaks from the trail. Cedar Basin, just a mile or so below Azalea Lake, features a meadow with a fine grove of Port Orford cedar, another regional endemic. Azalea Lake offers some campsites, which have some restrictions.

There are two trailheads to the Butte Fork. These directions take you to the upper trailhead. From the town of Jacksonville near Medford, take OR 238 to Ruch. From there follow County Road 859 (Applegate Road) south for 19 miles past Applegate Reservoir. At the "T" junction, turn left and go 1.3 miles to FR 1040. Just before the California-Oregon line, make a hard right to stay on FR 1040, which winds down and crosses the Middle Fork of the Applegate River. Continue along the river on FR 1040 to the Shoofly Trailhead, on the left near a ridge top.

9 Wild Rogue Wilderness

Rogue River, Wild Rogue Wilderness

THE ROGUE RIVER is probably Oregon's most legendary river, famous for the beauty of its rugged canyon, its whitewater rapids, and the fabulous silver throng of salmon and steelhead that once jammed the river's tributaries. The Wild Rogue Wilderness cradles the spectacular canyon of the Rogue River. The Siskiyou National Forest manages most of the designated wilderness, but some two-sevenths of the wilderness is under BLM jurisdiction.

The Rogue River has its origins in the Cascades near Crater Lake National Park. The powerful river is one of the few streams, along with its

LOCATION: 30 miles east of Gold Beach; 30 miles west of Grants Pass

SIZE: 35,818 acres

ELEVATION RANGE: 200 to 4,319 feet

MAJOR FLORA: Chaparral, Douglas fir, Pacific madrone

ADMINISTRATION: Siskiyou NF, Gold Beach RD, 541-247-3600; Medford BLM, 541-618-2200

BEST SEASON: March to June and September to November

GETTING THERE: From Merlin northwest of Grants Pass, drive the Merlin-Galice Road west to Galice, then follow signs to Grave Creek trailhead; continue northwest on the Grave Creek–Marial Back Country Byway to reach the wilderness boundary. From Gold Beach, drive east on FR 33 to Agress, then continue north about another 6 miles to the Foster Bar Trailhead.

northern neighbor the Umpqua, to have cut a path through the coastal mountain barrier. The river has carved a 4,000-foot-deep canyon through the Klamath Mountains to reach the Oregon Coast near Gold Beach.

The steep terrain is heavily forested with Douglas fir, Pacific madrone, and chaparral. At 4,319 feet, Mount Bolivar is the highest point in the wilderness and offers an expansive view from its summit. Away from the water, the land lies steep and dense with brush and poison oak. Few people—indeed, I would be surprised if more than a handful—try to hike the wilderness off-trail at any time of the year. The forest stands, dominated by Douglas fir in the wetter west, give way to oak and madrone in the east. Other species likely to be seen include sugar pine, knobcone pine, chinquapin, tan oak, flowering dogwood, bigleaf maple, and an occasional black oak. Understory species include Pacific rhododendron, azalea, and at higher elevations even some of the showy white blossoms of beargrass. The eastern two-sevenths of the Wild Rogue Wilderness were created in 1978 by the Endangered American Wilderness Act.

Despite the respective designations of Wild and Scenic River and Wilderness, jet boats from Gold Beach roar up and down the river as far upstream as Blossom Bar. The jet boats not only disturb the solitude of the canyon but also are a hazard for floaters, when the creation of large waves threatens to tip them over. They remain because of the economic clout of a few commercial jet-boat operations. Conservationists hope that someday this obnoxious commercial use will be ended, and the real protection of wilderness values such as tranquility and quiet will be returned to the river.

Like most of southwestern Oregon, the greatest precipitation occurs in the winter, with annual accumulations exceeding 80 to 90 inches at higher elevations. Though rain is common at low elevations, even in winter, the higher peaks are occasionally blanketed with snow. At low elevations, temperatures in winter are relatively mild, seldom dipping below freezing; during summer, however, temperatures often exceed 100 degrees in the canyon bottom. These temperatures make for enjoyable float trips, but argue against hiking the Rogue River Trail during July or August.

Geologically the Wild Rogue Wilderness is part of the larger Klamath Mountains subregion of southwestern Oregon. This landscape is composed of multiple slices of the Earth's crust that have been accreted onto the westward-moving North American continent. These slabs or slices are known as terranes. Each terrane owes its composition

Wild Rogue

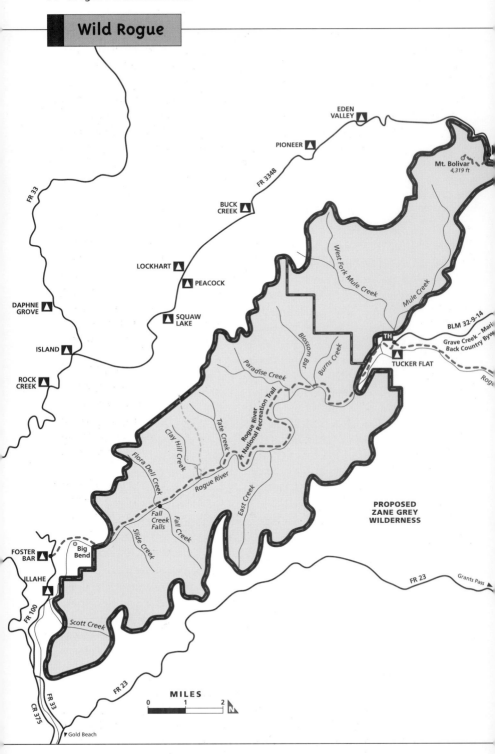

EDEN
VALLEY

PIONEER

FR 3348

Mt. Bolivar
4,319 ft

BUCK
CREEK

FR 33

West Fork Mule Creek

Mule Creek

LOCKHART

PEACOCK

DAPHNE
GROVE

SQUAW
LAKE

Blossom Bar

Burns Creek

BLM 32-9-14

Grave Creek – Marial
Back Country Byway

ISLAND

TH

Paradise Creek

TUCKER FLAT

Rogue

ROCK
CREEK

Rogue River
National Recreation Trail

Flora Dell Creek

Clay Hill Creek

Tate Creek

Rogue River

East Creek

PROPOSED
ZANE GREY
WILDERNESS

Fall
Creek
Falls

Fall Creek

FOSTER
BAR

Big
Bend

Slide Creek

FR 23

Grants Pass

ILLAHE

FR 100

Scott Creek

FR 33

FR 23

MILES

0   1   2

N

CR 375

Gold Beach

to a unique history and geographical origin, so that side-by-side terranes can have radically different geological composition. The Rogue River cuts through the Snow Camp terrane, a relict of a volcanic island group similar to those island archipelagoes seen in the South Pacific today. The cliffs and rocks exposed along the river include exposed volcanic dikes and magma chambers of ancient volcanoes. Gabbro, the intrusive equivalent of basalt that you can see throughout eastern Oregon, is also a common outcrop along the river. Another common rock here is andesite, the kind found on the major Cascade volcanoes like the Three Sisters or Mount Hood, and which occurs here at Blossom Bar, for instance. The difference in rock hardness among rock types results in differential erosion of each strata and is responsible for some of the larger rapids and falls on the river.

The wildlife of the Wild Rogue Wilderness includes common species like black-tailed deer, elk, mountain lion, black bear, and river otter. Ring-tailed cats reach their northern range limits in this area. Perhaps the most impressive aspect of the Rogue is the giant Chinook salmon that you can see in the river, often jammed up against cool water springs and side streams. The river also hosts coho salmon and steelhead, cut-throat, and rainbow trout. The Rogue's impressive steelhead runs were made famous by writer Zane Grey, who in 1926 purchased a cabin along its banks and fished it regularly. Nearly all salmon and steelhead runs are in decline with the habitat's degradation. The reduction in flows because of upstream irrigation has harmed the river's ability to support cold-water fish like salmon and trout.

Hikers should always hang food when in bear country, and those visiting the Wild Rogue Wilderness should do so as well. The bears often make a nightly circuit of designated campsites along the river, looking for opportunities. Remember, losing one's food to bears is not only a nuisance; it potentially creates a dangerous situation for future campers, since food-addicted bears are the ones most likely to attack people. Finally, food-addicted bears usually wind up dead at some point; so if for no other reason, think of the bears. They deserve your respect and cooperation.

There are several large roadless areas immediately adjacent to the Wild Rogue Wilderness. One of the largest is the proposed Zane Grey Roadless Area. Managed by the BLM, the Zane Grey area lies 25 miles east of Grants Pass and is contiguous with the Wild and Scenic Rogue Wilderness Area to the northwest, with its eastern flank near Grave Creek. The Rogue River National Recreation Trail passes through the entire length of this roadless area.

DAY HIKE: MOUNT BOLIVAR
One-way Length: 1.4 miles
Elevation Range: 3,160 to 4,319 feet
Difficulty: Easy

Mount Bolivar (4,319 feet) anchors the northeastern corner of the Wild Rogue Wilderness and provides a fantastic view down Mule Creek Canyon and the Rogue River Canyon. A sign at the trailhead even claims that one can see Mount Hood on a clear day. Unfortunately, in just about any other direction all you see is land scalped by logging. The long, long drive to the trailhead means this hike isn't likely to be crowded, despite its short length and exceptional view. The first part of the trail passes through alternating stretches of manzanita and old-growth Douglas fir forest as it switchbacks up the slope. Some sugar pine and knobcone pine are also scattered throughout. Pacific yew, a rare species this far south, also occurs here. Rhododendron and even beargrass in the understory provide a good floral display in June. The final push to the summit is more open, with manzanita and chinquapin.

From Grants Pass, take the Merlin exit off I-5 and drive the Merlin-Galice Road 23 miles. Cross the Rogue River and head up the mountain on gravel BLM Road 34-8-1. Follow this winding, narrow road for 15 miles. The road then joins the Whiskey Creek Road and becomes Road 32-7-19.3. A half mile later, the road turns into Road 32-8-31. Turn left toward Powers and proceed another 13.8 miles to the signed Mount Bolivar Trailhead on the left.

OVERNIGHT SHUTTLE HIKE:
ROGUE RIVER NATIONAL RECREATION TRAIL
One-way Length: 41 miles
Elevation Range: 200 to 545 feet
Difficulty: Strenuous

Though most people experience the Wild Rogue Wilderness by boat, for 40 miles the Rogue River National Recreation Trail passes through the wilderness. The trail follows the river canyon for its entire length and is often high above the river, providing outstanding views. Passing through old-growth forest, open meadows, and chaparral-covered slopes and among shady side canyons from Grave Creek to Illahe, the trail offers a continuously changing perspective on the river. Trail hikers and river floaters can choose from at least 40 primitive campsites along the river. Given the often-high temperatures that dominate the river canyon in summer, this hike is best done in the spring or fall. Springtime's abundant wildflower displays easily get the vote for best time of year. A winter hike, however, offers real solitude. Since numerous shuttle services are available for rafters floating the river, it's possible to pay for a car shuttle and make this a one-way hike.

The Rogue River National Recreation Trail follows the north bank of the river as it winds its way toward the Pacific Ocean. The western trailhead is at Foster Bar, about 30 river miles inland from the coastal town of Gold Beach. Grave Creek, the eastern trailhead, is about 30 river miles downriver from the town of Grants Pass.

Among the highlights of the river trail is Rainier Falls. Two miles from the Grave Creek trailhead, take a short side-trail down to the falls, one of the more difficult rapids on the river and a good place to watch rafts and kayaks plunging down the wild torrent. For those wanting to have a short day hike, this makes a good picnic and turnaround spot. At around 3 miles you reach Whiskey Creek, site of an old miner's cabin, now a national historic landmark. A good beach provides a nice swimming area. Black oaks shade the campsite. At mile 15.4, you'll reach Kelsey Creek, where you can find campsites. Mile 23 is the location of the Rogue

River Ranch, now owned by the BLM and on the National Register of Historic Places. At mile 24.4, you'll see Mule Canyon and a BLM-maintained ranger station. Tank up on water, as the next stretch of trail is hot and dry—but very scenic—as you walk above Mule Canyon, the narrowest part of the river. At mile 27.1, you'll pass Blossom Bar Creek, named for the numerous wild azaleas that grow here. Blossom Bar Rapid is another difficult passage that many boaters stop and scout before running. At mile 34.8, you'll pass Flora Dell Creek, boasting a 30-foot waterfall set in a shady canyon. At mile 41, you reach Illahe Campground, a developed site with toilets, water, and parking.

There are two trailheads. To reach the east trailhead, take the Merlin exit off of I-5 and drive 22 miles west on the Merlin-Galice Road to Grave Creek. Access the west trailhead from Gold Beach by driving 30 miles east on FR 33 to Agness. Continue beyond Agness to Foster Bar and the trailhead.

OTHER RECREATIONAL OPPORTUNITIES

The most popular way to experience the wilderness is to float the river by kayak or raft. The Rogue was one of eight rivers originally designated under the Wild and Scenic Rivers Act of 1968. The Wild section of the Rogue River begins at the mouth of Grave Creek, about 34 road miles northwest of Grants Pass. The river rages through 33 miles of Class III (or less) rapids but also includes roaring Rainie Falls (Class V) and breathtaking scenery at Mule Creek Canyon and Blossom Bar (both Class IV rapids). Most boaters take three to four days to float the Wild Rogue River. Foster Bar, the take-out, is 33 miles downriver from Grave Creek. Use of the Wild Rogue River is regulated during the spring and summer to protect the corridor from overuse and to provide a wild river experience. If you wish to run the river at this time, you must obtain a permit.

Inflatable kayaks rest along the Wild and Scenic Rogue River, Wild Rogue Wilderness

Cascade Range

The Cascades are the dominant physical feature in Oregon. They divide the state into two sections—the wet western third and the dry eastern two-thirds. Yet the Cascades are more like a broad plateau dissected by deep river canyons. The western part of the Cascades is called the "Old" or just "Western" Cascades. These 4,000- to 6,000-foot mountains are the eroded relics of once-high peaks. On the eastern slope are the "New" or "High" Cascades. Here the crest averages about 8,000 feet in elevation, but high volcanoes rise thousands of feet above the rest of the range. Some of these volcanoes are still active, including prominent peaks like Mount Hood, Mount Jefferson, Three Sisters, Diamond Peak, and Mount McLoughlin. There are no low passes across the Cascades—a geographical fact that proved a major obstacle to the settlement and development of Oregon. The only low-elevation route through the range is carved by the Columbia River at the Columbia Gorge.

In general, the western slope of the Cascades drops to the low-elevation Willamette, Umpqua, and Rogue Valleys. By contrast, the eastern slope of the range seldom dips below 3,000 or 4,000 feet except in the vicinity of the Columbia Gorge. Bearing the brunt of winter storms, the western slope often receives more than 100 inches of precipitation annually. In fauna and flora it greatly resembles the Coast Range ecoregion, with a few exceptions (Sitka spruce are absent here). Nevertheless, great forests of old-growth Douglas fir, western hemlock, and western red cedar cloak the low-elevation, forested slopes, grading into western white pine, mountain hemlock, lodgepole pine, Pacific silver fir, noble fir, and Alaska yellow cedar at the highest elevations. In the southern reaches of the Cascades, which tend to be drier, you begin to see more California species like Shasta red fir, sugar pine, white fir, and incense cedar. Understory species include bigleaf maple, red alder, vine maple, golden chinquapin, red huckleberry, rhododendron, and sword fern.

The eastern slope of the Cascades is dramatically different. In the northern part of the range near Mount Hood, the eastern slope is rather narrow, but as you move farther south toward Klamath Falls, the range broadens to become a high, forested plateau punctuated by volcanic peaks, with 8,364-foot Gearhart Mountain the highest summit. Other prominent peaks include 8,196-foot Yamsey Mountain and 7,134-foot Winter Ridge. This region also has some huge wetlands including Sycan Marsh and Klamath Marsh. Some have suggested that this triangular region, lying between

Middle and North Sister, glacial tarns, and moraines, Three Sisters Wilderness

Proxy Falls, Three Sisters Wilderness

Bend, Klamath Falls, and Lakeview, deserves a separate name of its own, but for the purposes of this book it will be included as part of the Cascades. The eastern slope is drained by the Hood and Deschutes Rivers and by the Klamath River system to the south.

The annual precipitation on landscapes immediately east of the Cascade Crest drops dramatically, with towns like Bend receiving less than 15 inches of precipitation annually. Indeed, the precipitation gradient between the Cascade Crest and areas like the Bend-Sisters region is among the greatest found in the United States over such a short distance.

This more arid climate favors species like lodgepole pine, white fir, ponderosa pine, and even juniper. Small patches of western larch, Engelmann spruce, and even Oregon white oak can be found east of the Cascades. Understory species here are simpler, with grouse huckleberry, beargrass, bitterbrush, and even chaparral found in the southern part of the range.

Though the Cascades have been the most heavily logged ecoregion of
Oregon after the Coast Range, some substantial differences exist between
the two. For one, public lands dominate in the Cascades, with national
forests and BLM lands comprising two-thirds of the land area. Oregon's
only national park, Crater Lake, is also found here. The other third is
mostly private timberland. In spite of the abundance of private land,
the number of people who actually live here is very small. Few towns
or communities exist up in the mountains. Most settlement is on the
fringes: in the Willamette, Umpqua and Rogue River Valleys to the west,
and in communities like Bend and Klamath Falls to the east.

Wildlife in this region is varied and includes various endangered species.
A couple of unique amphibian species here are the Larch Mountain salamander found in the Columbia Gorge, and the Oregon slender salamander,
endemic to Oregon, but one of the more common salamander species of
the old-growth western slope of the Cascades. Other sensitive amphibians
found here are the tailed frog, Cascade frog, and spotted frog.

When it comes to birds, the Cascades are famous for the spotted owl.
This region supports more of the birds than any other ecoregion in Oregon.
Dependent upon old-growth forests, its numbers have shrunk with the
rise in logging. Most spotted owls are found in forests more than 200 years
of age. They are not found in timberline forests of mountain hemlock or
in low-elevation ponderosa pine forests. Other species that depend on
older forests with plenty of snags include pileated woodpeckers and swifts.
The largest wintering roost of bald eagle in the coterminous United
States is found in the Klamath Basin, while boreal owls have been noted
near Mount Bachelor.

Common mammals of the Cascades include elk, deer, mountain lion, and
black bear. Rarer species include the wolverine, marten, and perhaps lynx.
Pronghorn antelope are occasionally spotted in the open forests east of
the Cascades.

Fish of the western slope of the Cascades include most of the major
species of salmon, including runs of coho and Chinook salmon and steelhead trout. In some streams bull trout persist, while rainbow along with
cutthroat trout are the dominant native trout. In the Klamath Basin, isola-
tion has created some endemic species, including the Lost River sucker
and shortnose sucker—both endangered species.

10 Badger Creek Wilderness

Lookout Mountain, Badger Creek Wilderness

LOCATION: 65 miles east of Portland

SIZE: 24,000 acres

ELEVATION RANGE: 2,100 to 6,525 feet

MAJOR FLORA: Oregon white oak–ponderosa pine woodlands, fir, subalpine meadows

ADMINISTRATION: Mount Hood NF, Barlow RD, 541-467-2291

BEST SEASON: April to November

GETTING THERE: From Hood River, drive OR 35 south approximately 30 miles to Robin Hood Campground. The wilderness lies to the east of OR 35 by way of the campground or various Forest Service roads.

THIS 24,000-ACRE WILDERNESS, just east of OR 35 south of Hood River, provides outstanding views of its nationally famous neighbor, Mount Hood. But it's not just Hood that is visible from the aptly named Lookout Mountain—on a clear day you are treated to vistas spanning a distance from Mount Rainier and Mount Adams in Washington south to the Three Sisters by Bend. Badger Creek Wilderness was created by the Oregon Wilderness Act of 1984.

Lying in the rain shadow of Hood, the wilderness receives an average of 70 inches of precipitation on its western slopes, while less than 20 inches is recorded at lower elevations on the eastern edge of the wilderness. The area falls in a transition zone between the High Cascades and the Columbia Plateau, with a diversity of vegetative types including oak–ponderosa pine woodlands, a relatively rare habitat type confined to the vicinity of the eastern edge of the Columbia Gorge.

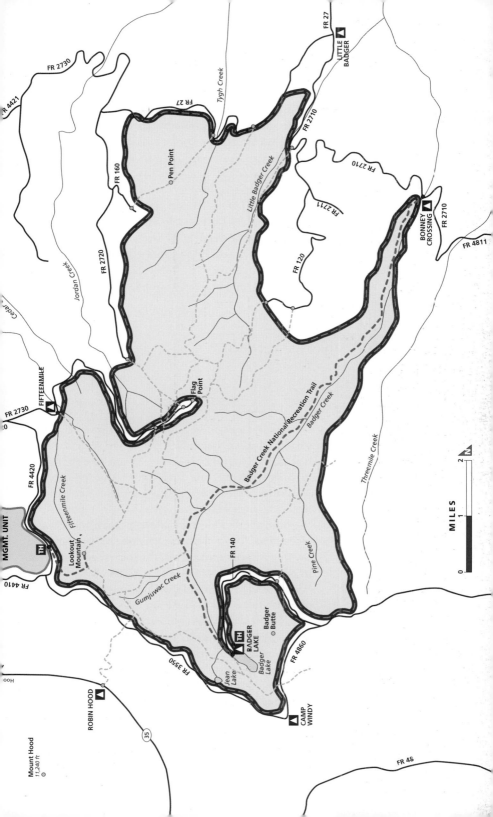

Numerous wildflower-filled meadows and rock gardens grace the higher elevations. Other tree species present include mountain hemlock, lodgepole pine, whitebark pine, western red cedar, grand fir, Engelmann spruce, Pacific silver fir, and subalpine fir.

As in most of the Cascades, volcanic rocks and flows dominate the area. Glaciers have carved the highest headwater areas along the western edge of the wilderness by Badger Lake, but most of the area was too dry and low for glaciers.

Three major drainages lie in the wilderness—Badger, Little Badger, and Tygh Creeks. Badger Creek drains Badger Lake and is reputed to have good fishing for rainbow trout. Badger Lake holds both rainbow and brook trout and is stocked annually. Wildlife in the area includes deer and elk. I found elk tracks in the mud during my hike.

About 55 miles of trails traverse the wilderness, including the Badger Creek National Recreation Trail, which follows the length of the creek in the wilderness. Very rough FR 3550 separates the western border of Badger Creek Wilderness from a substantial roadless area to the west that extends to OR 35. If this road were closed between Camp Windy and High Prairie, the wilderness could be expanded to the East Fork of the Hood River and OR 35.

DAY HIKE: LOOKOUT MOUNTAIN
One-way Length: 1.25 miles
Elevation Range: 5,900 to 6,500 feet
Difficulty: Moderate

The view from Lookout Mountain is one of the most spectacular in Oregon. Immediately west lies the hulking bulk of Mount Hood, while visible north and south are the high, glaciated Cascade volcanoes, including Mount Adams, Mount Rainier, Mount St. Helens, Mount Jefferson, and Three Sisters. More good news is that, in climbing to the rocky former lookout site, you pass through a series of subalpine meadows that are thick with wildflowers.

Most of the trail to the top of the mountain follows an old road, now a trail in the Badger Creek Wilderness. The trail grade is relatively gentle, and a sign at the trailhead even proclaims it wheelchair accessible. The trail eventually curves to the east, offering terrific views to the south across Badger Creek. Badger Lake is visible to the southwest, with Mount Jefferson and the Three Sisters beyond. You encounter Divide Trail, which continues east to Flag Point Lookout.

The Lookout Mountain trail switchbacks northwest up to the summit ridge. The trail passes a large, flat campsite area. With no water available, this is only useable early in the season when snow can be melted. The trail continues upward at a gentle grade, winding in and out among scattered whitebark pine, subalpine fir, and mountain hemlock. Views both north and south from this ridge are exceptional.

The trail intersects the old road, and the two continue up to the summit area where the old lookout once stood. The only remains are some cement foundations. The views, however, are still exceptional. Soak in the scenery for a while before retracing your steps back to the trailhead.

On the way down, be careful about missing the trail junction that leads back to the road. After you have come down the side hill with views of Mount Hood, you will pass a huge boulder that frames the mountain. Just after the boulder, watch closely for an unmarked trail that leads a short distance to the old road.

From Hood River, take OR 35 south to Dufur Mill Road (FR 44). Alternatively from Government Camp, go north on OR 35 until you pass Robin Hood Campground. Dufur Mill Road (FR 44) is another 2.5 miles beyond. Proceed on blacktop FR 44 for 3.8 miles to a sign for High Prairie and gravel FR 4410. Turn right (south) onto FR 4410 and drive about 5 miles to a "T" intersection. Turn left and proceed 200 yards to the trailhead and parking area.

DAY HIKE: BADGER CREEK NATIONAL RECREATION TRAIL #479
One-way Length: 12 miles
Elevation Range: 2,200 to 4,472 feet
Difficulty: Moderate

Badger Creek National Recreation Trail parallels Badger Creek from its source at Badger Lake, a water storage reservoir with a dam, to Bonney Crossing near the White River State Game Management Area—a major deer wintering refuge. Wildflowers are abundant, especially at lower elevations in April, May, and early June. Starting from Bonney Crossing, the trail proceeds through woodlands of oak and ponderosa pine. Five miles into the hike, the forest changes to Douglas fir–western hemlock, with cedar, spruce, and other mid-elevation species. At 5.7 miles you reach Pine Creek, a Badger Creek tributary and a nice campsite. Day hikers can turn around here. It's another 6.2 miles to Badger Lake. A number of additional campsites exist along the trail, so overnight backpacks are possible.

There are two potential trailheads. The lower end is at Bonney Crossing. To reach it from Hood River, go south on OR 35 about 2 miles past Bennett Pass to a right on FR 48 and to Rock Creek Reservoir. Turn left onto FR 4810, then take a right onto FR 4811, and a final right onto FR 2710 to the trailhead. To reach the upper end at Badger Lake, follow the same directions as above to FR 48, but turn left onto FR 4860 (Badger Lake Road), take it to FR 140, turn right, and drive the final 3.4 miles to 4,400-foot Badger Lake and the trailhead.

OTHER RECREATIONAL OPPORTUNITIES

Cross-country skiing into the wilderness is best from OR 35. You could climb 2.5 miles from Robin Hood Campground to Gumjuwac Saddle (1,700-foot climb) on Trail #480, then another 2 miles downhill to Badger Lake or 2.5 miles to Lookout Mountain. Conversely, you could ski from Bennett Pass over snow-filled FR 3550 to Camp Windy and then on to Badger Lake. A longer loop—probably best done as an overnight ski trip—would continue from Badger Lake up to Gumjuwac Saddle and down to Robin Hood Campground and OR 35.

‖ Boulder Creek Wilderness

Boulder Creek, Boulder Creek Wilderness

LOCATION: 50 miles east of Roseburg

SIZE: 19,100 acres

ELEVATION RANGE: 1,500 to 5,600 feet

ECOSYSTEMS: Ponderosa pine woodlands, Douglas fir, sugar pine, oak woodlands, bigleaf maple

ADMINISTRATION: Umpqua NF, Diamond Lake RD, 541-498-2531

BEST SEASON: April to November

GETTING THERE: From Roseburg, drive east on OR 138 for about 55 miles to Medicine Creek Road (FR 4775) and turn left (north). Almost immediately, turn west onto the Soda Springs Dam access road to a parking area 1.2 miles down this road.

BOULDER CREEK is a tributary of the legendary North Umpqua River, a famous steelhead and salmon stream. The North Umpqua borders the wilderness for several miles. Boulder Creek itself is a critical spawning site for anadromous fish. It tumbles between rapids, pools, and small waterfalls through a deep canyon.

The wilderness's low elevation makes it accessible throughout the year for hiking and exploring. Pine Bench, a forested plateau covered with ponderosa pine, is especially lovely in the spring when wildflowers are in their prime.

The ancient volcanics of the Western Cascades are exposed here in elaborate fashion. Within the wilderness lies the 1,420-acre Umpqua Rocks Geologic Area, which features basalt and andesite spires including Rattlesnake Rock, Old Man Rock, Old Woman Rock, and Eagle Rock. The basalts and volcanics were laid down some 30 million years ago by the volcanoes that created the Old Cascades. Pine Bench is a flat-topped ancient lava flow. Its origins, however, are much more recent: The bench was created when a basalt flow poured down the North Umpqua River Canyon several thousand years ago.

An annual precipitation of some 60 inches supports lush forests. Because of this abundant rainfall, an interesting aspect of this wilderness is the presence of ponderosa pine, a species typically found in low-precipitation zones east of the Cascades. The Pine Bench stand is said to be the largest tract of ponderosa pine west of the Cascade Crest in Oregon. Walking through Pine Bench, you might think you were someplace in the Blue Mountains of eastern Oregon. Much of the rest of the wilderness has forests of Douglas fir, incense cedar, white pine, noble fir, bigleaf maple, and other species. But the really special trees for me were the immense sugar pine. Sugar pine is common in California but rare this far north in Oregon. The tree's giant, 1- to 2-foot-long cones are very distinctive.

The Spring Fire that blazed across 16,500 acres in 1996 charred much of the wilderness. The startling rejuvenation and beneficial effect of wildfire is readily evident in many parts of the wilderness. Snags provide homes for woodpeckers and other birds. Downed logs support many small rodents and insects. New and young growth is sprouting everywhere.

The North Umpqua River is famous for its steelhead and Chinook salmon runs. The summer steelhead fishing is particularly well known. Rainbow trout also live in the river. Fly-fishing is permitted only in the stretch of water that flows past the Boulder Creek Wilderness.

Thirty miles of trail traverse the wilderness. The easiest is the North Umpqua Trail, which runs from Soda Springs along the river for 6 miles to a bridge by Eagle Rock Campground. You can hike this trail throughout the year. The Cinder Prairie Trail #1488 runs 6.2 miles from FR 3402 to Boulder Creek. This trail is no longer shown on some maps. Two trails run from Road 100 to Boulder Creek: the 2.2-mile Spring Mountain Trail #1553, and the 4-mile Boulder West Trail #1554.

DAY HIKE: BOULDER CREEK TRAIL #1552
One-way Length: 10.6 miles
Elevation Range: 1,600 to 5,400 feet
Difficulty: Moderate

The Boulder Creek Trail traverses the entire wilderness south to north, providing good access to the stream. The trail first switchbacks up to Pine Bench, traversing some oak woodlands—rare in this part of the Cascades. Once on Pine Bench, you intersect Bradley Trail #1491. The Boulder Creek Trail is relatively level for a way, then descends to cross Boulder Creek. Turn around here, unless you are inclined to stay overnight or have arranged a car shuttle. Continuing up Boulder Creek, the trail pulls away from the creek to climb a side hill but eventually rejoins the creek for a couple of miles. After the trail reaches the forks of Boulder Creek, it switchbacks up a ridge to continue at a more gentle slope for the remaining miles to FR 3810. Of the few campsites in this wilderness, one of the best is on Pine Bench

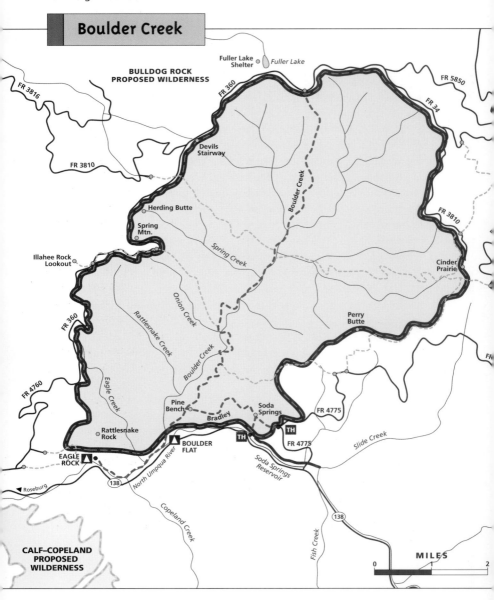

along the Boulder Creek Trail, where a small spring provides water near some flat ground for camps. The springs lie about 0.4 mile from the junction of Boulder Creek and Soda Springs Trails.

From Roseburg, take OR 138 east about 55 miles. Turn left onto FR 4775, then immediately turn left on FR 4775-011 for 2.6 miles on a very rough road to a parking area. Most people will likely find it better to park near the dam only 1.2 miles down this road and walk the rest of the way to the official trailhead, adding 1.5 miles to the hike.

LOOP HIKE: SODA SPRINGS–BOULDER CREEK
Trail Length: 4.6 miles
Elevation Range: 1,800 to 2,600 feet
Difficulty: Moderate

This loop allows you to hike across Pine Bench and back along the North Umpqua River, though it does not visit Boulder Creek at all without a small digression. The hike begins at the Soda Springs Trailhead parking area. To find the trail, you must walk under the aqueduct. Go 0.4 mile up Soda Springs Trail #1493. Don't be confused by the signs for North Umpqua Trail #1414, which shares the same path for a short distance, before the Soda Springs Trail heads north. The path will pass through beautiful Douglas fir forest with ferns. You soon pass Soda Springs, where tracks of elk and deer are common. At the next trail junction, turn left onto Bradley Trail #1491.

From here it is 1.5 miles to the Boulder Creek trail junction. You'll climb up the slope through the burnt snags from the Spring Fire. Note how many of the bigleaf maples are sprouting from their root crowns. As you approach Pine Bench, you'll pass some particularly large sugar pine. Once on the bench, the hiking is nearly level through open, grassy forests of ponderosa pine and Douglas fir. The persistence of pine here is likely a result of repeated fires, since ponderosa pine and sugar pine both require more open, drier forests to survive and are very good at surviving all but the most intense blazes.

To complete the loop from Boulder Creek Trail, turn left and head south. But you should probably take a moment to take in the view of the Boulder Creek valley by turning right and proceeding a short way up the trail to where you can walk to the edge of the canyon and see the rest of the drainage. Back at the trail junction, proceed down the hillside to the North Umpqua River, then left back up the river 1.7 miles to your starting point at the Soda Springs Trailhead.

Follow the same directions as for the Boulder Creek hike. From Roseburg, take OR 138 east about 55 miles, turn left onto FR 4775, then immediately turn left onto FR 4775-011; go 1.2 miles to the Soda Springs Trailhead, and park by the dam and aqueduct.

12 Bull of the Woods Wilderness

"Wood elves" by giant Douglas fir near Elk Creek, Bull of the Woods Wilderness

LOCATION: 70 miles southeast of Portland; 65 miles east of Salem

SIZE: 27,427 acres

ELEVATION RANGE: 2,400 to 5,558 feet

MAJOR FLORA: Douglas fir, western hemlock, Pacific silver, noble fir

ADMINISTRATION: Mount Hood NF, Estacada RD, 503-630-6861; Willamette NF, 541-225-6300

BEST SEASON: May to October

GETTING THERE: From Estacada, take OR 224 east about 26 miles to Ripplebrook Guard Station. A short distance beyond the station, turn right onto FR 46. Take this road just beyond River Ford Campground, and turn right onto FR 63. From here you'll find numerous options to get to various trailheads.

BULL OF THE WOODS WILDERNESS lies on the western slope of the Cascades, receiving the brunt of winter storms that drop more than 100 inches of precipitation here annually. Despite the heavy winter rains, summers are usually dry and delightfully cool. The abundant rain and snow support some of the finest forests left in the Old Cascades and provide a glimpse of what the entire western slope of the Cascades was like before industrial forestry scalped most of it. This is one of the lovelier wildlands in Oregon, yet it receives few visitors beyond the popular hikes to Bagby Hot Springs and Bull of the Woods Mountain. If you like forests, this is the place to be. "Bull of the woods" is a reference to the top woodman in a logging outfit.

Mossy streams, a dozen or so cirque lakes, and trees—big trees—define the area's charm. Douglas fir, western hemlock, western red cedar, and Pacific silver fir dominate the old-growth forests. Other species here include western white pine and an occasional Alaska cedar. Beargrass, rhododendron, and huckleberry are all common understory plants. The headwaters of the Collawash and Clackamas Rivers drain from the wilderness; these streams, along with Elk Creek and some of the lakes, offer fishing for trout. Elk, black-tailed deer, black bear, mountain lion, and coyote are among the larger mammals you may see. The old-growth forests are the haunts of the spotted owl and the varied thrush.

The Bull of the Woods region consists of old lava flows, tuff deposits, and other volcanic debris from eruptions that occurred between 50 million and 10 million years ago. Ice Age glaciation has left the mountains deeply carved and extremely rugged despite a relatively low elevation.

The 75 miles of trails in the wilderness allow plenty of opportunity for extended exploration. Further, Bull of the Woods Wilderness adjoins the 20,724-acre Opal Creek Wilderness (designated in 1998), allowing you to stretch out your wilderness experience if you wish. In fact, some 8,000 acres of the Bull of the Woods Wilderness were annexed to the Opal Creek Wilderness. Approximately 6,000 roadless acres lying along the eastern border of the wilderness and west of FR 46, plus several thousand more acres along the Hot Springs Fork near Bagby Hot Springs, should be added to the wilderness.

Glacier-carved Elk Lake, a popular camping area and the start of several trails into the wilderness, lies on the southern border. Beware that the final few miles of the road into Elk Lake are extremely rough—even in a 4WD, I found it unnerving to drive. Nevertheless, I have seen passenger cars at the lake—who knows how they got there!

Bagby Hot Springs lies along the Hot Spring Fork, just outside of the wilderness but within a roadless area and Forest Service Research Natural Area. The springs offer soothing soaks in wooden tubs. Note that no camping is allowed at the springs. The hike through the lovely old-growth forests all along the Hot Spring Fork practically to Silver King Lake are worth the effort, even if you don't spend any time at the springs.

DAY HIKE: BULL OF THE WOODS TRAIL #550
One-way Length: 3.3 miles
Elevation Range: 4,640 to 5,523 feet
Difficulty: Moderate

This trail is probably the most popular in the wilderness. It offers a nice, gradual climb along a ridge through lovely, old-growth Pacific silver fir forest to an isolated, rocky pinnacle that offers one of the best views in the entire Cascades. The trail only passes one potential water source, Terrace Spring, which was dry when I hiked the trail, so be sure to take plenty of water. Though most of the hike is through old-growth fir, a few isolated Alaska cedar stand along the trail. As you near the top of the mountain, the trail occasionally breaks out of the trees, offering fantastic views of Mounts Hood and Jefferson, plus Big Slide Mountain in the wilderness.

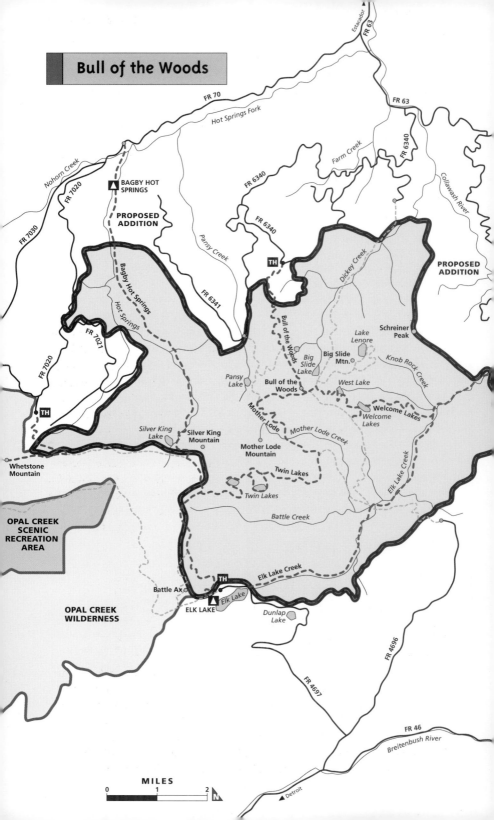

Bull of the Woods

The mountain is topped by a lookout built in 1939. On a clear day you can see most of the volcanic peaks, from Mount Rainier to the Three Sisters, not to mention the rugged ridges of the western Cascades. An outhouse on the edge of a cliff below the lookout offers what is possibly one of the best views of any such structure in the West, with the towering, glacier-clad slopes of Mount Jefferson directly outside the door.

From Estacada, take OR 224 east 26 miles to Ripplebrook Guard Station. A short distance beyond the station, turn right onto FR 46. Just beyond River Ford Campground, turn right onto FR 63. Take FR 63 to FR 6340 for a total of slightly more than 9 miles to the trailhead, on a short spur on the edge of a clear-cut.

DAY HIKE: WHETSTONE MOUNTAIN
One-way Length: 1.6 miles
Elevation Range: 3,950 to 4,969 feet
Difficulty: Moderate

This hike takes you to a peak along the western border of the wilderness overlooking the Little North Fork of the Santiam River in the Opal Creek Wilderness and Scenic Area. From the trailhead, the path first descends for a short way before climbing by switchbacks up to a ridgeline trail, then continues another 1.1 miles to the summit. The former fire lookout site on the rocky summit provides expansive views of the densely forested valleys of Opal Creek (though trees are beginning to obscure the view), plus more distant views of High Cascade volcanoes, including Mount Jefferson and the Three Sisters.

From Estacada, drive 26 miles on OR 224 to Ripplebrook Guard Station. Just beyond the station, turn right onto FR 46. Follow FR 46 to FR 63, turn right, and drive 3.5 miles to a right onto FR 70. Take FR 70 for 9 miles, following signs for the Whetstone Mountain Trail. Watch for and turn onto FR 7030. Drive 5.3 miles, then turn onto FR 7020 and drive less than a mile before coming to a final spur, FR 028, which ends in a parking area.

LOOP BACKPACK: BULL OF THE WOODS TRAVERSE
Trail Length: 25 miles
Elevation Range: 2,600 to 5,250 feet
Difficulty: Strenuous

This 2- to 4-day loop trip begins and ends at Elk Lake, a beautiful glacial lake immediately south of the Bull of the Woods Wilderness. The loop provides a wonderful overview of the wilderness. Potential side trips to several high peaks are available, as well as camping at glacial cirque lakes and among old-growth forests.

Start this loop at the Elk Lake Creek Trailhead at Elk Lake, elevation 3,750 feet. From the trailhead, descend 4 miles to the confluence of Battle Creek and Elk Lake Creek, passing through a beautiful old-growth forest with some large Douglas fir and western red cedar 5 to 6 feet in diameter. You'll find a good campsite here and several more along Elk Lake Creek. From the confluence, continue 2.7 miles down Elk Lake Creek Trail #559 to Welcome Lakes Trail #554. Ascend this trail, switchbacking up a ridge 2.6 miles to Welcome Lakes and more campsites. Climb out of the Welcome Lakes basin on Trail #554 to the ridge above Big Slide Lake and continue west past Bull of the Woods Mountain. If you don't mind the extra mileage, drop your packs here and make the 0.7-mile climb to the old fire lookout on the 5,523-foot mountain for some of the best views in the wilderness.

Whether you make the climb or not, continue on the ridge to Mother Lode Trail #558. This will lead you around the headwaters of Mother Lode Creek to a junction with Trail #573 to Twin Lakes, the preferred route. You can also continue 1.9 miles down Mother Lode Creek on Trail #558 to Elk Lake Creek by Battle Creek and hike the 4 miles back up Elk Lake Creek to Elk Lake. If you continue on to Twin Lakes, the best campsites lie at the upper lake. From Twin Lakes, the route climbs up to the ridge between Battle Creek and Battle Ax Creek, eventually reaching Bagby Hot Springs Trail #544. There are great views along this trail. Follow Trail #544 south 3.6 miles back to Elk Lake. Walk the dirt road along Elk Lake approximately a mile east back to the Elk Lake Creek Trailhead.

From Salem, drive OR 22 east to Detroit. In Detroit, turn left (east) onto Breitenbush Road (FR 46) and drive slightly more than 4 miles to a left onto easy-to-miss FR 4696. Go less than a mile on FR 4696, then bear left onto FR 4697. Drive about 6 miles to the lake. The last 1.5 miles are extremely rough; a 4WD is recommended, although I have seen passenger vehicles make it to the trailhead successfully by going very slowly.

Crater Lake National Park 13

Rabbitbrush near Steel Bay, Crater Lake National Park

CRATER LAKE IS ONE OF THE CROWN JEWELS of the Oregon Cascades. The lake is 1,932 feet in depth, making it the deepest in the United States and the seventh deepest in the world. No one who looks upon the lake can forget the intense blue of the water. And it's easy to understand why the lake is now protected as a national park. Only two roads besides Rim Drive access the park, so the majority of acreage is essentially wilderness, although not designated as such by Congress. But given the National Park Service's generally pro-protection management, for all intents and purposes Crater

LOCATION: 64 miles from Medford; 49 miles from Klamath Falls
SIZE: 183,000 acres
ELEVATION RANGE: 3,700 to 8,929 feet
MAJOR FLORA: Fir, mountain hemlock
ADMINISTRATION: National Park Service, Crater Lake, 541-594-3100
BEST SEASON: June to October
GETTING THERE: From Medford, take OR 140 and OR 62 north to the park.
From Klamath Falls, take US 97 and OR 62 north to the park.

Lake's backcountry is wilderness. As such, the park is an important link in the Cascade Crest of protected areas that stretches from Mount Hood south to the Mountain Lakes Wilderness near the California border.

Despite the fact that hundreds of thousands of people visit the park each year, few actually venture much beyond the park's Rim Drive and its viewpoints. The backcountry areas of the park are among the least used in the entire Cascades. In fact, in terms of nonmotorized recreation, the greatest use occurs in winter, when ski touring the Rim Drive becomes popular.

The caldera now filled with Crater Lake was created when a 12,000-foot stratovolcano, Mount Mazama, erupted and then collapsed in on itself. Ash from the eruption was carried as far as Nebraska. Ash on Crater Lake's Pumice Desert lies 50 feet deep! The eruption occurred an estimated 6,845 years ago. Since the formation of the caldera, other eruptions have created Wizard Island and associated features. Satellite cones on the flanks of Mount Mazama include Mount Scott, the Watchman, and Hillman Peak. Glaciers later scoured and gouged out U-shaped valleys such as Kerr Notch and Munson Valley. Inflow from springs and snowmelt created the lake. The lake's clarity reflects the limited input of sediments.

Crater Lake National Park receives an annual average of 69 inches of precipitation. The bulk of that falls as snow in winter. Indeed, the snow depth at Rim Village can reach 18 feet. The most abundant tree species is mountain hemlock. Other species found in the park include lodgepole pine, Shasta red fir, whitebark pine, and ponderosa pine at the lowest elevations.

Wildlife includes elk, deer, black bear, fox, porcupine, ground squirrel, chipmunk, pika, and marten. Although none existed in the past, six species of fish have been introduced into the lake. The three surviving species are rainbow trout, brown trout, and kokanee salmon.

The fiery creation of Crater Lake was noted by Native American legends. Some say that shamans even forbade others from visiting the crater. Pioneers and trappers didn't know of the site until 1853, when prospectors accidentally came upon it while searching for a mine. In 1886, the U.S. Geological Survey surveyed the area and sounded the depths of the lake. The half-ton boat employed for this purpose had to be hauled up the mountain and lowered by rope into the lake. Using a piece of pipe attached to piano wire, the team determined the depth to be 1,996, only slightly off from the official depth of 1,932 recognized today. Established in 1902, Crater Lake was the fifth designated national park in the country.

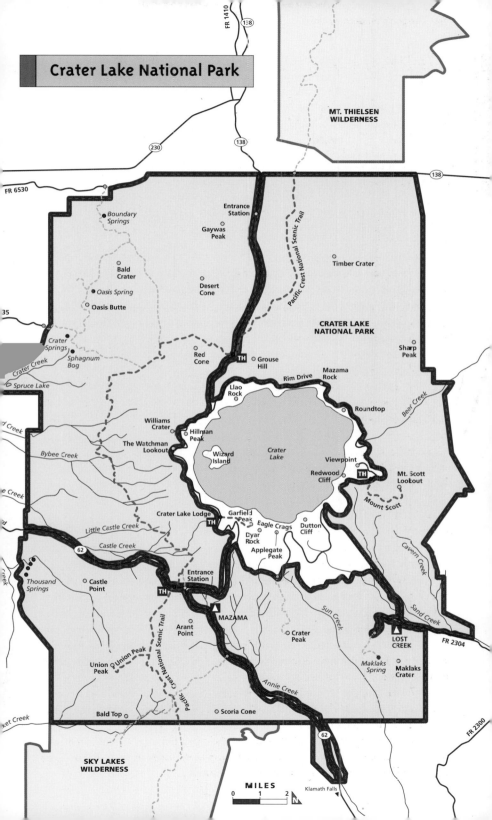

Crater Lake National Park

MT. THIELSEN WILDERNESS

FR 1410

138

230

138

138

FR 6530

35

Boundary Springs

Entrance Station

Gaywas Peak

Bald Crater

Oasis Spring

Oasis Butte

Desert Cone

Timber Crater

CRATER LAKE NATIONAL PARK

Pacific Crest National Scenic Trail

Crater Springs

Sphagnum Bog

Crater Creek

Spruce Lake

Red Cone

TH

Grouse Hill

Rim Drive

Mazama Rock

Sharp Peak

Llao Rock

Roundtop

Bear Creek

Williams Crater

Hillman Peak

The Watchman Lookout

Bybee Creek

Wizard Island

Crater Lake

Viewpoint

Redwood Cliff

TH

Mt. Scott Lookout

Mount Scott

Crater Lake Lodge

TH

Garfield Peak

Eagle Crags

Dutton Cliff

Dyar Rock

Applegate Peak

Little Castle Creek

Castle Creek

62

Cavern Creek

Thousand Springs

Castle Point

Entrance Station

TH

MAZAMA

Arant Point

Sun Creek

Crater Peak

Sand Creek

LOST CREEK

FR 2304

Union Peak

Pacific Crest National Scenic Trail

Maklaks Spring

Maklaks Crater

Bald Top

Scoria Cone

Annie Creek

62

FR 2300

SKY LAKES WILDERNESS

MILES

0   1   2

Klamath Falls

N

The park actually has few trails, since the road along the rim provides most visitors with all they desire from the park. The Pacific Crest Trail passes through the park, but it's essentially viewless along its entire route, with few sources of water. In fact, most of the park is trailless and thus a genuine wilderness for those with the skills to take advantage of its solitude.

DAY HIKE: MOUNT SCOTT
One-way Length: 2.5 miles
Elevation Range: 7,900 to 8,929 feet
Difficulty: Moderate

Mount Scott is the tenth highest peak in the Oregon Cascades. The summit is adorned with a lookout tower. Any peak with a lookout is bound to have a great view, and Mount Scott is no exception. From the summit you can see all of Crater Lake, north along the Cascades past Mount Thielsen, and south toward Mount Shasta. But Mount Scott's relatively sloping southeastern slope belies its real height. The first mile or so, the well-graded trail crosses relatively flat terrain, then begins to climb toward the summit via switchbacks. Once on top, enjoy the panorama, then return as you came.

From Medford, take OR 62 to Crater Lake National Park, turn north, and drive toward Rim Drive. Once at the rim, turn right (east) and drive 11 miles to the trailhead.

DAY HIKE: GARFIELD PEAK
One-way Length: 1.5 miles
Elevation Range: 7,090 to 8,054 feet
Difficulty: Moderate

Named for President Theodore Roosevelt's Secretary of the Interior, Mount Garfield boasts spectacular views of Crater Lake from the summit—and the hike getting there is also exceptionally beautiful. The trail begins behind the Crater Lake Lodge, climbing up through flowery meadows and forests of subalpine fir, whitebark pine, and mountain hemlock. Switchbacking as you climb toward the summit, enjoy ever more beautiful views. You eventually work your way up through whitebark pine to the rocky peak, where your view embraces Mount Shasta and Klamath Lake on the south and the blue waters of Crater Lake spreading out below almost beneath your feet.

From Medford, take OR 62 to Crater Lake National Park. Then turn north and drive toward Rim Drive. Once at the rim, turn left and drive to the Crater Lake Lodge parking area, where the trail starts.

DAY HIKE: UNION PEAK
One-way Length: 5.5 miles
Elevation Range: 6,180 to 7,709 feet
Difficulty: Strenuous

Most of this trail is viewless but easy hiking. The top of Union Peak does provide some vistas and is a worthwhile destination in its own right. From the trailhead, the route follows the Pacific Crest Trail #2000 south through sparse timber, mostly lodgepole pine and mountain hemlock forests. At 2.9 miles, you reach a trail junction. Turn west and hike 2.6 miles to the peak's rocky summit, guarded by cliffs. Views from the summit range up and down the Cascades, but Crater Lake itself is not visible.

From Medford, take OR 62 to Crater Lake National Park. At milepost 72, 1 mile before the south entrance to the park and near the summit of the highway, look for a pull-off for the Pacific Crest Trail #2000 and the trailhead.

OTHER RECREATIONAL OPPORTUNITIES

More backcountry activity takes place in winter than in summer, as the park is a popular ski destination. Rim Drive is closed in winter, providing an ideal ski corridor that circles the caldera, providing an ever-changing vista of the beautiful cobalt blue waters of the lake. Vehicle access is from OR 62 to parking near the Crater Lake Lodge. It is possible to ski in from the north, since OR 138 remains plowed all winter; however, the North Junction receives a considerable amount of snowmobile traffic. Since snowmobiles are restricted to the road, those wishing to travel off-road have an entire winter wonderland to themselves. The Pacific Crest Trail also leaves OR 138 just a mile from the North Junction. The trail in combination with the road makes for a good ski loop. Ski in on the PCT and then back out (and slightly downhill) on the road back to the North Junction.

14 Diamond Peak Wilderness

View of Diamond Peak from Summit Lake, Diamond Peak Wilderness

AN 8,744-FOOT CASCADE VOLCANO, Diamond Peak dominates this wilderness, although four other mountains here rise above 7,000 feet. The peak is surrounded by several sizable glacial lakes like Crescent, Odell, and Summit, plus numerous, smaller, glacial-cirque lakes, all within the wilderness boundary. Many of the larger lakes contain stocked trout populations, with brook trout and rainbow trout the most common species. Given the abundance of water—bigger lakes, pothole lakes, and small, water-filled depressions—mosquitoes can be fierce in early summer. Some 14 miles of the Pacific Crest Trail traverse the wilderness, in addition to 38 miles of other

LOCATION: 62 miles southeast of Eugene; 64 miles southwest of Bend
SIZE: 52,337 acres
ELEVATION RANGE: 4,790 to 8,744 feet
MAJOR FLORA: Lodgepole pine, mountain hemlock, noble and silver fir
ADMINISTRATION: Willamette NF, Middle Fork RD, 541-782-2283; Deschutes NF, Crescent RD, 541-433-3200
BEST SEASON: June to September
GETTING THERE: From Eugene, take OR 58 east through Oakridge to the wilderness, which lies just south of Willamette Pass. From Bend, take US 97 south to OR 58, then take OR 58 west to Willamette Pass.

trails. The highest-use areas—Marie, Divide, and Rockpile Lakes—are popular base camps for the climb up Diamond Peak.

Climbing Diamond Peak is no more than a long day hike. The views on top are spectacular. The nontechnical climb does require boulder hopping, so sturdy shoes are necessary. Most people approach the climb from Emigrant Pass near Summit Lake. From the parking area to the summit is a 6-mile but several-thousand-foot climb, so give yourself plenty of time, and bring plenty of water, since water sources are scarce on the peak. Those not wanting to rush the climb will camp at Rockpile or Marie Lake and ascend the mountain from their base camp, cutting down considerably on the length of the hike.

Diamond Peak is a basaltic andesite shield volcano less than 100,000 years old. The central core cone is surrounded by lava flows. A vent on its northern summit produced the first lava flows on the mountain. This was followed by a second vent on the southern summit that also released more lava. Then glaciers carved away at the mountain's sides, creating cirque basins. Glaciers still cling to the mountain slopes.

Forests of mountain hemlock, lodgepole and western white pine, and silver, noble, and other true firs cover most of the wilderness. The summit of Diamond Peak rises above timberline. Wildlife here reflects that found elsewhere along the Cascade Crest: black bear, Roosevelt elk, black-tailed deer, mountain lion, snowshoe hare, red squirrel, and various bird species.

DAY HIKE: YORAN LAKE
One-way Length: 4.3 miles
Elevation Range: 4,800 to 5,950 feet
Difficulty: Moderate

Yoran Lake offers nice views of Diamond Peak and fishing for brook and rainbow trout. The Yoran Trail begins at the west end of Odell Lake and ends at Yoran Lake. This gradually climbing trail starts in a forest of Engelmann spruce, silver fir, and noble fir. At about a mile, you encounter a wet meadow. The trail continues to a mountain hemlock–white fir forest with small openings near the lakes. Some heavily used campsites exist on the lake for those interested in staying the night.

Diamond Peak

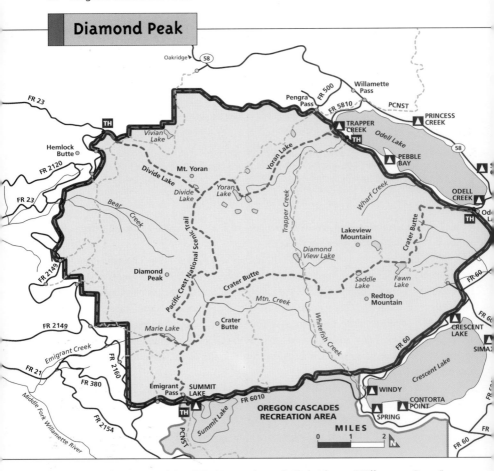

From Eugene, drive OR 58 east through Oakridge to Willamette Pass. Just beyond the pass is the turnoff for FR 5810, which leads around the west end of Odell Lake to the Yoran/Trapper Trailhead. The trailhead is about 2 miles from OR 58.

DAY HIKE: DIVIDE LAKE
One-way Length: 4 miles
Elevation Range: 5,330 to 6,390 feet
Difficulty: Moderate

Glacially carved, blue-green Divide Lake reflects three different peaks in its waters, including 7,100-foot Mount Yoran and 8,744-foot Diamond Peak. The hike to it is relatively easy, passing several other small lakes en route including Notch Lake. Most of the hike is along a ridge that provides occasional views of the mountains. Huckleberry is abundant along the route in August; mosquitoes are a plague in July. The trail goes 0.6 mile to a trail junction. Continue left past Notch Lake for 0.4 mile to another junction—stay right and follow the Mount Yoran Trail 3.2 miles to Divide Lake.

From Eugene, take OR 58 to the turnoff for Hills Creek Reservoir just 1 mile beyond Oakridge. Go 0.5 mile on FR 21, then proceed straight ahead on FR 23. Follow this road for 19.5 miles to Hemlock Butte Pass. Just beyond the pass is a sign for the trailhead, a few hundred yards up a spur road.

OVERNIGHT HIKE: CRATER BUTTE TRAIL TO MARIE LAKE
One-way Length: 14.3 miles
Elevation Range: 4,850 to 6,200 feet
Difficulty: Moderate

This makes a nice two- to three-day overnight hike, passing through some beautiful forest with occasional views of Diamond Peak. Meadows rim a portion of Marie Lake's shoreline; views of Diamond Peak require a short climb upslope. The lake makes a good destination for backpackers. The Crater Butte Trail begins at the east end of Odell Lake near Odell Lake Resort. The trail starts in Douglas fir–white fir–mountain hemlock forest, then grades into lodgepole pine and back to a mountain hemlock–noble fir forest. It passes by junctions for Fawn, Saddle, and Stag Lakes, all providing potential overnight camping. At 13.7 miles, it reaches the Pacific Crest Trail. From this junction it is 0.5 mile to Marie Lake. Marie Lake sits at 6,100 feet and contains brook trout.

From Eugene, take OR 58 east beyond Willamette Pass to the turnoff for Odell Creek Campground and Odell Lake Resort, on the southeastern shore of the lake. The trailhead begins near the lodge.

Diamond Peak at sunset, Diamond Peak Wilderness

SHUTTLE HIKE: PACIFIC CREST TRAIL #2000
One-way Length: 18.2 miles
Elevation Range: 5,100 to 7,100 feet
Difficulty: Strenuous

This section of the Pacific Crest National Scenic Trail (PCT) lies between Emigrant Pass (Summit Lake) and Willamette Pass. The trail goes around the eastern base of Diamond Peak near timberline at about 7,100 feet. Diamond Peak has been deeply cut into by glaciers, leaving sharp divides (aretes) separating great bowls (cirques). Basaltic lava and volcanic cinders and ash make up this stratovolcano. The PCT passes a number of lakes, including Yoran and Marie, which are short distances from the trail.

These directions get you to the southern trailhead near Emigrant Pass. From Eugene, take OR 58 just beyond Oakridge to FR 21. Take FR 21 south to Hills Creek Reservoir. Continue around the reservoir and drive about 31 miles to FR 2154. Follow signs for Summit Lake and FR 6010. Go around Summit Lake to the Emigrant Pass parking area. To reach the northern trailhead, take OR 58 to Willamette Pass.

OTHER RECREATIONAL OPPORTUNITIES

Most of the Diamond Peak Wilderness is far from paved access roads; it's essentially inaccessible in winter except to hardy adventurers intent on a major expedition. Access to the north side of the wilderness is available from the Gold Lake Snow Park on OR 58 near Willamette Pass. One of the easier skis is the short trip to Midnight Lake. Beginning at the Gold Lake Snow Park, it is 2.7 miles one way. Longer trips along the PCT beyond Midnight Lake are possible. Snowshoeing or skiing in from the Crescent Lake Lodge to Fawn Lake is also a popular winter trek.

Gearhart Mountain Wilderness   15

Cliffs by The Dome, Gearhart Mountain Wilderness

THIS IS ONE OF THOSE ISOLATED WILDLANDS so far off the beaten track that few ever visit it. The area features lovely, open forests interspersed with occasional meadows. As one of the higher summits in southeastern Oregon, the broadly sloping 8,364-foot summit of Gearhart Mountain is visible from all directions. The Gearhart Mountain Wilderness was first given protection as a Wild Area in 1943, a Forest Service administrative designation. Congress included it as one of the original wilderness areas established under the 1964 Wilderness Act. The 1984 Oregon Wilderness Act enlarged the wilderness by 4,144 acres to its current size of 22,833 acres.

Gearhart Mountain is an old "volcanic eruptive center" made up of andesitic lavas. This ancient volcano was then cut and scoured by glaciers. Evidence

LOCATION: 12 miles northeast of Bly; 40 miles northwest of Lakeview

SIZE: 22,833 acres

ELEVATION RANGE: 5,900 to 8,364 feet

MAJOR FLORA: Ponderosa pine, Douglas fir, white fir, whitebark pine, chaparral

ADMINISTRATION: Fremont NF, 541-947-2151

BEST SEASON: June to October

GETTING THERE: From Bly, take OR 140 east 13 miles to FR 3660, and turn left by Quartz Mountain Snow Park. Drive 13 miles, then turn right onto FR 34. Drive a very short distance, turn left onto FR 012, go past Corral Creek Campground, and look for the trailhead sign.

for this past glaciation can be seen in both the U-shaped canyons of Gearhart Creek and Dairy Creek, and in the glacial cirques found at the heads of some of the wilderness's drainages. Ash from Mount Mazama (Crater Lake) covers the ground to a depth of 2 feet. There is only one water body in the wilderness, 18-acre Blue Lake. Gearhart Marsh, a large meadow-wetlands, lies northwest of Blue Lake.

Gearhart Mountain stands east of the Cascades in a region that has a more continental climate. Winters are cold but often clear. Annual precipitation varies from 30 to 40 inches depending on elevation. Nearly all precipitation comes as snow, and at least one measuring device collected 100 inches at 7,000 feet near Deming Creek. In summer, the daytime temperatures can be warm, even hot. But skies are usually clear, except for occasional afternoon thundershowers.

The vegetation reflects the climate on the drier east side of the Cascades. This includes open ponderosa pine forests grading into white fir, and lodgepole pine at the middle elevations. Whitebark pine is found on the highest ridges, while aspen is common along the edges of meadows. Two rare plants in the wilderness are blue-leaved penstemon and green-tinged paintbrush.

Wildlife includes elk, deer, black bear, mountain lion, coyote, marmot, and other forest species of eastern Oregon. Blue Lake is stocked annually with trout.

The proposed Dead Horse Rim Wilderness lies just east of the Gearhart Mountain Wilderness on the eastern side of FR 3372. The proposed Coleman Rim Wilderness lies just to the southeast across FR 34. Both roadless areas, if protected, would add considerably to the biological value of all three areas.

OVERNIGHT BACKPACK OR ONE-WAY SHUTTLE: GEARHART MOUNTAIN TRAIL #100
One-way Length: 13.5 miles
Elevation Range: 6,340 to 8,120 feet
Difficulty: Moderate

The Gearhart Mountain Trail traverses the wilderness north-south. Few people hike the trail end to end; rather, they hike partway and return the same way. If you're interested in hiking, the Wild and Scenic North Fork of the Sprague River provides access to Blue Lake and fishing. If you're interested in views, the Lookout Rock entrance quickly gains elevation to rocky outcrops that provide expansive views. The Palisades—10 acres of convoluted rock outcrops, balancing rocks, and deeply incised, rock-walled mazes—is less than a mile from the Lookout Rock Trailhead.

Beyond the Palisades lies the Dome, a 300-foot-high rock monolith. If you continue 4.7 miles from the trailhead, you'll reach a saddle at 7,930 feet with great views of Gearhart Mountain. Another 1.3 miles farther up the trail, you'll come to the Notch, a break in the rocky cliffs that lead up to the north face of Gearhart Mountain. From the Notch, it's another 4 miles to Blue Lake and 6.8 miles to the North Fork Trailhead on FR 015. For those only interested in fishing Blue Lake, it is easiest to start at the North Fork Trailhead. Blue Lake is only 2.8 miles down along an easy trail.

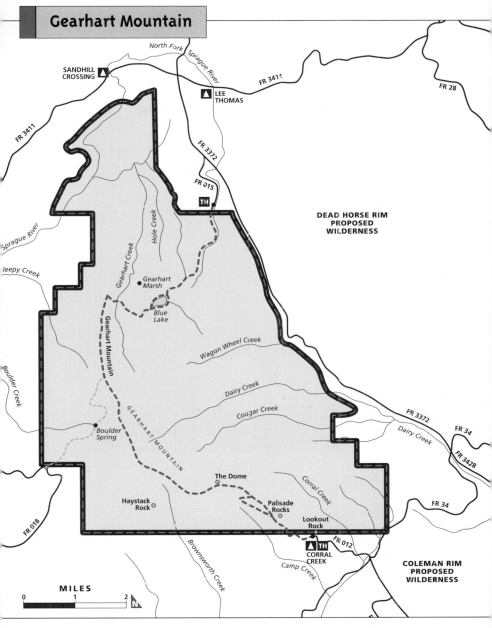

Gearhart Mountain

To reach the Lookout Rock Trailhead from Bly, head east on OR 140 for 0.5 mile, turn left on Campbell Road, go 0.5 mile to FR 34, and turn right. Drive 15 miles on FR 34 to FR 012. Turn left and follow the road 2 miles to the trailhead by Corral Creek Campground. To reach the North Fork Trailhead from Bly, go east on OR 140 0.5 mile to Campbell Road, turn left, go 0.5 mile to FR 34, and turn right. Drive 19 miles to FR 3372, turn left, and proceed 9 miles to FR 015. Turn left and follow FR 015 for 2 miles to the trailhead.

16 Mark O. Hatfield (Columbia) Wilderness

East Fork Eagle Creek, Hatfield (Columbia) Wilderness

LOCATION: 30 miles east of Portland

SIZE: 39,000 acres

ELEVATION RANGE: 1,200 to 4,736 feet

MAJOR FLORA: Old-growth Douglas fir–western hemlock, silver fir, western red cedar

ADMINISTRATION: Mount Hood National Forest, Hood River RD, 541-352-6002; Columbia River Gorge National Scenic Area, 541-386-2333

BEST SEASON: Year-round, but higher elevations are closed until May

GETTING THERE: From Portland, drive I-84 east 36 miles. Exit at Cascade Locks onto US 30, from which numerous trails start. The wilderness is also accessible from Hood River via I-84 and US 30.

THIS WILDERNESS PROTECTS the higher reaches of the 80-mile-long, more than 4,000-foot-deep Columbia River Gorge. This chasm is unique in cutting through the entire Cascade Range—most rivers start at the crest of the range and flow westward. This spectacular landscape has the greatest concentration of waterfalls in the country—77 on the Oregon side alone—including Multnomah Falls, the second highest year-round waterfall in the United States. Besides waterfalls and stately old-growth forests, vantage points in the wilderness offer fantastic views of the Columbia River from numerous cliff-face promontories. Some 90 miles of trails across the wilderness provide ample opportunities for exploration, including 14 miles of the

Pacific Crest Trail (PCT). Many of these trails are extremely steep, with some rising as much as 3,700 feet over the course of 5 to 6 miles.

As the only low-elevation gap in the Cascades, the gorge is a major transportation corridor, with an interstate highway, a state highway, a railroad, and smaller roads all squeezed into the limited amount of flat ground along the Columbia River. The gap in the mountains also transports weather: Well over 100 inches of precipitation falls on the slopes of the Cascades above Portland, although as you move eastward the amount of precipitation gradually diminishes. By the time you reach the middle of the gorge at Cascade Locks, there are "only" 75 inches of precipitation. Hood River, at the gorge's eastern entrance, receives a relatively scant 29 inches of precipitation annually.

Most of this moisture comes as rain at lower elevations, but snow accumulates to great depths at higher elevations. The vegetation responds to these changes with moist, fern-lined forests of Douglas fir and western hemlock in the west gradually giving way to Oregon white oak and ponderosa pine in the east. More than a dozen rare plants are endemic to the gorge, most of them residing on cliffs, including Columbia kittentails, long-bearded hawkweed, Howell's bentgrass, Columbia Gorge arnica, and Barrett's penstemon.

Wildlife found here includes elk, black-tailed deer, black bear, mountain lion, pine marten, bald eagle, spotted owl, and the Larch Mountain salamander, which is found only in this region. Salmon spawn in the lower reaches of some of the streams outside of the wilderness, but waterfalls and cascades prevent salmon from migrating very far upstream.

Wildlands supporters were greatly offended when in 1996 the 39,000-acre wilderness was renamed the Mark O. Hatfield Wilderness by Congress for the long-time Oregon senator. Hatfield was one of the most ardent foes of wilderness ever to represent Oregon in Congress. True, Hatfield did sponsor wilderness legislation, but generally only for "rock and ice" areas. He fought against every wilderness proposal bill for sites with large trees that could otherwise serve timber industry interests. His sponsorship of Oregon wilderness legislation in 1984 was motivated more by the effort to free up lands for logging than by any genuine concern for Oregon's forests, watersheds, or wildlife. (Because of a conservationist lawsuit against the Forest Service's second Roadless Area Review Evaluation, roadless lands at that time could only be released for timber harvest by an act of Congress, effectively requiring legislators to pass some kind of wilderness bill.) Furthermore, through the use of congressional riders and huge taxpayer-funded subsidies to the timber industry, Hatfield did much more to destroy than to protect Oregon's old-growth forests and wilderness through wilderness designation. A more appropriate legacy for the former senator would be a sign on the largest clear-cuts in the state commemorating his efforts to erase Oregon's natural heritage. Despite the official name, for the rest of this book, the wilderness will be referred to by its original name—the Columbia Wilderness.

The Columbia Wilderness reflects major geological events that define the Pacific Northwest's distinctive topography. The rocks that make up the cliffs and mountains were created some 6 to 17 million years ago, when huge basalt flows spread out from volcanoes in the Columbia Basin to the east. A hard, black rock, basalt is exposed in the many cliff faces throughout the gorge. Known as the Columbia River basalts, more than 300 individual lava flows account for the region's basalt coverage, but the majority of flows occurred between 16.5 and 15.5 million years ago and are called the Grande Ronde basalts (after the fine examples of these flows in the Grande Ronde River Canyon of eastern Oregon). Composing the bulk of the cliff surfaces we see today in the Columbia River Gorge, these lava flows also formed the flat-topped plateaus common in the wilderness, as well as the waterfalls for which the gorge is famous.

Ice Age glaciers carved out small cirques, or bowl-like basins, on some of the north-facing slopes. But the Ice Age had another greater geological impact on the gorge. After glaciers moving south into present-day northern Idaho dammed up what is now the Clark Fork of the Columbia River, giant floods repeatedly inundated the gorge. The huge glacial lake created at the dam would periodically burst, sending huge, catastrophic floods down the Columbia River. These walls of water scoured the basalt canyons of what is now eastern Washington, creating the scablands. Floodwaters raced down the Columbia Gorge, a bottleneck, backing up waters to a depth of 800 feet. What is now Crown Point was under water. The present gorge was only created in the last 2 million years, as the Cascade Range was uplifted and the river cut down through the rock.

Indian tribes often traveled through the river gorge, a natural transportation corridor. Although several rapids and even falls had to be portaged, Indians in canoes readily ran the river to tidewater. Explorers Lewis and Clark were the first whites to enter the gorge, recording sightings of elk, black bear, and California condor here. England established a major fur trading outpost in 1825 at Fort Vancouver (on the site of present-day Vancouver, Washington), the first permanent white settlement in the area, as part of its powerful, fur-trading Hudson's Bay Company. Trappers and traders traveling to Fort Vancouver noted the mild climate of the Willamette Valley and its fertile soils, and soon people from across the United States were making the six-month trek from Independence, Missouri, to Oregon City on the Oregon Trail.

The gorge became the last obstacle for the would-be settlers to overcome: It was so narrow and rough that they could not construct a road through it. Some immigrants dismantled their wagons and built rafts that were floated through the treacherous rapids (now under reservoir waters) of the gorge. In 1845, Barlow Road was constructed around Mount Hood, providing an alternative means for immigrants to get to the Willamette Valley and allowing most people to avoid the gorge route.

Most of this historic area became part of the Mount Hood National Forest. Although the Columbia Wilderness was designated as part of the 1984 Oregon Wilderness Bill, local concerns about overdevelopment outside of the wilderness persisted. In 1986, the 292,500-acre Columbia River Gorge National Scenic Area was created, including both wilderness and non-wilderness lands in the gorge area. The goal of the scenic area is to bring about compatible growth and development within developed areas, and protection of the gorge's scenery and wildlife.

Conservationists are proposing that 44,000 additional acres comprising the lower-elevation lands between the existing wilderness and US 30 be added to the existing wilderness. This new 83,000-acre wilderness, including Horsetail Falls and Larch Mountain, would be renamed the Columbia Gorge Wilderness.

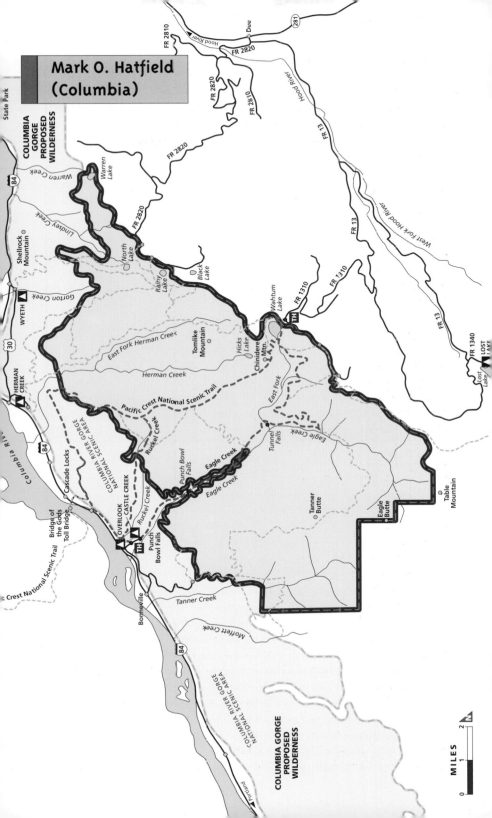

Mark O. Hatfield
(Columbia)

Campfire, Hatfield (Columbia) Wilderness

DAY HIKE: PUNCH BOWL FALLS–EAGLE CREEK TRAIL
One-way Length: 2.1 miles
Elevation Range: 120 to 400 feet
Difficulty: Moderate

Punch Bowl Falls is one of the loveliest waterfalls in the gorge. Falling over a 10-foot lip, the falls drop into a giant, swirling green pool draped in moss and ferns. The spectacular hike to Punch Bowl is along a beautiful stream past numerous waterfalls on Eagle Creek Trail #440. Beyond the falls, the upper part of this trail lies within the official wilderness boundary (technically the waterfall is not within the wilderness, but since the canyon on either side of the trail is, we can include it). Cut from streamside cliffs, the trail can be a problem for those are made uneasy by sheer drop-offs. Small children should be kept under control and close to the parents.

From Portland, go east on I-84 to Exit 41. If you're coming from Hood River on I-84, you must take Exit 40, then go east on I-84 East to Exit 41. The Eagle Creek Trailhead and trail to Punch Bowl Falls are less than a mile off the interstate, just beyond the fish hatchery.

DAY HIKE: CHINIDERE MOUNTAIN
One-way Length: 1.9 miles
Elevation Range: 3,950 to 4,673 feet
Difficulty: Moderate

This short hike begins as an amble through some old-growth noble fir forest and ends with outstanding vistas on the mountain summit. Begin by hiking down to Wahtum Lake, then take the Pacific Crest Trail (#2000) along the west side of the lake, but continue toward the outlet of the lake and the Eagle Creek Trail. From the lake outlet, it is 1.3 miles up the 4,673-foot mountain via switchbacks to an outstanding view at a former lookout site. There are terrific wildflower displays on the southwestern slope of the mountain in July. On a clear day, volcanoes from Mount Rainier to Mount Jefferson are visible from the peak.

From Hood River, follow the Hood River Highway (OR 281) and signs for Tucker County Park and proceed to Dee. At Dee, turn right onto FR 13, which leads to Lost Lake. After about 6 miles, take the right fork on FR 13 and follow it to a right onto FR 1310, which leads to the trailhead.

LOOP HIKE: EAGLE CREEK–PACIFIC CREST TRAIL
Trail Length: 30 miles
Elevation Range: 400 to 4,200 feet
Difficulty: Strenuous

This 3- to 4-day loop combines the Eagle Creek Trail, the Pacific Crest Trail (PCT), and a short hike on a connector trail between Cascade Locks and the Eagle Creek Trailhead. The route provides a good introduction to the Columbia Wilderness's special charms, including plenty of waterfalls, old-growth forests, and vistas. The first day is spent on Eagle Creek, passing waterfalls like Punch Bowl, Metlako, and Tunnel Falls. There's a camp just beyond Tunnel Falls at 7.2 miles.

On day two, continue uphill along the East Fork of Eagle Creek to beautiful Wahtum Lake where you can find numerous campsites, good fishing for brook trout, and abundant huckleberry. Wahtum Lake is 13.3 miles from the Eagle Creek Trailhead. Day three, head northbound on the PCT. It's mostly downhill from here, but you'll need to camp somewhere between Wahtum Lake and Cascade Locks, unless you can manage 15 miles plus the 2.5-mile connector in one day. The last day hike is from the PCT via connector Trail #400 back to your vehicle at Eagle Creek Trailhead. A shortcut is to take the Ruckel Creek Trail #405 from the PCT back to your car.

From Portland, go east on I-84 to Exit 41. From Hood River, drive I-84 West, take Exit 40, then turn back east on I-84 to Exit 41. The Eagle Creek Trailhead is less than a mile from the interstate, just beyond the fish hatchery.

17 Menagerie Wilderness

Trout Creek, Menagerie Wilderness

ONE OF THE SMALLEST designated wilderness areas in Oregon, Menagerie Wilderness was created by the 1984 Wilderness Act. A series of rocky spires and pinnacles, particularly Rooster Rock, attract climbers from throughout the region. Views include the snow-covered peaks of the Three Sisters. Two main drainages meander through the area, Trout Creek and Keith Creek.

The Douglas fir–western hemlock forest here burned in 1870 in a 10,000-acre blaze. Understory plants include salal, sword fern, vine maple, and Oregon grape. Small pockets of old-growth exist at Trout Creek and

LOCATION: 18 miles east of Sweet Home
SIZE: 5,033 acres
ELEVATION RANGE: 1,600 to 3,900 feet
MAJOR FLORA: Douglas fir, western hemlock, western red cedar
ADMINISTRATION: Willamette National Forest, Sweet Home RD, 541-367-5168
BEST SEASON: April to November
GETTING THERE: From Sweet Home, take US 20 east 18 miles to the Trout Creek Trailhead on the north side of the highway.

Keith Creek. Giant chinquapin and red-barked Pacific madrone grow on the rocky summit ridge.

The rocky spires along the ridgeline consists of basalt and other igneous rocks from the volcanoes that created the western Cascades. These spires were once conduits that carried geothermal waters up through the volcanoes. More resistant to erosion, the slightly harder rock of these ancient conduits has endured.

The two trails in the wilderness both lead to Rooster Rock. Trout Creek Trail #3405 is slightly longer than the steeper Rooster Rock Trail #3399.

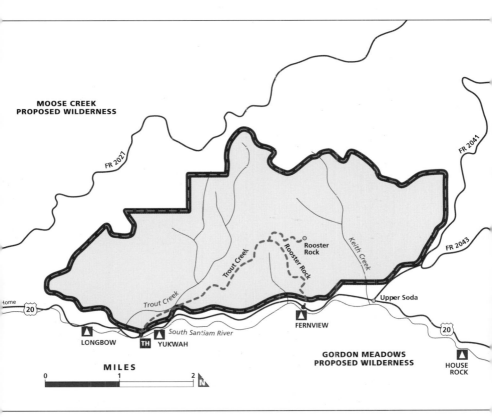

DAY HIKE: ROOSTER ROCK TRAIL #3399
One-way Length: 2.0 miles
Elevation Range: 1,300 to 3,567 feet
Difficulty: Moderate

A knoll that provides magnificent views at the top of the ridge, Rooster Rock is also a rock climbing destination. The first part of this trail climbs slowly for 0.9 mile, then more steeply for another 0.6 mile to its junction with the Trout Creek Trail. From here it is another half mile to the top of the ridge.

From Sweet Home, take US 20 east for 20 miles. No parking is available at the trailhead, so park on the side of the highway and walk back to the trailhead.

DAY HIKE: TROUT CREEK #3405
One-way Length: 2.8 miles
Elevation Range: 1,234 to 3,567 feet
Difficulty: Moderate

This smooth, graded trail gradually but steadily ascends through the 130-year-old trees of the wilderness to the rocky summit of Rooster Rock. A half mile from Rooster Rock, the Trout Creek Trail joins the Rooster Rock Trail for the final push to the base of Rooster Rock.

From Sweet Home, take US 20 east 18 miles to the Trout Creek Trailhead, on the north side of the highway.

Middle Santiam Wilderness 18

Middle Santiam River, Middle Santiam Wilderness

THE SELDOM-VISITED Middle Santiam Wilderness, created by the 1984 Oregon Wilderness Act, protects one of the few large remaining stands of ancient forest in the heavily logged western Cascades. Trees older than 450 years are common. Indeed, some believe that this wilderness and the surrounding roadless lands contain the largest continuous tract of old-growth forest left in the Cascades. Forest species include Douglas fir, western hemlock, western red cedar, noble fir, and bigleaf maple. Sugar pine, with 12- to 20-inch cones, reach their northern limits here. Forests with old-growth characteristics such as downed, woody debris, snags, and fallen logs are common. The highest peak in the wilderness is 4,965-foot Chimney Peak, a former lookout site. From its summit, views of the entire upper Santiam drainage are possible, as are the High Cascades volcanoes from Mount Thielsen to Mount Hood.

LOCATION: 60 miles east of Salem

SIZE: 8,542 acres

ELEVATION RANGE: 1,600 to 5,022 feet

MAJOR FLORA: Old-growth Douglas fir, western hemlock, noble fir

ADMINISTRATION: Willamette NF, Sweet Home RD, 541-367-5168

BEST SEASON: June to November

GETTING THERE: From Albany on I-5, take US 20 east through Sweet Home and Cascadia to FR 2041 at Upper Soda. Turn left on FR 2041 and proceed to the trailhead.

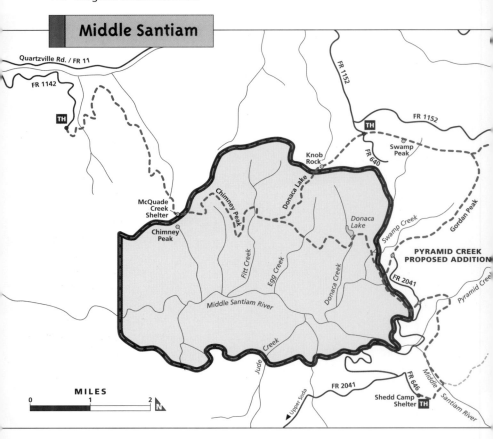

The soils in this area are particularly unstable. The line of cliffs by Donaca Lake are the result of an ancient landslide. Indeed, one of the original access roads into the wilderness was closed as a consequence of landslides. Logging such unstable slopes results in high sediment loads in the area rivers and is one of the major factors contributing to declining salmon and trout populations. The green-pooled Middle Santiam River flows through the center of the wilderness and is known as one of the most productive wild trout fisheries in the state. Rainbow trout are abundant, but only Donaca Lake supports cutthroat trout.

Wildlife species common in the Cascades are found here, including elk, black-tailed deer, black bear, mountain lion, marten, and snowshoe hare. Some spotted owls also live here, along with populations of Pacific newt, Cascades frog, long-toed salamander, and the boreal toad.

Surrounding the Middle Santiam Wilderness are some 16,000 roadless acres including Pyramid Creek, scene of anti-logging demonstrations in the early 1990s. Today, thanks to these efforts, most of the Pyramid Creek drainage remains roadless and could be added to the Middle Santiam Wilderness someday.

Despite its small size, the wilderness boasts three trails. McQuade Creek Trail accesses the northwestern corner of the wilderness, Chimney Peak Trail the southeastern corner, and Gordan Peak Trail the northeastern corner.

DAY HIKE: DONACA LAKE–CHIMNEY PEAK TRAIL
One-way Length: 5 miles
Elevation Range: 2,300 to 4,965 feet
  Difficulty: Strenuous

The first part of this hike lies within the proposed Pyramid Creek addition to the Middle Santiam Wilderness and passes through magnificent old-growth forests. From the trailhead the trail switchbacks for 0.75 mile to the Middle Santiam River by Shedd Camp Shelter. There is a wonderful pool here for swimming. The trail crosses the Middle Santiam River (no bridge) and continues upslope through old-growth. Eventually you descend down to Pyramid Creek, where you'll find a beautiful campsite. Those interested in only a short hike can turn around here; otherwise, cross the stream and head uphill to FR 2041, closed by a landslide near the Middle Santiam River. The trail enters the wilderness area just beyond the road and soon reaches the junction with Gordan Peak Trail #3387. Continue straight ahead to Donaca Lake. Most people go no farther than the lake, but the trail continues on to the base of Chimney Peak, once the site of a lookout.

From Sweet Home, take US 20 east to Upper Soda (there's only a restaurant). Turn left on FR 2041 (Soda Fork Road). Stay on FR 2041, passing many side roads and clear-cuts. After crossing a pass, continue downhill to a short spur of FR 646 to FR 647 and the trailhead parking.

LOOP BACKPACK: DONACA LAKE
  Trail Length: 15.8 miles
Elevation Range: 3,500 to 4,800 feet
    Difficulty: Strenuous

This loop takes you through the majestic old-growth of the Middle Santiam and of the Pyramid Creek proposed addition to the wilderness. Trout-filled Donaca Lake makes a good overnight campsite. From the parking area you can travel either way, but for the sake of this description, start by heading west, skirting the talus slopes of Knob Rock. Enter the Middle Santiam Wilderness and continue a total of 3.2 miles from the trailhead to a junction with Chimney Peak Trail #3382. At this junction, turn left and go approximately 2.2 miles to Donaca Lake, where you'll find several campsites. From Donaca Lake, continue east on Chimney Peak Trail and cross Swamp Creek to reach the junction with Gordan Peak Trail #3387. Turn left onto Gordan Peak Trail and follow this 3.5 miles toward Gordan Peak. At the junction with Swamp Peak Trail #3401, turn left again and go 2.2 miles back over 4,835-foot Swamp Peak to your starting point.

From Sweet Home, drive east on US 20 for 4 miles and turn left on FR 11 (Quartzville Road). Travel 35 miles up the Quartzville Road and turn right on FR 1152. Travel 3.2 miles to spur Road 640, turn right, and continue 1.2 miles to the trailhead.

19 Mount Hood Wilderness

Wildflowers on Vista Ridge, Mount Hood Wilderness

GIVEN ITS OVERALL MAJESTIC APPEARANCE, combined with good year-round access from Portland, Oregon's largest city, it's not surprising that this is one of the most popular wilderness areas in Oregon. The namesake 11,240-foot, glacier-clad mountain—the highest peak in the state—stands alone, rising above its surroundings in stately splendor. Though plenty of people hike, ski, or backpack in this wilderness, what makes it different from most other wilderness areas in the state is first-rate climbing. One of the major glacier-clad peaks in the country, Hood attracts a national following of climbers who are challenged by the mountain's height and slopes. But visitors

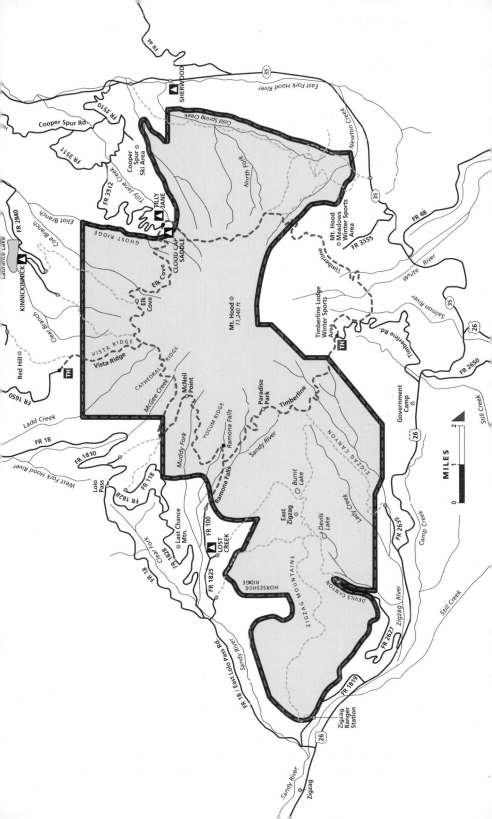

LOCATION: 25 miles east of Portland

SIZE: 47,160 acres

ELEVATION RANGE: 1,800 to 11,240 feet

MAJOR FLORA: Alpine meadows, noble fir, Douglas fir, grand fir, subalpine fir, Pacific silver fir, lodgepole pine, mountain hemlock

ADMINISTRATION: Mount Hood National Forest: Information Center, 503-622-7674; Hood River RD, 541-352-6002

BEST SEASON: June to October

GETTING THERE: From Portland, take US 26 east through Sandy and on to Zigzag. The wilderness begins just after the intersection of FR 18 (East Lolo Pass Road) and US 26.

should not approach the mountain lightly. With broken volcanic rock that provides few solid foot- and handholds, glaciers and steep snowfields to cross, and stormy weather the norm, Mount Hood also has one of the highest accident rates of all the Earth's peaks.

Mount Hood is still considered an active volcano, and sulfurous steam is often seen near the summit. Indeed, Hood is one of the major volcanoes of the Cascade Range, having erupted repeatedly for hundreds of thousands of years, most recently during two episodes in the past 1,500 years. The last episode ended shortly before the arrival of Lewis and Clark in 1805. Recent eruptions are related to the growth and collapse of lava domes.

The other major influence upon Hood's appearance has been glaciation. At least twelve named glaciers and snowfields now cover the volcano. During the past Ice Age between 29,000 and 10,000 years ago, all of these glaciers were much larger, with their terminus lying at the 3,000-foot level or even lower. Today most glaciers are found at 6,500 feet or higher. Outwash from these Ice Age glaciers filled what is today the Hood River Valley near Parkdale, contributing to its present-day flat surface.

Much of the area's annual precipitation of 150 inches (western slope) falls as snow between October and April; summers tend to be dominated by clear, dry weather. The heavy precipitation feeds a lower-elevation forest of Douglas fir with understory of Oregon grape, salal, rhododendron, and huckleberry. Higher-elevation forests include silver fir, noble fir, whitebark pine, and mountain hemlock. Grand fir is common on the drier east side. But the real attractions of Hood are the extensive subalpine and alpine flower gardens at higher elevations. Filled with lupine, paintbrush, western pasqueflower, Cascade aster, white avalanche lily, and beargrass, these natural gardens encircle the peak and provide a *Sound of Music* atmosphere for hikers who reach these floral displays.

The Mount Hood area was first set aside by the Forest Service as a 14,800-acre Primitive Area. In 1940, its size was reduced slightly and it was reclassified as a Wild Area—an early precursor of the wilderness designation. It was then incorporated as one of the original Wilderness Areas designated by Congress in the 1964 Wilderness Act.

More than 10,000 climbers a year come seeking the summit, making Mount Hood the most visited snow-clad peak in America. Most climbers begin at Timberline Lodge on the south side of the mountain, near the ski area. Taking off above the ski lifts, climbers can usually make it to the top and back in less than 10 hours. At least 12 other routes up the mountain have been well established. Those just seeking a close-up look at glaciers should hike up the 3-mile Cooper Spur Trail from Cloud Cap Saddle Campground.

Some 30 trails provide access to all sides of the mountain and wilderness. The 38-mile Timberline Trail that encircles the mountain rivals the Wonderland Trail of Mount Rainier and is one of the most famous footpaths in the state.

A total of 165,000 additional acres of roadless lands surrounding Mount Hood are proposed as new additions to the wilderness. These include the Still Creek area with Tom, Dick, and Harry Mountain, as well as the Twin Lakes Roadless Area.

DAY HIKE: ELK COVE
One-way Length: 4 miles
Elevation Range: 5,150 to 5,860 feet
Difficulty: Moderate

Elk Cove is a flower-filled meadow with outstanding views of Mount Hood. Along the trail to Elk Cove, you'll also pass many other flowery meadows, plus enchanting Compass Creek Falls. From Cloud Cap Saddle Campground, find a billboard by the Timberline Trail. Go right onto Trail #600. The trail continues at more or less the same elevation to Compass Creek Falls, approximately 2 miles from the trailhead. Then it descends toward Coe Branch and climbs slightly back to Elk Cove. If you wish to camp, avoid the meadows and camp among the trees on a spur trail 100 yards downhill.

The trailhead at Cloud Cap Saddle Campground is at the end of FR 3512. From Hood River, take OR 35 south to the right-hand turnoff for Cooper Spur Ski Area. Drive the Cooper Spur Road to FR 3511, following signs for the campground, then turn left on FR 3512, and take the road to its end.

DAY HIKE: RAMONA FALLS
One-way Length: 3.3 miles
Elevation Range: 2,460 to 3,460 feet
Difficulty: Moderate

The 120-foot Ramona Falls looks like a wide curtain as it drops across a cliff face of columnar basalt in a dark wood. It is one of the most popular destinations in the wilderness. Rhododendron crowd the stream, providing for a particularly beautiful hike in June when they are in bloom. The first part of the trail follows the Wild and Scenic Sandy River, a glacial stream with a characteristic milky color (a result of glacial flour). After a mile, cross a temporary bridge placed across the river each spring. Almost immediately, you meet a trail junction. One is a horse trail—the quickest way to the falls. It proceeds up the valley, following the Sandy River until it diverts a half mile through the woods to the falls. The other option is slightly longer. The trail turns uphill to rise for 0.6 mile to the Muddy Fork, where you turn right to follow the banks of Ramona Creek 1.8 miles to the falls.

From Portland, drive US 26 east to Zigzag, and turn left onto East Lolo Pass Road (FR 18). Go about 5 miles to FR 1825, turn right, and go 2.7 miles to FR 100, a short spur that leads to the trailhead.

DAY HIKE: VISTA RIDGE
One-way Length: 2.5 miles
Elevation Range: 4,600 to 5,700 feet
Difficulty: Moderate

Vista Ridge starts out along an old road that soon turns into a trail. You come to a trail junction in 0.4 mile; turn right and continue in a mountain hemlock forest with a series of long switchbacks that take you up the ridge. You may begin to wonder how it got its name. Be patient. Eventually the forest begins to break up into tree islands with small meadows. At 2.1 miles, you reach another trail junction. The views are superb at this point. Mount Hood is squarely in front of you. Mounts Rainier, Adams, and St. Helens can be seen to the north. Flowers cover the ridge. This makes for a good place to have lunch and turn around. If you have more energy, you can turn left here to Elk Cove or right to Cairn Basin—both offer good campsites for those interested in making this into an overnight backpack.

From Portland, take US 26 east to Zigzag, and turn left onto East Lolo Pass Road (FR 18) toward Hood River. Stay on FR 18 to FR 16 and continue to follow signs for Vista Ridge, still 9 miles distant. The last part of the route is on FR 1650 and leads to a parking area.

LOOP HIKE: TIMBERLINE TRAIL #600
Trail Length: 41 miles
Elevation Range: 2,800 to 7,300 feet
Difficulty: Strenuous

Completely encircling glorious Mount Hood, the Timberline Trail is for many the ultimate hiking trail in Oregon. Generally staying at or near timberline, the trail provides outstanding vistas, wonderful strolls through countless flowery meadows, and the chance to camp with in-your-face views of Hood's glacier-clad cone. Although some people race along the trail, completing it in two days, it's probably best to take four days to complete the tour. Another option is to take one or more of the 21 trails that intersect the main trail, which allow you to walk a smaller segment. Keep in mind that because of overall high elevation, snow will block many parts of the trail, particularly on the north slope, until mid-July. The best time to hike the trail is in August and September.

The trail's difficulty arises from the necessity of crossing many stream and river channels that have carved deep canyons into the slope of the mountain. Hikers experience more than 9,000 feet of elevation change along the length of the trail. Further, many stream crossings will be difficult, especially those with headwaters in the glaciers. As the day warms and glacial ice and snow begin to melt, these streams can grow dramatically in size. For instance, between Cairn Basin and Cooper's Spur you'll encounter 13 stream crossings, and most are bridgeless. If you reach a crossing that appears treacherous, think about waiting until the following morning to attempt it. Note also that early in the season, it's best to take an ice ax for crossing steep, snowy slopes, particularly around daybreak when the snow may be crusted and hard.

Most people start at Timberline Lodge and proceed west on the Pacific Crest Trail #2000 (PCT), which also serves as the Timberline Trail for a distance. It is 10.2 miles to Ramona Falls, with crossings of Zigzag, Little Zigzag, and Sandy canyons. Those with time might want to visit Paradise Park, a flowery meadow that loops off of the PCT at about 3.7 miles. A designated campsite lies south of Ramona Falls.

From Ramona Falls, most people journey to Cairn Basin. Contour around Yocum Ridge to the Muddy Fork, then go up and over Bald Mountain, which provides great vistas across flowery meadows. Shortly after crossing the mountain, at about 5.5 miles from Ramona Falls, the PCT and Timberline Trail part company. To continue on the Timberline Trail, head east toward Cairn Basin.

The third day takes you around the northern portion of the mountain. The trail drops from Cairn Basin to Eden Park, then over Vista Ridge. Take in superb views of the mountain and the volcanoes to the north, including Rainier, Adams, and St. Helens. You'll pass Elk Cove, with radiant, flower-studded meadows, views of Mount Hood, and several nice campsites. After crossing more streams, you will arrive at Cloud Cap Saddle, where you'll find a trailhead complete with a small lodge and campground. This is a good place to terminate the hike if you're short on time, since a paved road leads to the campground from the Hood River Valley. Unless you want to camp in a regular campground, it's best to continue on to Cooper Spur, where some majestic, if stony, alpine campsites lie on the slope of Mount Hood.

It is 12.3 miles from Cooper Spur to Timberline Lodge. The vistas, east to the Cascades and south to volcanoes including Mount Jefferson and the Three Sisters, make this a great day of scenery. Watch out for the crossing of Newton Creek at 4.5 miles from Cooper Spur. After crossing the White River headwaters, which can also be troublesome, you eventually rejoin the PCT on Boy Scout Ridge and then have less than 2 more miles to Timberline Lodge and the end of the loop trip.

To get to the most popular trailhead at Timberline Lodge on the south slope of Mount Hood, take US 26 east from Portland to Government Camp, and follow signs.

OTHER RECREATIONAL OPPORTUNITIES

With two plowed and paved roads providing access to the high country, plus a dozen plowed snow parks, cross-country skiing is popular in the winter. The best skiing is available at Timberline Lodge. The Timberline Trail toward Zigzag Canyon is a popular route. The trail from Hood River Meadows to Elk Meadows is another good path, with great views of the mountain on a clear day. Off-trail routes lead from Bennett Pass Snow Park into the wilderness. Marked ski trails are widespread; check with the Forest Service for trail maps and descriptions.

20 | Mount Jefferson Wilderness

Three-Fingered Jack looms above Marion Lake, Mount Jefferson Wilderness

ONE OF THE LARGER WILDERNESS AREAS in Oregon, Mount Jefferson Wilderness is also one of the most scenic, occupying the north-central portion of the Cascades east of Salem. The Warm Springs Indian Reservation borders it to the northeast. The icy, glacier-clad volcanic cone of photogenic Mount Jefferson, Oregon's second highest mountain at 10,497 feet, is visible from any high point in the wilderness. Five glaciers mantle Mount Jefferson's slopes, and the wilderness also contains the striking, 7,841-foot Three Fingered Jack, an older, more highly eroded volcano. Most of the high country in this wilderness is wide open, almost like a park, with scattered tree cover, long talus

LOCATION: 25 miles west of Sisters; 48 miles east of Sweet Home
SIZE: 111,177 acres
ELEVATION RANGE: 3,000 to 10,497 feet
MAJOR FLORA: Lodgepole pine, Douglas fir, western hemlock, noble fir, Pacific silver fir, white pine, subalpine fir, ponderosa pine, mountain hemlock, whitebark pine
ADMINISTRATION: Willamette NF, Detroit RD, 503-854-3366; Deschutes NF, Sisters RD, 541-549-7700; Mount Hood NF, Clackamas RD, 503-630-8700
BEST SEASON: June to October
GETTING THERE: From Sisters, drive 25 miles west on US 20 to Santiam Pass. From Sweet Home, drive 48 miles east to Santiam Pass.

slopes, rocky outcroppings, alpine meadows, and year-round patches of snow. Wildflower meadows abound at higher elevations, and with more than 150 lakes, this wilderness is a justifiably popular recreation destination.

One of the 13 volcanoes of the High Cascades, the pyramid-shaped peak was named in 1806 by the Lewis and Clark expedition for President Thomas Jefferson. The Mount Jefferson vicinity was first designated a Forest Service Primitive Area in 1930. In 1933, it was expanded to 83,033 acres. When the passage of the 1964 Wilderness Act instantly upgraded many of Oregon's primitive areas like the Three Sisters to designated wilderness, the Mount Jefferson area was left out in the cold. But four years later, a Mount Jefferson Wilderness of more than 100,000 acres was officially designated and later enlarged to its present 111,177 acres

The first recorded ascent of Mount Jefferson was in 1888, when E. C. Cross and Ray Farmer scaled the mountain via the south ridge. The climb remains a technical challenge, primarily due to poor rock and an abundance of ice. Most climbs involve some snow or glacier travel, so ice axes and crampons are mandatory. The glaciers are large enough to present problems with crevasses, but they are not as extensive as those on Mount Rainier and other peaks farther north. The most popular climbing routes are on the north side and are accessed by the Whitewater Trail and Jefferson Park. Others climb the southwestern side of the mountain from a base camp at Pamelia Lake.

Mount Jefferson is a stratovolcano, basically a large cone of andesite atop a basalt foundation. The oldest rocks in the mountain are more than 3.9 million years old, but the lava that composed the Mount Jefferson cone began to erupt about 680,000 years ago—and has continued to do so periodically for hundreds of thousands of years. Ash from a particularly massive eruption, some 100,000 to 35,000 years ago, has been detected as far away as Arco, Idaho. Although its last eruptive episode was about 15,000 years ago, Mount Jefferson—like Mount St. Helens—is still capable of further large, explosive events.

The upper cone of Mount Jefferson is composed of dacite lava flows and domes. At the time of its most recent eruptions, most of the mountain was also sheathed in glaciers, so eruptions caused major mudflows when the molten rock melted the overlying ice. The most recent lava flows in the Mount Jefferson area are basaltic lava flows. Hot springs at Breitenbush just outside of the wilderness suggest that hot magma is still relatively close to the surface.

Once a small cinder cone that erupted some 300,000 years ago, Three Fingered Jack is the other major volcano in the wilderness. You can see these old lava flows as the red, orange, and gray layers in the west-facing wall of the mountain. A second major eruption occurred some 250,000 years ago, when the mountain reached an estimated height of 9,000 feet. The last eruption occurred some 200,000 years ago. This resulted in the creation of a basalt magma plug that now makes up the northern shoulder of the mountain. Glaciers then eroded away the flanks of the volcano, leaving behind just a jagged piece of the southern slope of what was once a major Cascade volcano.

As with most of the Cascades, annual precipitation is heavy, with an average of 75 inches recorded for this area. But like most of western Oregon, nearly all of that precipitation occurs as snow in the winter. Summers tend to be sunny, warm, and dry. The areas east of the Cascade Crest is considerably drier and sunnier, even in winter, making for good cross-country skiing conditions.

The abundant precipitation supports a diverse plant community. Except for above-timberline areas and a few basins with extensive subalpine meadows, nearly all of the wilderness is heavily cloaked in forests. The most common tree species are Douglas fir, silver fir, subalpine fir, western white pine, sugar pine, white fir, mountain hemlock, lodgepole pine, ponderosa pine, and western red cedar. Understory species include vine maple, beargrass, huckleberry, and Pacific rhododendron.

Wildlife includes elk, deer, black bear, mountain lion, and coyote. Despite the name Grizzly Creek, no grizzlies remain in the wilderness. Also, there are no mountain goats, though there is a Goat Mountain. Yellow-bellied marmots and pikas are common in rocky areas. At Marion Lake once, I had a river otter on my fly rod seize a rainbow trout I had hooked. The otter broke off the line and got away with the fish.

Paulina Creek, Mount Jefferson Wilderness

The wilderness is laced with 190 miles of trails, including a 40-mile stretch of the Pacific Crest National Scenic Trail #2000 (PCT). Many consider this stretch to be the best section of the trail in Oregon. Popular entry points include Summit Lake Trail #4014 from US 20 at the south end; from the west, Duffy Lake Trail #3427 off FR 2267; Marion Lake Trail #3436 off FR 2255; Pamelia Lake Trail #3439 off FR 2246, 13 miles southeast of Detroit; and Whitewater Trail #3429 off FR 2243. Breitenbush Lake is approached from the north. Popular east-side entry points are Cabot Lake Trail #3437 from FR 1234 at Jack Lake, and Jefferson Lake Trail #4001 from FR 1292.(If you wish to avoid crowds, skip the larger lakes accessed by short trails.)

Cross-country skiing in the wilderness area is difficult, since most of the access roads are snowed under, and long approaches are necessary before you even reach the wilderness boundary. Plowed-road access is limited to the Santiam Pass area, where you can find good skiing from the Santiam Snow Park. The PCT is sometimes skied, as is the 2.2-mile trail to Square Lake, which features views of Three Fingered Jack, but none are maintained ski trails, so plan on breaking your own trail. Those interested in winter camping can ski to Santiam Lake, a good overnight ski destination on a relatively level trail. Begin at the Santiam Snow Park, take the PCT about 1.7 miles to a junction, then bear left for another 3.4 miles to Santiam Lake, which offers great views of Three Fingered Jack—if the weather is clear.

Special regulations apply to this wilderness, including restrictions on group size, and even limited entry to some camping areas. Contact the Forest Service to learn about current rules.

DAY HIKE: MARION LAKE #3436
One-way Length: 2.5 miles
Elevation Range: 3,360 to 4,130 feet
Difficulty: Easy

Marion Lake is one of the most popular destinations in the wilderness, and for good reason. It is the largest lake in the wilderness, at 350 acres, and full of trout. Moreover, there are terrific views of Three Fingered Jack and Mount Jefferson from various points around the shoreline. And finally, it is a very short hike from a parking lot. Even so, if you don't like crowds, and don't like camping in places that look something like a hard-packed parking lot, then you'd best consider going someplace else. Or hike to the lake in the middle of the week just to look around and enjoy the view, when the mile-long lake doesn't make a bad day-hike destination.

The trail climbs gently in 1.3 miles to Lake Ann, where camping is banned. Continue on the trail another 0.7 mile to Marion Lake. If you want to stretch out the hike, consider climbing another 2.6 miles to the summit of Marion Mountain, a former lookout site that offers great views of Mount Jefferson. Other trails that connect from Marion Lake allow for longer loops and even overnight destinations.

From Salem, take OR 22 68 miles east to Marion Forks, then turn left (east) on FR 2255 and drive slightly more than 5 miles to the trailhead at its end.

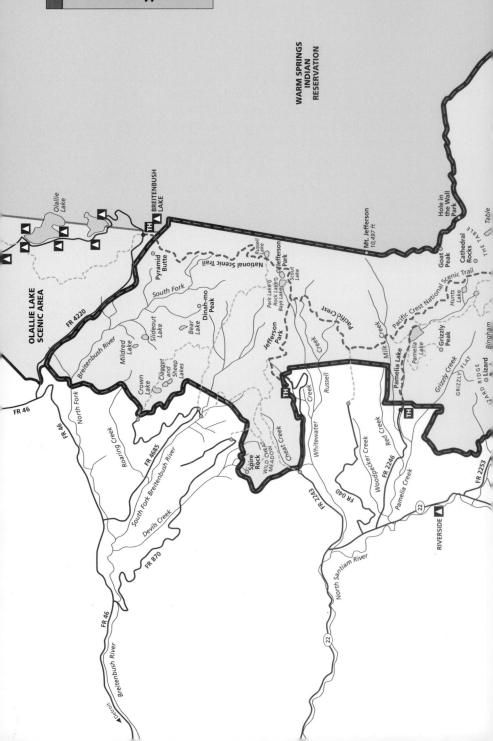

Mount Jefferson

OLALLIE LAKE SCENIC AREA

Olallie Lake

BREITENBUSH LAKE

WARM SPRINGS INDIAN RESERVATION

Hole in the Wall Park

Mt. Jefferson 10,497 ft

Russell Lake

Jefferson Park

Scout Lake

THE TABLE

Table

Cathedral Rocks

Goat Peak

Pacific Crest National Scenic Trail

National Scenic Trail

Pyramid Butte

Park Lake
Rock Lake
Bays Lakes

South Fork

Dinah-mo Peak

FR 4220

Breitenbush River

Slideout Lake

Bear Lake

Mildred Lake

Jefferson Park

Pacific Crest

Hunts Lake

Grizzly Peak

Clagget and Sheep Lakes

Crown Lake

Milk Creek

Grizzly Creek

Pamelia Lake

Pamelia Lake

GRIZZLY FLAT

LIZARD RIDGE

FR 46

North Fork

Roaring Creek

Russell Creek

Creek

TH

Bingham

Lizard

FR 46

FR 4685

South Fork Breitenbush River

Spire Rock

WILD CHEAT MEADOW

Cheat Creek

Whitewater

Russell

Creek

Woodpecker Creek

Red Creek

FR 2246

Pamelia Creek

TH

FR 2253

FR 870

Devils Creek

FR 2243

FR 040

North Santiam River

22

RIVERSIDE

FR 46

Breitenbush River

Detroit

22

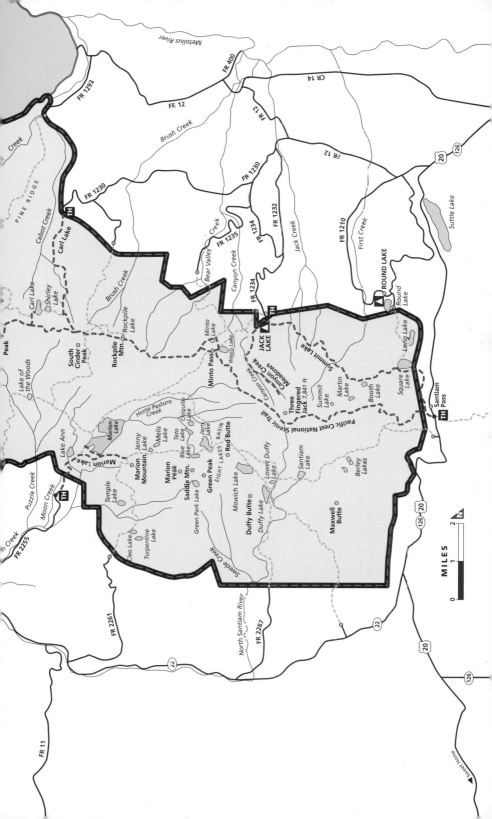

OVERNIGHT HIKE: JEFFERSON PARK
One-way Length: 5.1 miles
Elevation Range: 4,100 to 5,880 feet
Difficulty: Moderate

Jefferson Park is one of the premier scenic places in Oregon, a lake-studded basin with islands of mountain hemlock interspersed with vast wildflower meadows full of paintbrush, lupine, and heather, all overshadowed by the imposing presence of Mount Jefferson. If there's a more beautiful spot in Oregon, I haven't seen it yet. As you might imagine, many others feel the same way, so if you're looking for a quiet weekend of solitude, this may not be the place for you. Luckily for me, in three different trips to Jefferson Park I've yet to camp in the basin with another person or even encounter many people on the trail. One way to avoid crowds is to camp outside of the basin, but plan on hiking farther as a consequence.

A strong hiker may make this into a day hike, but bear in mind that a day hike requires a more-than-10-mile round-trip walk—and a climb of almost 2,000 feet. Most of the elevation gain occurs in the first part of the trail as it switchbacks up through old-growth Douglas fir forest to the Sentinel Hills and a trail junction on the ridge crest at 1.5 miles. From here the climbing is more moderate as the trail traverses the side of the ridge, crosses a saddle, and maintains a fairly level path into the basin. Enjoy terrific views of Mount Jefferson along this stretch of trail. You will encounter several popular lakeside campsites but may want to choose a less crowded site away from the lakes.

From Salem, take OR 22 about 62 miles to the Whitewater Road (FR 2243) and turn left (east). Drive 7.4 gravel miles through former forests (clear-cuts) to the trailhead.

DAY HIKE: PAMELIA LAKE #3439
One-way Length: 2.1 miles
Elevation Range: 3,100 to 3,890 feet
Difficulty: Easy

Pamelia Lake lies in a glacier bowl surrounded by dense forests with Mount Jefferson rising regally beyond. So dramatic is the scene that it reminds me of something out of the Canadian Rockies. Given the short hike and great scenery, it's not surprising that this is a popular trail. Go elsewhere if you seek solitude. The trail winds through a beautiful, mossy forest with vine maple and rhododendron as understory next to bubbling Pamelia Creek. Follow the lakeshore to the right for a fine prospect. The best view, however, is a cliff-side vista about 2 miles up the trail to Grizzly Peak.

From Salem, drive OR 22 east about 64 miles to Pamelia Road (FR 2246). Turn left (east) and go 6.7 miles to trailhead.

SHUTTLE HIKE: SUMMIT LAKE TRAIL #4014
One-way Length: 7.5 miles
Elevation Range: 4,900 to 5,400 feet
    Difficulty: Moderate

The first part of this trail is along the Pacific Crest Trail #2000. Summit Lake Trail #4014 runs around the eastern side of Three Fingered Jack from the PCT to the Jack Lake Trailhead. It continues on to Minto Pass, where it rejoins the PCT again. This hike offers a nice leg stretcher while passing several lakes en route. Arrange for a shuttle pick-up at Jack Lake Trailhead at the end of FR 1211.

From Sweet Home, drive US 20 east to Santiam Pass and a parking area for the Pacific Crest Trail and Summit Lake Trail. To reach the pick-up at Jack Lake Trailhead, drive US 20 east of Santiam Pass for 8 miles to a large sign that reads "Wilderness Trailheads." Take FR 12 to FR 1230, drive 1.5 miles, then turn left onto FR 1234 and drive to its end.

DAY HIKE: CARL LAKE
One-way Length: 5 miles
Elevation Range: 4,540 to 5,500 feet
    Difficulty: Moderate

Beautiful Carl Lake lies in a glacial basin below a rocky ridge. The trail climbs gently uphill as far as Cabot Lake but then begins to rise seriously via switchbacks to Carl Lake, which hosts cutthroat trout and a few brook trout.

Take US 20 east of Santiam Pass for 8 miles to a large sign that reads "Wilderness Trailheads." Take FR 12 to FR 1230, and follow it 8.3 miles.

DAY HIKE: CANYON CREEK MEADOWS
One-way Length: 2 miles
Elevation Range: 5,130 to 5,520 feet
    Difficulty: Easy

Full of lupine and red paintbrush with the rugged face of Three Fingered Jack rising above, Canyon Creek Meadows is gorgeous in summer. The hike winds up through lodgepole pine forests, passing several small ponds, and eventually drops down to Canyon Creek and the meadows. If you wish, hike another 0.7 mile to the upper meadows, which are even more dramatic.

Take US 20 east of Santiam Pass for 8 miles to a large sign that reads "Wilderness Trailheads." Take FR 12 to FR 1230, drive 1.5 miles, then turn left onto FR 1234 to reach Jack Lake Trailhead

SHUTTLE BACKPACK: PACIFIC CREST TRAIL–
MOUNT JEFFERSON TRAVERSE
One-way Length: 39.8 miles
Elevation Range: 4,300 to 6,900 feet
Difficulty: Strenuous

This section of the PCT is considered by many to be the most scenic segment of the trail in Oregon. For most of its length it remains at or near timberline, passing through countless subalpine meadows and past dozens of lakes. The first 7 miles traverses the west side of Three Fingered Jack. Then it follows the Cascade Crest, switchbacking across the crest before crossing the shoulder of Mount Jefferson and passing through beautiful, lake-studded Jefferson Park. Then the trail rises over Park Ridge to the exit at Skyline Road. Because Skyline Road is so rough, it is recommended that you continue another 6 miles to Olallie Lake in the Olallie Lake Scenic Area, where the access road is far better.

The southern trailhead lies along US 20 at Santiam Pass. The northern terminus is at the very rough Skyline Road on the edge of the Olallie Lake Scenic Area.

To reach the northern end from Salem, drive OR 22 east to Detroit, then take the Breitenbush River Road (FR 46) east and up the North Fork of the Breitenbush River. At the top of a pass, turn right onto FR 4220 (Skyline Road) and drive to the trailhead at Breitenbush Lake.

Horsepackers, Mount Jefferson Wilderness

Mount Thielsen Wilderness 21

Mount Thielsen, Mount Thielsen Wilderness

THE 55,100-ACRE MOUNT THIELSEN WILDERNESS straddles the crest of the Cascades just north of Crater Lake National Park. It lies at the headwaters of the Umpqua River and is surrounded on the north and west by the Oregon Cascades Recreation Area. The highest peak is 9,182-foot Mount Thielsen, a highly eroded volcano whose needlelike summit is often called the "lightning rod of the Cascades." Because of its isolated, elevated position, Mount Thielsen has indeed received more than its share of lightning strikes.

For some, the spirelike peak suggests that of the Matterhorn in the Alps. In fact, the origins of both distinctive mountains were similar. Thielsen is the remnant of a 100,000-year-old volcano's core plug—a former shield volcano of basaltic andesite built atop a broad pedestal

LOCATION: 65 miles east of Roseburg

SIZE: 55,100 acres

ELEVATION RANGE: 5,400 to 9,182 feet

MAJOR FLORA: Mountain hemlock, lodgepole pine, western white pine, whitebark pine

ADMINISTRATION: Deschutes NF, Crescent RD, 541-433-3200; Umpqua NF, Diamond Lake RD, 541-672-6601; Winema NF, Chemult RD, 541-365-7001

BEST SEASON: June to October

GETTING THERE: From Roseburg, take OR 138 east for 75 miles. Several trailheads for Mount Thielsen lie along OR 138 near Diamond Lake.

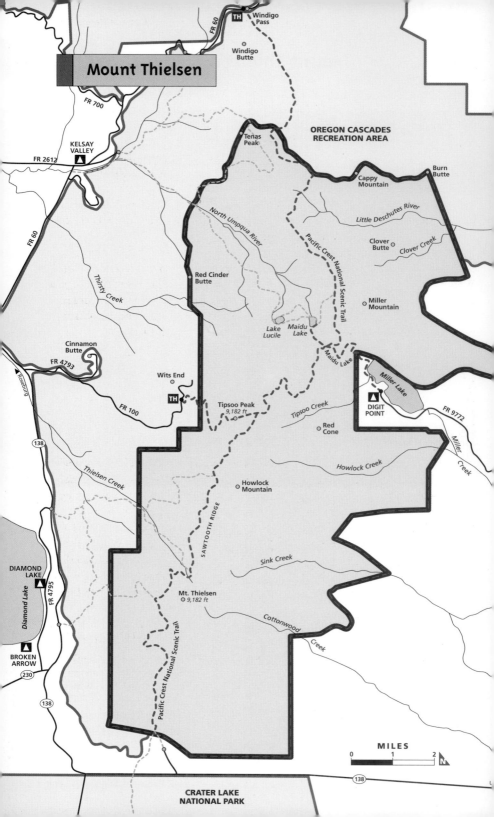

Mount Thielsen

TH Windigo Pass

Windigo Butte

FR 700

FR 60

KELSAY VALLEY

FR 2612

OREGON CASCADES RECREATION AREA

Tenas Peak

Cappy Mountain

Burn Butte

Little Deschutes River

North Umpqua River

Pacific Crest National Scenic Trail

Clover Butte

Clover Creek

Red Cinder Butte

Thirsty Creek

Miller Mountain

Lake Lucile

Maidu Lake

Cinnamon Butte

FR 4793

Maidu Lake

Miller Lake

Wits End

FR 100

TH

Tipsoo Peak
9,182 ft

Tipsoo Creek

DIGIT POINT

FR 9772

Miller Creek

Roseburg

138

Thielsen Creek

Red Cone

Howlock Creek

Howlock Mountain

SAWTOOTH RIDGE

Sink Creek

DIAMOND LAKE

FR 4795

Mt. Thielsen
9,182 ft

BROKEN ARROW

Diamond Lake

230

Cottonwood Creek

138

Pacific Crest National Scenic Trail

MILES

0   1   2

N

138

CRATER LAKE NATIONAL PARK

of older lava—that was carved by Ice Age glaciers into its current form. The peak is remarkable even at a distance for its colorfully interbedded, pyroclastic rocks that dip away from the jagged spire of the central plug. Mount Thielsen's age is approximately 290,000 years, making it much older than less eroded Cascade volcanoes like the Three Sisters or Mount Jefferson. More recently, the entire area was buried under Mount Mazama ash, which erupted from vents at Crater Lake National Park and has buried the area in as much as 60 feet of ash. Fulgurite, a coating that creates carrotlike tubes in rocks hit repeatedly by lightning, is abundant on the peak—a sign that the summit area has been struck many times.

Spanning the Cascade Crest, the wilderness receives from 60 to 80 inches of precipitation annually, most of it as snow in the winter months. Summer days are dry and usually sunny. Winters can be cold and very cloudy.

Plant communities are not particularly diverse. The area is heavily forested, primarily with lodgepole pine at lower elevations and mountain hemlock higher up. Whitebark pine grows near timberline. Scattered here and there are western white pine and occasional Pacific silver fir. Understory consists of huckleberry and other shrubs.

Wildlife is scarce, but you may occasionally encounter elk, mule deer, black bear, coyote, marmot, and snowshoe hare, along with gray and Steller's jays.

DAY HIKE: TIPSOO PEAK
One-way Length: 3.1 miles
Elevation Range: 6,500 to 8,031 feet
Difficulty: Moderate

Tipsoo Peak Trail penetrates the heart of the wilderness, switchbacking up to the summit of 8,031-foot Tipsoo Peak, an old volcanic cone. Along the way, the trail passes through some lovely, old-growth mountain hemlock forest before breaking out into a few small meadows near the summit. I did encounter a few beautiful sugar pine close to the trailhead. The view from the top is spectacular. You can look south directly to Mount Thielsen rising dramatically above the rest of the terrain. A pumice desert and lovely Tipsoo Meadows lie directly below your perch. To the north you can see Diamond Peak, Maiden Peak, the Three Sisters, and even a small portion of Mount Washington. I encountered elk tracks and fresh mountain lion tracks on my hike.

From Roseburg, take OR 138 east about 75 miles toward Diamond Lake. About 5 miles before reaching the lake, turn left onto Cinnamon Butte Road (FR 4793). At 1.7 miles, stay right on Road 100 for another 3.2 miles to the end of the road and an obvious wide spot and trailhead.

SHUTTLE BACKPACK HIKE: PACIFIC CREST TRAIL #2000
One-way Length: 30.4 miles
Elevation Range: 5,900 to 7,560 feet
    Difficulty: Strenuous

This section of the Pacific Crest Trail (PCT) traverses the entire north-south length of the Mount Thielsen Wilderness and allows you to sample a small portion of the proposed Oregon Cascades Wilderness as well. The easiest trailhead to find is the southern one by Crater Lake. The trail enters the wilderness in 1.2 miles, passing through forests of lodgepole pine and mountain hemlock, with only occasional views to the south or toward Mount Thielsen. But the grade is easy, and it's very pleasant hiking. You pass west of Mount Thielsen and reach Thielsen Creek at 8.3 miles. At 11 miles, you hike west of Howlock Mountain. At 13.2 miles, cross the Cascade Crest at 7,560 feet, the highest point along the PCT in Oregon and Washington. Then continue east of Tipsoo Peak; at 26.4 mile, the trail leaves the wilderness to enter the proposed Oregon Cascades Wilderness. It is another 4 miles to Windigo Pass.

There are two trailheads. To reach the southern trailhead, drive OR 138 east from Roseburg to Crater Lake National Park. The trailhead lies along the northern boundary of the park as you head toward US 97. Reach the northern trailhead by driving OR 138 east for 73.5 miles from Roseburg toward Diamond Lake. Turn left onto FR 60 (Windigo Pass Road) toward Lemolo Lake. Continue on FR 60 past Lemolo Lake for 6.7 miles to the Windigo Pass Trailhead.

DAY HIKE: MAIDU LAKE
One-way Length: 2.9 miles
Elevation Range: 5,600 to 6,180 feet
    Difficulty: Moderate

Few trails lead into the Mount Thielsen Wilderness from the eastern side of the Cascades, but the hike from Miller Lake to Maidu Lake is one and makes for a nice, easy introduction to the wilderness. From the trailhead, you'll first skirt the shore of Miller Lake. After 0.8 mile, you'll reach a trail junction. Turn left and follow Evening Creek as the trail climbs 2.1 miles up through a lodgepole pine forest to a junction with the Pacific Crest Trail. Continue straight, crossing the PCT and then descending to Maidu Lake.

From Chemult, go 0.5 mile north on US 97 to Miller Lake Road (FR 9772), and take it 12 miles to the Digit Point Campground and trailhead.

Mount Washington Wilderness   22

View of Mount Washington from Big Lake,
Mount Washington Wilderness

MOUNT WASHINGTON is the ultimate "rocks and ice" wilderness. With the majority of the acreage strewn with lava flows and rubble, and the rest mostly noncommercial lodgepole pine stands, the designation of the Mount Washington Wilderness wasn't controversial. However, some forested areas with ponds, and a total of 28 lakes, do exist here, in the southwestern corner and in the north near Big Lake. Lying on the crest of the Cascades just south of Santiam Pass and north of McKenzie Pass, the so-called Black Wilderness is named for Mount Washington, its highest peak at 7,794 feet. The Pacific Crest National Scenic Trail, which extends for 16.6 miles through the wilderness, is the primary trail, starting from the northern boundary

LOCATION: 15 miles west of Sisters

SIZE: 52,516 acres

ELEVATION RANGE:
3,200 to 7,794 feet

MAJOR FLORA: Mountain hemlock, lodgepole pine, ponderosa pine, whitebark pine

ADMINISTRATION: Willamette NF, McKenzie RD, 541-822-3381; Deschutes NF, Sisters RD, 541-549-7700

BEST SEASON: July to October

GETTING THERE: From Sisters, or from the south, take OR 242 (Old McKenzie Highway) to McKenzie Pass; the Pacific Crest Trail #2000 is to the west of Dee Wright Observatory. From the north, take US 20 to a right onto FR 2690 (Big Lake) by Santiam Pass.

Mount Washington

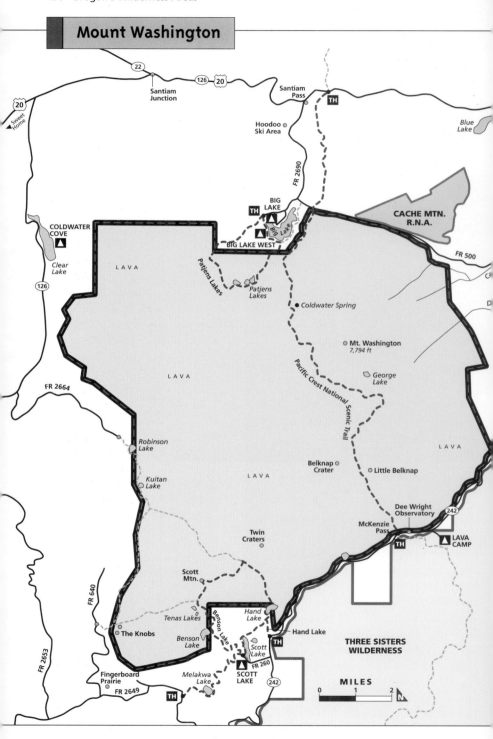

22

126 20

Santiam
Junction

Santiam
Pass

TH

20

Sweet
Home

Hoodoo
Ski Area

Blue
Lake

FR 2690

BIG
LAKE

TH

CACHE MTN.
R.N.A.

COLDWATER
COVE

BIG LAKE WEST

Big Lake

FR 500

Clear
Lake

126

L A V A

Patjens Lakes

Patjens
Lakes

Coldwater Spring

Mt. Washington
7,794 ft

L A V A

George
Lake

FR 2664

L A V A

Robinson
Lake

Pacific Crest National Scenic Trail

L A V A

Kuitan
Lake

L A V A

Belknap
Crater

Little Belknap

Dee Wright
Observatory

242

McKenzie
Pass

TH

LAVA
CAMP

Twin
Craters

Scott
Mtn.

FR 640

Tenas Lakes

Benson Lake

Hand
Lake

Hand Lake

THREE SISTERS
WILDERNESS

The Knobs

Benson
Lake

Scott
Lakes

TH

FR 2653

Fingerboard
Prairie

Melakwa
Lake

SCOTT
LAKE

FR 260

242

FR 2649

TH

MILES

0   1   2

N

near Big Lake and extending to the southern boundary near the Dee Wright Observatory. Nevertheless, the overall barrenness of the majority of the wilderness probably contributes to its overall low recreational use.

With few trees or even pasture, the area was largely bypassed by history. Most people had as much reason to go here as to the moon. In 1872, a wagon road was constructed over the Cascades at present-day McKenzie Pass, a road later graveled and finally paved by the 1930s. McKenzie Pass was named after the river, which in turn took its name from Donald McKenzie, a partner in John Jacob Astor's fur company who had explored the Willamette Valley in 1812. The first recorded climb of the rocky pinnacle of Mount Washington was not until 1923, when six boys from Bend managed to reach the top.

The Mount Washington Wilderness was originally set aside by the Forest Service as a Wild Area in 1957. When the 1964 Wilderness Act was signed into law, the Mount Washington Wilderness was designated as one of the original wilderness areas.

The main feature of the wilderness is its geological displays. The vast majority of the lava flows here do not actually originate from Mount Washington; rather they are from Belknap, a newer, younger shield volcano. Belknap erupted as recently as 1,400 years ago, and its lava tongues cover 98 square kilometers on the crest of the Cascades. The first of recent eruptions occurred prior to 2,900 years ago, when basaltic lavas moved about 6 miles eastward from the growing shield. A second eruptive phase began 2,883 years ago and produced the Little Belknap shield on the east flank of the Belknap Crater. Basaltic andesite lavas poured forth from a central vent during the third phase 1,495 years ago, creating most of the modern Belknap Crater.

Like all of the Cascades, Mount Washington Wilderness receives the bulk of its precipitation as snow in winter. Summers are typically warm and dry. Though forests do cover the area, the bulk of the tree cover is lodgepole pine. Some ponderosa pine grows at the lowest elevation on the east side, while Douglas fir is found on the western slope. Mountain hemlock occasionally forms tree islands amidst the lava flows. Huckleberry, beargrass, and rhododendron make up the understory plants here. Wildlife is limited here to a few deer and elk, along with very limited numbers of black bear and mountain lion that may wander through the area. Smaller mammals include pika, marten, snowshoe rabbit, marmot, and ground squirrel.

LOOP HIKE: PATJENS LAKES
Trail Length: 6 miles
Elevation Range: 4,450 to 4,800 feet
Difficulty: Easy

The loop hike around Patjens Lakes climbs so little that it's an excellent hike for families with small children, with views of Mount Washington along the trail. Although listed as a day hike, the abundance of water at the Patjens Lakes, along with plenty of flat campsites, makes this an easy overnight excursion as well. The trail passes through lodgepole pine forest broken up by an occasional meadow filled with beargrass in July. Ripe huckleberry are abundant in August. Of the three Patjens Lakes, the last on the loop is the largest. The lakes were named for Henry Patjens, who grazed sheep here at the turn of the century. The last part of the loop brings you along a roadless shore of Big Lake.

Drive US 20 to Santiam Pass, then turn south on FR 2690 toward the Hoodoo Ski Area, following signs for Big Lake Campground. The trailhead lies near Big Lake West Campground.

DAY HIKE: HAND LAKE
One-way Length: 0.5 mile
Elevation Range: 4,800 to 5,000 feet
Difficulty: Easy

Hand Lake is a short, easy hike from the highway, permitting access to a wonderful meadow often decked with flowers in summer. The lake has a lava flow on its eastern border, and an old wooden shelter near the western end. Frogs are abundant around the lake.

Drive northeast on OR 242 toward McKenzie Pass; between mileposts 72 and 73, just past the Scott Lake Road turnoff, watch carefully for a pullout on the south side of the road, opposite a trail sign on the north side.

DAY HIKE: BENSON LAKE
One-way Length: 1.4 miles
Elevation Range: 4,820 to 5,200 feet
Difficulty: Easy

It is a short 1.4 miles through lodgepole pine forests to the lake. The lake holds brook trout that bite readily to flies. It is only another 1.1 miles to Tenas Lakes, which hold cutthroat, brook, and rainbow trout. All these lakes are great for family hikes with small children.

Drive OR 242 toward McKenzie Pass. Some 5.6 miles west of McKenzie Pass, between mileposts 72 and 73, turn off onto Scott Lake Road (FR 260), and go 1.5 miles to the trailhead.

SHUTTLE BACKPACK: PACIFIC CREST TRAIL #2000
One-way Length: 16.6 miles
Elevation Range: 4,700 to 6,100 feet
Difficulty: Strenuous

The Pacific Crest Trail is the major path through this wilderness, much of it through lava flows or lodgepole pine forests, although you will also cross the western flank of Mount Washington. A strong hiker could do the entire route in one long day, but be sure to take plenty of water, as few water sources exist along the route. Coldwater Spring, 9 miles from the McKenzie Pass trailhead, is one of these sources.

The south end of the trail begins by the Dee Wright Observatory on OR 242 at McKenzie Pass. The northern end is along US 20 at Santiam Pass.

Mountain Lakes Wilderness 23

Mount Carmine from Whiteface Peak, Mountain Lakes Wilderness

IF YOU WANT TO SEE what Crater Lake will look like in a few tens of thousands of years, visit the Mountain Lakes Wilderness today. The wilderness's highest mountain was created from a volcanic caldera, or collapsed cone, similar to the event that created Crater Lake. Beginning more than 2 million years ago, multiple eruptions built up a 12,000-foot mountain. Then the mountain erupted with unusual intensity, emptied its magma chambers, and imploded in upon itself, leaving behind the caldera. Later, the caldera was carved and scoured by Ice Age glaciers. These glaciers helped to breach the caldera's rim, carving out eight prominent peaks from the former volcanic cone, and also created the lakes that give the wilderness its name. The highest point in the wilderness is Aspen Butte, 8,208 feet high.

The 23,071-acre Mountain Lakes Wilderness was one of three Oregon areas originally protected in the 1930s part

LOCATION: 40 miles east of Medford

SIZE: 23,071 acres

ELEVATION RANGE: 4,700 to 8,208 feet

MAJOR FLORA: Mountain hemlock, Shasta red fir, whitebark pine

ADMINISTRATION: Winema National Forest, Klamath RD, 541-885-3400

BEST SEASON: June to October

GETTING THERE: From Medford, drive east on OR 140 to Lake of the Woods. Several wilderness trailheads lie south of OR 140 just beyond Lake of the Woods.

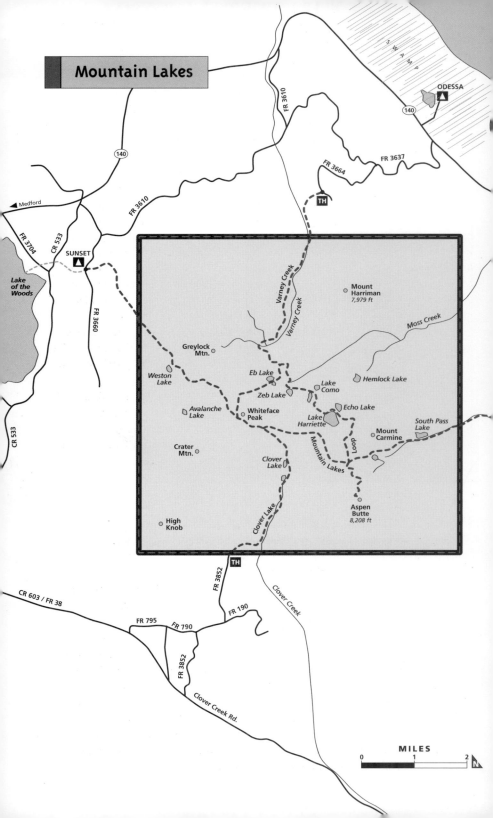

of the Forest Service system of Primitive Areas. With the passage of the 1964 Wilderness Act, it became one of the original designated wilderness areas in the National Wilderness System. Its borders form a perfect square, demonstrating that political boundaries, not ecological considerations, went into its designation. This small wilderness attracts less attention than its nearby neighbors, like the Sky Lakes Wilderness and Crater Lake National Park, so those looking for solitude might consider hiking here.

Like most of the southern Cascades, the majority of the region's 40 to 50 inches of annual precipitation comes in winter as snow, while summers are remarkably dry except for an occasional thundershower. Summer days can be warm, but never hot, while the nights nearly always cool down for comfortable sleeping temperatures.

Forests are dense, with scattered ponderosa pine at the lowest elevations grading into white fir, then mountain hemlock and Shasta red fir, with occasional patches of aspen, lodgepole pine, and Pacific silver fir. Whitebark pine grows on the ridge tops. Meadows are uncommon. Wildlife is typical of the Cascades and includes mule deer, black bear, coyote, red squirrel, snowshoe hare, and other forest species. Bald eagles are occasionally spotted here because of the proximity of Mountain Lakes Wilderness to Klamath Lake Basin wildlife refuges.

Like other such areas in Oregon, significant roadless lands adjoin this wilderness, on the west, south, and north. In total, more than 11,000 acres could be added to the wilderness boundaries to create a much larger wildlands, enhancing its biological value as a refuge.

Mountain Lakes Wilderness is easy to reach. The hub of the maintained trail system is the Mountain Lakes Loop Trail in the core of the wilderness. It traces an 8.2-mile path around the caldera rim. You can reach it from the north by way of the Varney Creek Trail (4.4 miles); from the west on the Mountain Lakes Trail (6.3 miles); or from the south by way of the Clover Creek Trail (3.3 miles).

DAY HIKE: CLOVER LAKE
One-way Length: 2.2 miles
Elevation Range: 5,300 to 6,700 feet
Difficulty: Easy

This is a short, easy sampling hike of the Mountain Lakes Wilderness and begins from the least crowded trailhead in the wilderness. It is also the shortest way to reach Aspen Butte, the highest peak in the wilderness.

From the trailhead, the route passes through lovely forest for a half mile to reach Clover Creek. Then the trail follows this beautiful stream as it alternatively runs through dense forest and open, flower-spangled meadows. Some 1.5 miles from the trailhead, the path crosses Clover Creek. Notice how the valley changes its character and shape just beyond this point, from a narrow, V-shaped canyon into a broad, U-shaped valley, reflecting the sculpting influence of the Clover Creek Glacier that flowed off of Whiteface Peak. At mile 2.2, you reach Clover Lake, a shallow but exquisite, jade-colored pool that reportedly supports brook trout. After enjoying the lake and views, you can turn around here.

For those with more energy, continue up the trail beyond the lake another 1.5 miles to the junction with the Mountain Lakes Loop Trail #3727. It's some 2 more miles east to the Aspen Butte Trail junction with glorious views of the wilderness and Lake Harriette. Climb one more mile to the top of 8,208-foot Aspen Butte, the highest point in the wilderness. A duck on the loop trail marks the turnoff for this unofficial trail to the summit.

From Medford, go east on OR 140 to the FR 3601 turnoff for Lake of the Woods. Turn right (south) and go about 7 miles on FR 3601 and County Road 533 to County Road 603, also known as FR 38 or Clover Creek Road. Turn left and proceed 5 miles to FR 3852. Turn left and continue 3 miles to the trailhead.

OVERNIGHT BACKPACK: VARNEY CREEK TRAIL #3718 TO LAKE HARRIETTE
One-way Length: 6.7 miles
Elevation Range: 5,500 to 6,900 feet
Difficulty: Moderate

Many consider Lake Harriette to be one of the most beautiful lakes in Oregon. That's debatable, but it's certainly lovely and the largest and most popular lake in Mountain Lakes Wilderness. The first part of Trail #3718 follows Varney Creek and crosses the wilderness boundary about one mile from the trailhead. Then, about 1.4 miles south of the trailhead, the route crosses to the west side of the creek, providing views of 7,979-foot Mount Harriman as you enter the former caldera. At slightly more than 4 miles, the trail crosses over a 6,600-foot notch in the rim of the caldera to enter the lakes basin and connect with the Mountain Lakes Loop Trail #3727. Turn left (east) here and continue on the loop trail. Less than a mile from this junction is Lake Como, the first of several lakes on the loop. After passing a second, unnamed lake, the trail traverses another pass at 6,900 feet to drop into the Lake Harriette basin, where lovely campsites abound.

This hike can be extended into a wonderful 17.1-mile loop that passes a number of lakes, crosses passes, and provides a fine overview of the Mountain Lakes Wilderness. From Harriette Lake the trail climbs 1.5 miles to a pass, then another 0.4 mile along a cliffy rim to the highest point on the hike at 7,580 feet. From here, the trail descends 2 miles through a mountain hemlock forest to the junction with the Clover Creek Trail. Continue right at the junction for another 0.7 mile to another pass by Whiteface Peak. If you have some extra time, the scramble up the peak to the south of the pass is relatively easy and offers fine views of the wilderness, Klamath Lake, and Mount McLoughlin. From the pass it's another 1.4 miles to Zeb and Eb Lakes, two small potholes where you can camp before you reach the junction with the Varney Creek Trail, which you then follow back to the trailhead.

From Medford, drive east 47 miles on OR 140 toward Klamath Falls. Opposite the Odessa Campground, turn right (south) onto FR 3637 for Varney Creek Trail. Drive 2 miles to FR 3664, turn left, and go another 2 miles to the trailhead.

Opal Creek Wilderness and Scenic Recreation Area

Opal Creek, Opal Creek Wilderness

OPAL CREEK is one of the most beautiful streams in western Oregon. It flows into the Little North Fork of the Santiam River. A limpid blue color, the creek pours over water-rounded boulders and among lichen-shrouded, old-growth Douglas fir forests. The wilderness and scenic area protecting the Opal Creek drainage was created in 1996 and established in 1998. It lies immediately east of the Bull of the Woods Wilderness and includes about 8,000 acres of lands formerly part of that wilderness. Elkhorn Creek, a major tributary here of the Little North Santiam, was also designated a Wild

LOCATION: 50 miles northeast of Salem

SIZE: 20,724 acres in wilderness; 13,408 acres in scenic area

ELEVATION RANGE: 1,600 to 4,600 feet

MAJOR FLORA: Old-growth Douglas fir

ADMINISTRATION: Willamette National Forest, Detroit RD, 503-854-3366

BEST SEASON: April to November

GETTING THERE: From Salem, drive east on OR 22. Ten miles beyond the Stayton exit, bear left onto well-marked North Fork Road. This county road becomes FR 2209 at the forest boundary, which it parallels along the western portion of the wilderness.

and Scenic River. Both Elkhorn Creek and the Little North Santiam River support steelhead runs.

Opal Creek Wilderness boasts steep, rugged, forested hillsides. The eastern portion of the area encompasses the headwaters of two major creeks, Battle Ax and Opal, which join and flow into Little North Santiam River. The western portion of the area is dominated by two prominent peaks, Whetstone and Henline Mountains, both former fire lookout sites.

Opal Creek flows through the Western Cascades, volcanic rock formed between 24 and 16 million years ago. Glaciers carved the upper reaches of Battle Ax and Opal Creeks, creating U-shaped valleys.

Annual precipitation exceeds 100 inches annually, but nearly all of that moisture comes in winter as snow at higher elevations, and as gentle soaking rains at lower elevations along the Little North Santiam River. Summers are usually clear and sunny, with delightfully cool nights.

The heavy precipitation supports lush forests of Douglas fir, Pacific silver fir, and western hemlock. One Douglas fir along the road to Jawbone Flat is known as the Governor Gus Gibbs tree. It is 270 feet tall and more than a thousand years old! Many other "younger" trees, only 500 to 750 years old, are also scattered throughout the valley. Western red cedar and Pacific yew occur in wet lowlands, while higher ridges support stands of Engelmann spruce and mountain hemlock. Common hardwoods include bigleaf maple and red alder. Understory vegetation includes huckleberry, vine maple, and Pacific rhododendron. Wildlife includes black bear, elk, deer, coyote, marten, spotted owl, dipper, and pileated woodpecker.

Anyone visiting the peaceful setting of Opal Creek would never guess that the drainage was the scene of pitched battles for more than a decade between those who wanted to log the drainage's huge trees and those set on saving the old-growth forests. The Opal Creek drainage proper encompasses approximately 6,700 acres. Of this area, approximately 610 acres were logged between 1965 and 1975, long before the controversy over timber harvest developed. All of those acres were high on the ridgelines at the head of the drainage. There has never been any harvest near Opal Creek itself.

The film *Rage Over Trees* brought attention to the Opal Creek cause, generating public support for protection. In response, Congress placed a moratorium on timber

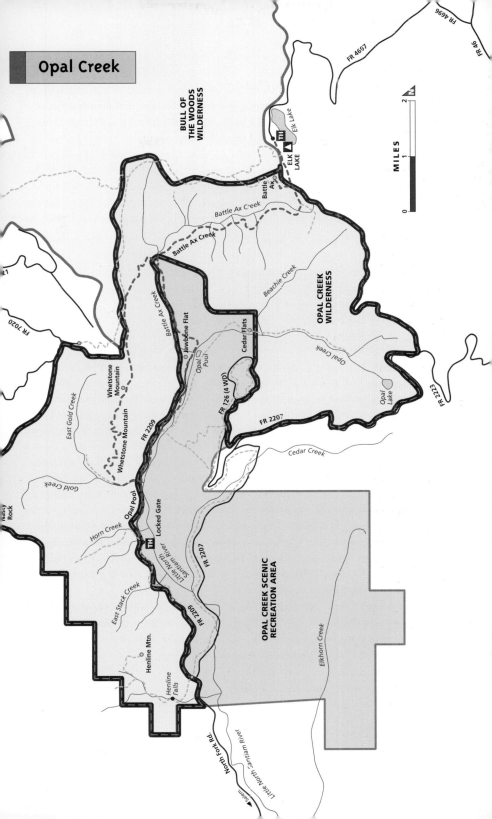

Opal Creek

BULL OF
THE WOODS
WILDERNESS

OPAL CREEK
WILDERNESS

OPAL CREEK
SCENIC
RECREATION AREA

FR 4696

FR 4697

FR 49

Elk Lake

ELK
LAKE

Battle Ax

Battle Ax Creek

Battle Ax Creek

Battle Ax Creek

Beachie Creek

Opal Creek

Opal
Lake

FR 2223

Jawbone Flat

Opal
Pool

Cedar Flats

FR 126 (4 WD)

FR 2207

Cedar Creek

FR 2207

Whetstone Mountain

Whetstone
Mountain

FR 2209

East Gold Creek

Gold Creek

Nasty
Rock

Opal Pool

Horn Creek

Locked Gate

TH

Little North Santiam River

East Stack Creek

FR 2209

Henline Mtn.

Henline
Falls

Elkhorn Creek

North Fork Rd.

Little North Santiam River

Salem

FR 7020

FR 2207

MILES

0 1 2

N

cutting in the drainage. In 1996, the Omnibus Parks and Public Lands Management Act established protection for the entire upper Little North Santiam River, which includes Opal Creek. As for Opal Creek itself, the upper portion of the drainage was allocated as "wilderness" and is managed in accordance with the Wilderness Act of 1964. The lower reaches were included in the newly designated Opal Creek Scenic Recreation Area. Neither of these designations permit commercial timber harvest.

The Henline Falls–Ogle Mountain, Henline Mountain, and Nasty Rock trailheads lie along the North Fork Road. Access the eastern or "interior" portion of the wilderness from the gated end of FR 2209. Only foot and horse travel is permitted beyond the gate. This former mining access route continues to parallel the wilderness boundary. Whetstone Mountain, Opal Creek–Kopetski, and Battle Ax Creek trailheads lie along this route.

DAY HIKE: OPAL POOL
One-way Length: 3.5 miles
Elevation Range: 1,950 to 2,200 feet
Difficulty: Moderate

This gentle hike mostly follows an old mining road to Jawbone Flat, then continues on by trail to Opal Pool, an enchanting spot of clear, green water. Bikes are allowed on the road as far as Jawbone Flat. The trail passes through exceptionally large 700-year-old Douglas fir and other large trees, offering frequent glimpses of the gin-clear, blue-green waters of the Little North Santiam River. You will come to the deserted Mertin Sawmill at about 2 miles up the road. To view the Cascada de los Niños (Waterfall of the Children), go behind the mill and follow the short path to the stream. Besides being a beautiful sight to ponder, the 30-foot falls is a barrier to the upstream migration of steelhead. Just beyond this point, the road forks. Stay left and continue on the old road another 1.1 miles to the historic mining town of Jawbone Flat. Most of the buildings here were constructed between 1929 and 1933. To get to Opal Pool, continue through Jawbone Flat, cross Battle Ax Creek, and go right a quarter mile to the scenic gorge and gemlike Opal Pool. If you want to continue beyond this point, you can reach a grove of giant red cedar another 2 miles up the Opal Creek Trail.

From Salem, drive east on OR 22. Ten miles beyond the Stayton exit, bear left onto well-marked North Fork Road. This county road becomes FR 2209 at the forest boundary, which it parallels along the western portion of the wilderness. The hike begins at a locked gate and parking area.

SHUTTLE HIKE: ELK LAKE TO LITTLE NORTH SANTIAM RIVER
One-way Length: 10.9 miles
Elevation Range: 1,800 to 4,700 feet
Difficulty: Strenuous

This hike offers an easy, one-way downhill trek for those who arrange a shuttle. The drive into Elk Lake is difficult and long, but glacier-carved Elk Lake is worth seeing. If you begin at Elk Lake, you must drive to the western end to find the trailhead. The first 1.5 miles follow an old road west through meadows and trees along the slope of Battle Ax Mountain. The route crosses a low saddle between Battle Ax Mountain and Mount Beachie. At the saddle, Trail #3340 switchbacks to the top of Battle Ax Mountain, an old lookout. It's worth taking the time to climb the peak for the outstanding view of the surrounding wilderness and High Cascade peaks visible from this point. Whether you climb the mountain or not, continue over the saddle. From this point, the path becomes a real foot trail, Battle Ax Creek Trail #3339, launching downhill along the side of Battle Ax Creek Valley through lovely old-growth forests. It's 6.7 miles from the pass to Jawbone Flat, a collection of old mining buildings dating to the 1930s. From here, follow the old mining road 3 miles past giant, 500-year-old Douglas fir and out to the lower trailhead.

To reach the upper trailhead from Salem, drive OR 22 east 52 miles to Detroit. Bear left (east) onto Breitenbush Road (FR 46) and go 4.3 miles to paved FR 4696. The road is on the left and easy to miss! Go less than a mile, turn left onto gravel FR 4697, and drive another 4.5 miles to a junction. Stay left on FR 4697 for another 1.5 miles to Elk Lake. (This last stretch is extremely rough, narrow, and difficult to turn around in. I recommend a 4WD vehicle, although I have seen passenger vehicles make it to the trailhead successfully by going very slowly.)

To reach the lower trailhead on the Little North Santiam River, see directions to the Opal Pool Day Hike, opposite.

LOOP OVERNIGHT BACKPACK: WHETSTONE MOUNTAIN
Trail Length: 14.5 miles
Elevation Range: 1,800 to 4,969 feet
Difficulty: Strenuous

This strenuous, 14.5-mile loop takes you to one of the high points of the Opal Creek Wilderness, drops you down into the fine, old-growth forests along Battle Ax Creek, then follows the Little North Santiam River back to your starting point. If you are going to make it an overnight trip, remember that there are few camping spots with water until you reach Battle Ax Creek, since most of the first part of the trip is on a ridge top.

From the locked gate, continue east up the old mining road along the Little North Santiam River, crossing the bridge over Gold Creek en route. Just beyond the creek on your left, take Trail #3369, which winds up an old road toward Whetstone Mountain. You'll reach a fork a mile up this road; turn right to continue the climb up Whetstone Mountain, passing through forest of noble and Pacific silver fir to the summit ridge. From the old lookout site on top of Whetstone Mountain, scan the horizon to see the Three Sisters and other high peaks of the Cascades. For those wishing to make it a day trip, the summit of Whetstone makes a good turnaround point for an 11-mile round-trip trek.

For those looking to do the entire loop, continue east on Trail #3369 for 0.8 mile, then turn right at the junction of Trails #546 and #3369. In 0.4 mile, reach another fork in the trail and take another right, continuing on Trail #3369. This 1.8-mile section of the trail is strewn with down trees and drops 2,000 feet before reaching Battle Ax Creek. Cross the creek, then go right onto Trail #3339. Follow it downstream toward Jawbone Flat, watching for a sign indicating Opal Pool. Take the time to walk the short spur trail leading to a view of lovely Opal Pool. Continue down the road through Jawbone Flat and out to the trailhead.

To reach the trailhead, see directions to the Opal Pool Day Hike, p. 146.

Lichen-shrouded mountain hemlock

Oregon Cascades Recreation Area 25

Dawn over Summit Lake, Oregon Cascades Recreation Area

THE LARGEST UNPROTECTED ROADLESS area left in the Cascades, Oregon Cascades Recreation Area (OCRA) spans 157,000 acres across the Cascade Crest. It provides an integral link and biological corridor between the Diamond Peak Wilderness and the Mount Thielsen Wilderness; the OCRA nearly surrounds the latter on its northern end. Much of the terrain is rolling and heavily forested. Summit Lake, the largest water body here, borders the area's northwestern corner, but numerous small lakes and potholes dot the northern end of the OCRA. Volcanic peaks also mark the landscape; at 7,664 feet, Cowhorn Peak is the highest.

LOCATION: 70 miles east of Roseburg

SIZE: 157,000 acres

ELEVATION RANGE: 4,300 to 7,664 feet

MAJOR FLORA: Pacific silver fir, lodgepole pine, mountain hemlock, Douglas fir

ADMINISTRATION: Deschutes, Umpqua, and Willamette NF: Crescent RD, 541-433-3200

BEST SEASON: June to October

GETTING THERE: From Eugene, drive OR 58 east 41 miles to Oakridge. Just a mile east of Oakridge, turn right onto FR 21, drive 31 miles, and turn left onto FR 2154, following signs for Timpanogas Lake. Just before reaching the lake, turn left and go 2 miles. For Windigo Pass, continue on FR 2154 beyond Timpanogas Lake, following signs toward Diamond Lake. Continue to Lemolo Lake, then turn left onto FR 60 and go 7.6 miles.

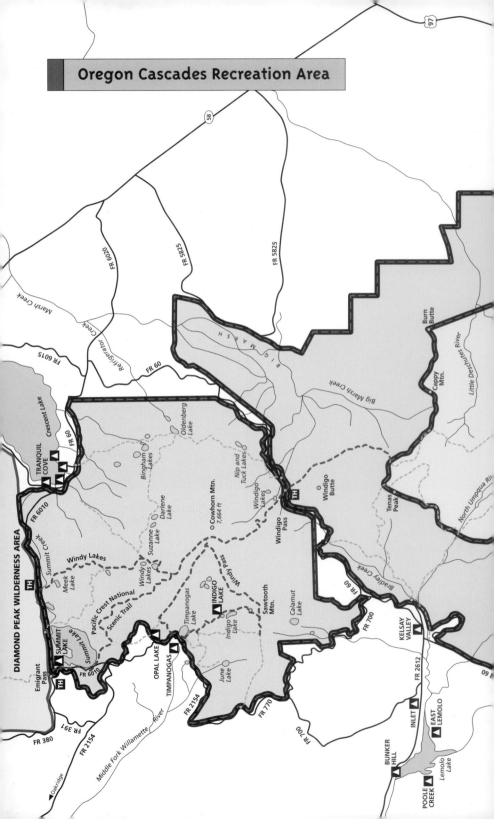

Oregon Cascades Recreation Area

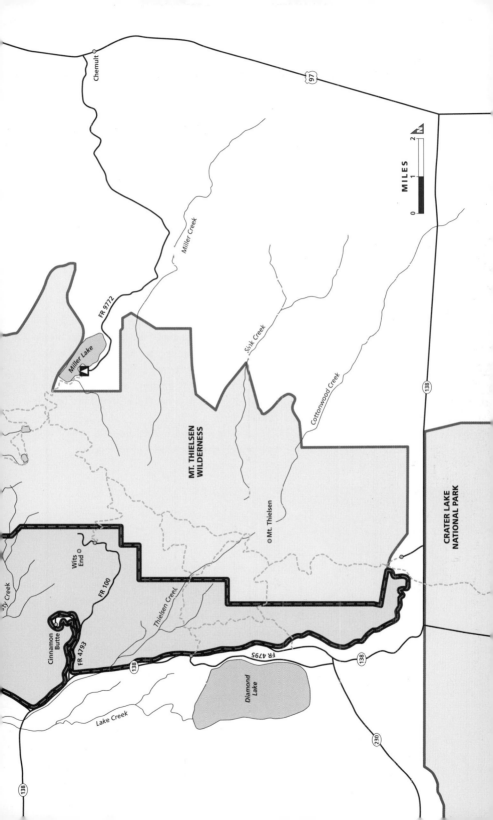

The OCRA was originally proposed for wilderness protection during the debates preceding the passage of the 1984 Oregon Wilderness Act. In yet another move by former Senator Mark Hatfield to reduce the amount of designated wilderness in the state, Oregon Cascades was instead designated a Recreation Area. The main reasons for this designation appeared to be the chance to keep the area open for some future potential timber harvest and to permit ORV use, particularly by snowmobiles. Primitive, gravel FR 60 slices the area in half, connecting Crescent Lake on the east with OR 138 on the west.

The OCRA is one large, exposed stretch of volcanic features. Cones and old lava flows dot the landscape. Cowhorn and Sawtooth Mountains were both stratovolcanoes later sliced up by Ice Age glaciers. Glaciers also scooped out the many lakes and ponds in the uplands, as well as the U-shaped upper valley of the North Umpqua River.

The climate of the OCRA is similar to that of other Cascades wildlands. Annual precipitation ranges up to 80 inches or more at higher elevations, with most of the moisture coming as snow in the winter. Summer days tend to be warm and sunny with almost no rainfall, while evenings are cool.

Wildlife consists of black bear, deer, elk, snowshoe rabbit, marten, and other small mammals. A number of the lakes scattered throughout the area support brook trout, rainbow trout, and other fish. Summit Lake is reported to contain lake trout along with brook and rainbow trout, but fishing is extremely difficult, and the lake's productivity is low. Forests dominate the area, with the majority of timber consisting of Pacific silver fir, mountain hemlock, and lodgepole pine. Huckleberry and beargrass are two common understory species here.

The Pacific Crest Trail (PCT) provides a main thoroughfare across these wildlands. The few other trails here access some of the lakes and higher peaks.

SHUTTLE HIKE: PACIFIC CREST TRAIL FROM WINDIGO PASS TO EMIGRANT PASS
One-way Length: 12.7 miles
Elevation Range: 5,600 to 7,200 feet
Difficulty: Moderate

The PCT provides the major access to the OCRA. The stretch between Emigrant Pass and Windigo Pass follows the Cascades Divide, accessing some of the higher peaks in the area. The trail passes close to the top of 7,664-foot Cowhorn Mountain, which is composed of layers of basaltic lava and volcanic ash. Glaciers have carved the ridge into basins.

To reach Emigrant Pass from Eugene, drive OR 58 east 41 miles to Oakridge. Just a mile east of Oakridge, turn right onto FR 21, drive 31 miles, and turn left onto FR 2154, following signs for Timpanogas Lake. A few miles before reaching the lake, turn left onto FR 391; at the next junction, turn right onto FR 380 and go about a mile. For Windigo Pass, continue on FR 2154 about 5 miles beyond Timpanogas Lake. Veer south onto FR 770. After about 2 miles, turn left onto FR 700 and continue south to FR 60, then turn left and go about 5 miles.

DAY HIKE: WINDY LAKES
One-way Length: 5.7 miles
Elevation Range: 5,580 to 6,220 feet
Difficulty: Moderate

This hike takes you to a collection of four lakes near Cowhorn Mountain that offers beautiful campsites among old-growth mountain hemlock. The trail begins in a lodgepole pine forest. You soon cross Summit Creek, the outlet of Summit Lake. After a half mile you reach Meek Lake, where there is a lovely campsite. Continue past numerous ponds and tarns (great for mosquitoes), climbing gradually uphill to a trail junction by an unnamed lake, some 3 miles from the trailhead. Bear left for another 1.6 miles, passing North Windy Lake, to another trail junction by East Windy Lake. To reach the South Windy Lake, continue another 0.9 mile southward. Good campsites abound at all the lakes. South Windy Lake is reported to hold cutthroat trout, while brook trout inhabit the other lakes.

From Eugene, take OR 58 east 77 miles to a right-hand turn, about 8 miles past Willamette Pass, onto FR 60 to Crescent Lake. Follow FR 60 along the lakeshore to FR 6010, which leads to Summit Lake. Follow FR 6010 (a very rutted road but passable if driven slowly) for nearly 4 miles to the Meek Lake Trailhead.

Summit Lake, Oregon Cascades Recreation Area

DAY HIKE: INDIGO LAKE
One-way Length: 2.2 miles
Elevation Range: 5,320 to 5,920 feet
Difficulty: Easy

Indigo Lake rests in a forested glacial bowl below Sawtooth Mountain, which rises more than a thousand feet above, providing a dramatic backdrop for the blue-green lake. The hike starts at Timpanogas Lake, where a nice Forest Service campground makes a good base of operations for numerous day hikes here. The trail climbs up by switchbacks through mountain hemlock forest to a four-way junction. To reach the lake, continue left for 1.2 miles, passing en route through a small meadow. You can camp at the lake, but the area has been heavily impacted. If you want to extend the hike, take the trail from the lake heading northeast to the ridge on the shoulder of Sawtooth Mountain, and connect with the Windy Pass Trail. Views from the ridge are expansive.

From Eugene, drive 41 miles on OR 58 to Oakridge. Just a mile east of Oakridge, turn right onto FR 21, drive 31 miles to FR 2154, turn left, and follow signs for 9.3 miles to Timpanogas Lake.

OTHER RECREATIONAL OPPORTUNITIES

The only suitable boating in this area is on gin-clear Summit Lake. Nearly as crystalline as nearby and better known Waldo Lake, Summit Lake is absolutely gorgeous. Road access is limited to the lake's western and northern shores, leaving most of the lakeshore wild and undisturbed. Canoeing and kayaking on the lake with Diamond Peak hanging on the northern horizon is an unforgettable experience. This is one of the more beautiful areas for nonmotorized water recreation in Oregon.

Rogue–Umpqua Divide Wilderness 26

Fall color along Fish Lake in the
Rogue–Umpqua Divide Wilderness

THIS LONG AND SKINNY WILDERNESS
stretches along some rugged peaks in the
Western Cascades. Wildflower meadows
abound, and some glacially carved lakes
also adorn the landscape. The Rogue–
Umpqua Divide Wilderness feeds both
its namesake rivers and was created in
1984 by the Oregon Wilderness Act.

Like the rest of the Old Cascades,
the peaks of the Rogue–Umpqua Divide
Wilderness date back further than the
higher, younger peaks of the High
Cascades. Ancient volcanoes deposited
these rocks some 23 to 16 million years
ago. Some of the highest peaks were

LOCATION: 56 miles northeast of Medford;
10 miles northwest of Crater Lake National Park

SIZE: 33,000 acres

ELEVATION RANGE: 2,300 to 6,783 feet

MAJOR FLORA: Douglas fir, mountain hemlock,
incense cedar, sugar pine, lodgepole pine,
Pacific silver fir, noble fir, occasional meadows

ADMINISTRATION: Rogue River NF, Prospect
RD, 541-560-3400; Umpqua NF, Diamond Lake
RD, 541-498-2531

BEST SEASON: June to September

GETTING THERE: From Medford, take OR 62
toward Crater Lake National Park. Bear left
at the junction onto OR 230 toward Diamond
Lake. Numerous trailheads lie just off this road.
From Roseburg, take OR 138 east 76 miles to
Diamond Lake; about 5 miles north of the
Crater Lake National Park entrance, bear right
(southwest) onto OR 230 to access numerous
trails close to the highway.

glaciated. However, the largest lake here, Fish Lake, was created not by glaciation but by an ancient landslide.

Plant communities include ancient old-growth Douglas fir forests mixed with large incense cedar and sugar pine. As you climb higher, Shasta red fir, Pacific silver fir, and subalpine fir forests are intermixed with mountain hemlock. There are even a few stands of Alaska yellow cedar, rare this far south in Oregon. Meadows bloom with beargrass and anemone.

Wildlife includes such regular Cascades species as black bear, bobcat, coyote, elk, deer, and smaller mammals like marten, red squirrel, and pika.

Recreation here consists mostly of hiking and backpacking. Reaching the wilderness boundaries in winter for ski touring is difficult because of the long approaches on snow-covered logging roads.

> **DAY HIKE: ABBOTT BUTTE**
> One-way Length: 3.6 miles
> Elevation Range: 5,100 to 6,131 feet
> Difficulty: Moderate

This trail follows old roads, and then a trail, to an abandoned lookout. The first part of the trail travels northeast, then east through mountain hemlock forest around Quartz Mountain to Windy Gap at 5,100 feet. Here the path heads northeast a half mile to Sandy Gap, where you can enjoy great views of the Cascades. About 1.3 miles from Sandy Gap, the trail crosses an old road. Turn right and follow the abandoned road a mile to the top of the butte, where views are somewhat obscured by trees.

From Medford, drive northeast on OR 62 toward Crater Lake. About 6 miles past the Prospect Ranger Station, turn left onto FR 68. Drive about 12 miles to a pass with a sign for the Rogue–Umpqua Divide Trail.

> **DAY HIKE: FISH LAKE**
> One-way Length: 1.5 miles
> Elevation Range: 3,370 to 4,000 feet
> Difficulty: Easy

This is one of those hikes where you will spend far more time driving backroads to get to the trailhead than it takes to hike to your destination. The good thing is that the drive is beautiful in its own right, so you probably won't mind doing it. From the trailhead, amble downhill through a forest of Douglas fir, incense cedar, and ponderosa pine. A forest fire charred much of the route, but like most fires, the burn did not kill most of the larger trees. The time goes quickly and soon you are at Fish Lake, the largest lake in the Rogue–Umpqua Divide Wilderness. The best campsites for those staying overnight are at the lake's northern end. As its name implies, the lake holds fish, mostly rainbow trout and brook trout, which occasionally attain lengths of 20 inches.

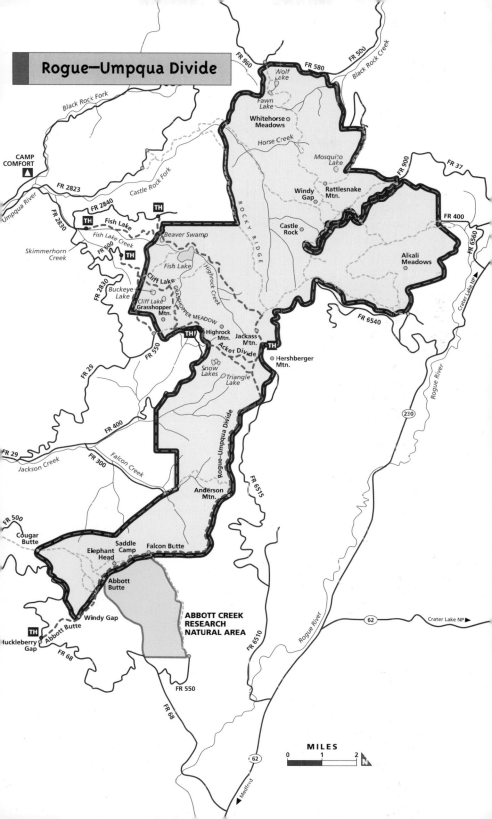

Rogue–Umpqua Divide

FR 960

FR 580

FR 503

Black Rock Creek

Nolf Lake

Fawn Lake

Whitehorse
Meadows ○

Horse Creek

Mosquito Lake

FR 900

FR 37

Black Rock Fork

CAMP
COMFORT ▲

FR 2823

Castle Rock Fork

Windy
Gap ●

Rattlesnake
Mtn.

FR 400

Umpqua River

FR 2830

FR 2840

TH

Fish Lake

Fish Lake Creek

TH

Beaver Swamp

Castle
Rock

FR 6560

Crater Lake NP

Skimmerhorn Creek

FR 600

TH

Fish Lake

ROCKY RIDGE

Alkali
Meadows ●

FR 2830

Buckeye Lake

Cliff Lake

Highrock Creek

FR 6540

Cliff Lake ●
Grasshopper
Mtn.

GRASSHOPPER MEADOW

Grasshopper Creek

TH/

Highrock
Mtn.

Jackass
Mtn. ●

FR 550

Acker Divide

TH

Hershberger
Mtn. ●

FR 29

Snow Lakes

Triangle Lake

FR 400

Rogue–Umpqua Divide

230

Rogue River

FR 29

Falcon Creek

FR 300

Anderson
Mtn. ●

FR 6515

Jackson Creek

FR 500

Cougar
Butte ●

Saddle
Camp

Elephant
Head ●

Falcon Butte ●

Abbott
Butte ●

TH

Windy Gap

Abbott Butte

**ABBOTT CREEK
RESEARCH
NATURAL AREA**

FR 6510

Rogue River

62

Crater Lake NP ▶

Huckleberry
Gap

FR 68

FR 550

FR 68

MILES

0   1   2

N

62

▶ Medford

From Roseburg, drive I-5 south to Canyonville (Exit 98). Then follow the Tiller-Trail Highway (OR 227) 23 miles east to Tiller. Just beyond Tiller, turn left onto FR 46 (which becomes FR 28) for South Umpqua Falls. Go about 24 miles to a right onto FR 2823, go another 2.4 miles, bear right onto FR 2830, and continue a scant 2 miles to the Fish Lake Trailhead. When you get to the trailhead sign, veer left and go another 4.6 miles on FR 2840 to the Beaver Swamp Trail at a second Fish Lake Trailhead, which makes for a shorter hike to the lake.

DAY HIKE: BUCKEYE AND CLIFF LAKES
One-way Length: 1.7 miles (to Cliff Lake)
Elevation Range: 3,620 to 4,190 feet
Difficulty: Easy

The hike on Trail #1578 to Buckeye and Cliff Lakes is very popular, in part because the lakes lie in scenically attractive mountain bowls, and in part because of the relatively short hike involved. The trail begins at a low-elevation trailhead (3,620 feet) among ponderosa pine and sugar pine stands. As you gain in elevation, the forest gradually changes to Douglas fir and mountain hemlock. Just 0.2 mile from the trailhead, you reach a "T" junction; proceed left. It is 0.7 mile to the wilderness boundary and then another 0.5 mile to Buckeye Lake, passing en route the junction with Acker Divide Trail #1437. Cliff Lake is just 0.3 mile beyond Buckeye Lake. The scenic cliffs on Grasshopper Mountain, an old scarp resulting from a massive landslide, overlook both lakes.

For those wanting a longer hike, it's another 1.9 miles up to the former lookout site on 5,523-foot Grasshopper Mountain. You can make an even longer loop by continuing beyond Grasshopper Mountain to Grasshopper Meadow and Acker Divide Trail #1437. This stretch of trail preserves the most magnificent old-growth Douglas fir, incense cedar, and sugar pine in the entire wilderness. Continue on Acker Divide Trail to the trailhead, then go right on Trail #1437 back to the junction with the Buckeye Lake Trail #1578. For those base-camping at either of the lakes, numerous other hiking options exist, including day hikes to Fish Lake or Grasshopper Meadows.

From Roseburg, drive I-5 south to Canyonville (Exit 98). Then follow the Tiller-Trail Highway (OR 227) 23 miles east to Tiller. Just beyond Tiller, turn left onto FR 46 (which becomes FR 28) for South Umpqua Falls. Go about 24 miles to FR 2823, turn right, and follow signs for the Skimmerhorn Trailhead. After 2.4 miles, turn right by Camp Comfort Campground onto FR 2830, proceed about 4 miles to a left onto FR 600, and drive nearly 2 more miles to the trailhead.

OVERNIGHT BACKPACK: ROGUE–UMPQUA DIVIDE TRAIL

One-way Length: 27 miles

Elevation Range: 3,700 to 6,250 feet

Difficulty: Strenuous

This 3- to 4-day backpack requires a shuttle to do. The recommended beginning trailhead is the Beaver Swamp Trail, leading to Fish Lake at the northwestern corner of the wilderness, with an exit onto FR 68 by Huckleberry Gap on the southern end. Along the route, you'll pass plenty of flower-studded meadows and lakes and have a number of opportunities to climb higher peaks for expansive views. For the most part, this wilderness area receives little use. Other than around the few lakes that attract day hikers and fishers, solitude is easily obtained.

Briefly, the route begins at the Beaver Swamp Trailhead, circles around Fish Lake (where there are good campsites), and proceeds up on Rocky Ridge and over Jackass Mountain, providing ample views. The trail continues south, staying right along the wilderness border, which is the watershed divide, and circles around Hershberger Mountain. The views from the summit of this former lookout site are worth the extra climb to the top. Some have compared the flowery meadows around Hershberger's base to those found at Mount Rainier. From Hershberger Mountain, the trail continues south past Anderson Mountain, another abandoned lookout site, and around Elephant Head Mountain and Abbott Butte to the end near Windy Gap and your vehicle (or ride) on FR 68.

To reach the trailhead, see directions for the Fish Lake Day Hike (opposite).

27 | Salmon-Huckleberry Wilderness

Old-growth Douglas fir along the Salmon River, Salmon-Huckleberry Wilderness

NESTLED IN THE WESTERN SLOPES of the Old Cascades just south of Mount Hood, this wilderness is named for two physical features—the Salmon River and Huckleberry Mountain. The two natural wonders to which these features refer—salmon and huckleberries—are also abundant here. The highlight of this wilderness is undoubtedly the deep, waterfall-filled canyon of the 40-mile-long Salmon River, a federally protected Wild and Scenic River with headwaters on Mount Hood; the other major drainage here is Eagle Creek, a tributary of the Clackamas River. Salmon and steelhead runs and wild cutthroat trout live in both streams. Plaza Lake, near the southern border, is

LOCATION: 30 miles east of Portland
SIZE: 44,600 acres
ELEVATION RANGE: 1,400 to 4,877 feet
MAJOR FLORA: Old-growth Douglas fir, western hemlock, western red cedar, Pacific silver fir at higher elevations
ADMINISTRATION: Mount Hood National Forest, Zigzag RD, 503-622-3191
BEST SEASON: April to November
GETTING THERE: Drive US 26 east from Portland to Zigzag, then turn right (south) onto FR 2618 up the Salmon River into the heart of the wilderness.

the only lake in the wilderness. This fact is offset by old-growth forest and ridge-top summits with outstanding views of Mount Hood and other peaks of the High Cascades.

The magnificent old-growth Douglas fir and western hemlock forests along the lower stretches of the Salmon River and Eagle Creek are sustained by 80 to 100 inches of annual precipitation. Indeed, old-growth forests outside of the wilderness on the lower parts of Eagle Creek are currently the center of a controversial timber sale that would log part of this pristine drainage. Noble fir is common at higher elevations. Moss-draped bigleaf maple and red alder are common at lower elevations. Understory vegetation includes Pacific rhododendron, vine maple, salmonberry, bunchberry, sorrel, sword fern, beargrass, and huckleberry. Some of the highest ridges have open, flowery meadows.

Composed of 10-million-year-old volcanic rocks, the mountains of the Salmon-Huckleberry Wilderness have been eroded down to relatively smooth ridgelines. Devils Peak and Salmon Butte are both eroded stubs of these ancient volcanoes. During the Ice Age, glaciers plucked and gouged the headwaters, creating broad, U-shaped valleys and small cirques on some of the peaks and ridges. Though the ridges are smooth, the slopes are steep and heavily forested.

Wildlife here reflects the usual Cascades species, including black bear, elk, black-tailed deer, mountain lion, and coyote, along with runs of steelhead and Chinook salmon in the streams. The summer steelhead fishing on the Salmon River is considered to be excellent. Deer and elk winter along the typically snow-free lower portion of the Salmon River.

Because of the low elevation of the major stream valley, the wilderness is accessible to hikers year-round. Though most people hike the lower parts of the Salmon River, you should consider hiking one of the five ridgeline trails if the weather is clear. All offer outstanding views, particularly Huckleberry Mountain and Hunchback Mountain. Devils Peak and Salmon Butte are both former lookout sites.

Several significant roadless areas adjoin the Salmon-Huckleberry Wilderness. In particular, the entire northern slope of Hunchback Mountain and Devils Peak down to Still Creek and FR 2612 is roadless and should be added to the wilderness. Another 4,600 acres of roadless lands lie along the South Fork Eagle Creek and Eagle Creek drainages. The historic Old Baldy Trail winds through this area and into the Salmon-Huckleberry Wilderness. This low-elevation area is also critical winter range habitat for deer and elk.

DAY HIKE: SALMON RIVER TRAIL #742
One-way Length: 3.5 miles
Elevation Range: 1,600 to 2,400 feet
  Difficulty: Easy

The 14-mile-long Upper Salmon River Trail is probably the most heavily used path in the wilderness. It provides access to some of the best old-growth Douglas fir and western hemlock forests in the state. Truly immense trees can be seen along this trail. Waterfalls abound along the river, but you can't see most of them from the trail. In the first 2 miles, the trail more or less stays along the river, passing through a forest of giant Douglas fir, western red cedar, and western hemlock. You don't reach the wilderness boundary until you have hiked some 1.5 miles along this trail, a good example of how Oregon's politicians like former Senator Mark Hatfield sought to keep merchantable timber out of wilderness. Conservationists hope that future wilderness additions will provide protection for these monster trees. At Rolling Riffle Camp, a flat area with numerous tent sites, the trail climbs up above the river, offering few glimpses of the inner gorge and various waterfalls. At 3.5 miles, the trail climbs up on a bluff that offers a vista of the Salmon drainage. Day hikers can turn around here.

For those inclined, opportunities abound for longer hikes. Camp overnight at Goat Creek, some 4.8 miles from the trailhead, or at a sizable site by the river at 8.3 miles from the trailhead. Other smaller campsites lie elsewhere along the trail. If you can arrange a shuttle, you could hike the entire Salmon River Trail from an upper trailhead just off the highway by Government Camp and past Trillium Lake.

From Portland, go east on US 26 to Zigzag. Turn right (south) onto Salmon River Road (FR 2618) and follow it 4.9 miles to the trailhead, located where pavement ends and the road crosses a bridge over the river.

DAY HIKE: HUCKLEBERRY MOUNTAIN
One-way Length: 5.3 miles
Elevation Range: 1,200 to 4,300 feet
  Difficulty: Strenuous

Four trails climb up Huckleberry Mountain, though two begin on private lands. The two best routes are Boulder Ridge, described here, and a second slightly longer trail via Cheeney Creek. Both are steep. Though it's possible to use both trails as part of a loop, you need either to arrange a short shuttle or to lock a bicycle at one trailhead; you can pedal back to your vehicle without undue effort. The view from the top of Huckleberry Mountain is worth any extra effort involved.

The first part of the trail crosses a bridge over the Salmon River and soon begins switchbacking up the side of Boulder Ridge. At 2.3 miles, you attain a good view of Mount Hood. Those not inclined to do the entire hike to the summit can turn around here. Otherwise, continue to follow Boulder Ridge at a slightly less steep angle up to the summit of the Huckleberry Mountain.

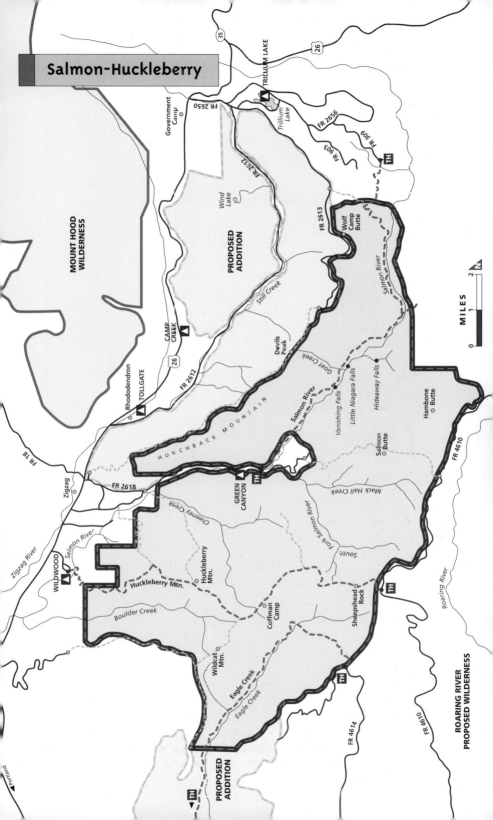

Salmon-Huckleberry

MOUNT HOOD WILDERNESS

PROPOSED ADDITION

Government Camp

Trillium Lake

FR 2650

FR 2656

FR 2612

FR 309

FR 903

Wind Lake

Still Creek

Wolf Camp Butte

Salmon River

FR 2613

Goat Creek

Devils Peak

Rhododendron

TOLLGATE

CAMP CREEK

26

FR 2612

HUNCHBACK MOUNTAIN

Salmon River

Vanishing Falls

Little Niagara Falls

Hideaway Falls

Hambone Butte

Salmon Butte

FR 4610

Zigzag

FR 18

FR 2618

GREEN CANYON

Cheeney Creek

Mack Hall Creek

Zigzag River

Salmon River

WILDWOOD

Huckleberry Mtn.

Huckleberry Mtn.

South Fork Salmon River

Shepshead Rock

Boulder Creek

Coffman Camp

Wildcat Mtn.

Eagle Creek

Eagle Creek

Roaring River

FR 4614

FR 4610

ROARING RIVER PROPOSED WILDERNESS

PROPOSED ADDITION

Portland

MILES

0 1 2

From Portland, drive east on US 26 toward Zigzag. Just before Wildwood (some 3 miles west of Zigzag), turn right into the BLM's Wildwood Recreation Site to a picnic area and trailhead.

DAY HIKE: EAGLE CREEK TRAIL #501
One-way Length: 4.7 miles
Elevation Range: 1,600 to 2,200 feet
Difficulty: Moderate

A low-elevation drainage, Eagle Creek is accessible year-round, and this hike takes you through beautiful old-growth forests. The first part of the hike is actually outside of the wilderness and the site of controversial logging plans. Activists have been fighting Forest Service plans to log the old-growth in this drainage for several years, and conservationists are proposing that these lands be added to the Salmon-Huckleberry Wilderness.

Eagle Creek Trail #501 passes through old-growth western red cedar, western hemlock, and Douglas fir forest, with a mossy bigleaf maple understory. About 2 miles into the hike, you come to the first access to the creek and a nice campsite. The trail then continues along the creek for another 1.5 miles to another campsite, a good place to turn around or to stay overnight.

From Estacada, take OR 224 north 4 miles toward Portland to the Eagle Fern County Park exit. Take Wildcat Mountain Road east 2 miles, turn right onto Eagle Fern Road, go about 2.5 miles east, and bear right onto George Road. Follow George Road about 6 miles, turn right onto SE Harvey Road, and drive another 2.5 miles—ignoring multiple secondary side roads. Park just before a right fork of the road begins to descend down a steep, overgrown road that once led to an old trailhead, and walk the old road down into the Eagle Creek Valley.

Sky Lakes Wilderness 28

Fourmile Lake and Pelican Butte from Mount McLoughlin, Sky Lakes Wilderness

MORE THAN 200 TARNS, ponds, and lakes dot this aptly named, wooded sanctuary that straddles the crest of the Cascades just south of Crater Lake National Park. Fourmile Lake, along the wilderness's southern boundary, spans more than 750 acres. And rising above all and visible from nearly all points in the wilderness is 9,495-foot Mount McLoughlin, one of the Oregon Cascades' highest volcanoes. The wilderness is long and narrow, averaging 6 miles wide by 27 miles long. The Pacific Crest Trail traverses its entire length. The glaciated U-shaped valley of the Middle Fork of the Rogue is the lowest point in the wilderness and offers hiking by May; most trails in the wilderness, however, are snow-covered until July.

LOCATION: Along the Cascade Crest 40 miles northeast of Medford

SIZE: 113,590 acres

ELEVATION RANGE: 3,500 to 9,495 feet

MAJOR FLORA: Shasta red fir, mountain hemlock, lodgepole pine, whitebark pine, western white pine, sugar pine

ADMINISTRATION: Rogue River NF, Butte Falls RD, 541-865-2700; Winema NF, Klamath RD, 541-885-3400

BEST SEASON: June to September

GETTING THERE: From Medford, drive OR 140 east to Fish Lake Summit. Just past the summit, turn north for Fourmile Lake and other trailheads.

The summit of Mount McLoughlin is a popular destination for hikers. The superlative view from the peak provides vistas from Crater Lake to Mount Shasta in California. A "trail" of sorts goes all the way to the top, and no technical skill is required to reach the summit. But numerous pathways leading down through the boulder fields near the top can sometimes confuse hikers on the descent, making it difficult to find the main hiking trail once down in the trees. The actual elevation gain is more than 4,000 feet, so 4 to 5 hours are needed to complete the ascent.

Like many High Cascades volcanoes, Mount McLoughlin consists of basaltic andesite lava flows. From some directions, the mountain has a perfect, Fuji-like symmetrical cone; viewed from the north or east, however, a hollow on the face of the volcano is obvious. The hollow was carved by Ice Age glaciers that excavated the northeast face into a cirque. Like most other major drainages within Sky Lakes Wilderness, Seven Lakes Basin and the deep canyon of the Rogue River's Middle Fork were carved by massive ice fields that blanketed the highest elevations of the Cascades. With the onset of warmer climate, local glaciers virtually disappeared some 12,000 years ago.

Compared to other Cascade volcanoes, Mount McLoughlin is relatively young, with the bulk of its main cone less than 200,000 years old, and many lava flows on its flanks are thought to be between 30,000 and 20,000 years old. The bowl-like basin exposes steeply dipping layers of pyroclastic breccia, tuff, and numerous interlayered lava flows that compose the walls of the cirque, providing a window into McLoughlin's geological formation.

Mount McLoughlin isn't the only volcano to erupt within what is now the Sky Lakes Wilderness. Minor lava eruptions and mud flows occurred at places like Big Bunchgrass Butte and Imagination Peak. And Goosenest Mountain, a volcanic cone on the northeast corner of the wilderness, is another recent eruption. All these eruptions were overshadowed by the explosion and subsequent collapse of Mount Mazama some 6,700 years ago. Some of the vast amount of rock and ash blown into the air landed in the northern portion of Sky Lakes Wilderness, creating the pumice-covered "Oregon Desert."

The climate of the Sky Lakes Wilderness is typical of that of the Cascades as a whole. Summers tend to be nearly rainless with warm, dry days dominating. Nights are reasonably cool but seldom cold. Annual precipitation averages 40 inches at midelevations and can exceed 80 or 90 inches at higher elevations, but nearly all of this comes as snow in the winter months. The snowpack often lasts until July.

Vegetation comprises a significant amount of old-growth forest with occasional wet meadows and even some chaparral. Dominant species are Shasta red fir, mountain hemlock, white fir, and lodgepole pine, along with lesser amounts of whitebark pine, western white pine, and chinquapin, among others. Grouse huckleberry, huckleberry, and bearberry are among the typical shrubs found here.

Common Cascades wildlife inhabit the area, such regulars as mule deer, elk, black bear, coyote, yellow-bellied marmot, marten, coyote, and pika. Goshawks and spotted owls are known from the area. Mosquitoes are abundant.

Several significant roadless areas border the wilderness. At the southeast corner lies the 11,000-acre Pelican Butte Roadless Area, which also borders the Klamath Marsh National Wildlife Refuge on the east. Named for 8,036-foot Pelican Butte, the Pelican Butte area is heavily forested with white fir, Shasta red fir, and mountain hemlock. An old road leads to the top to a former lookout site.

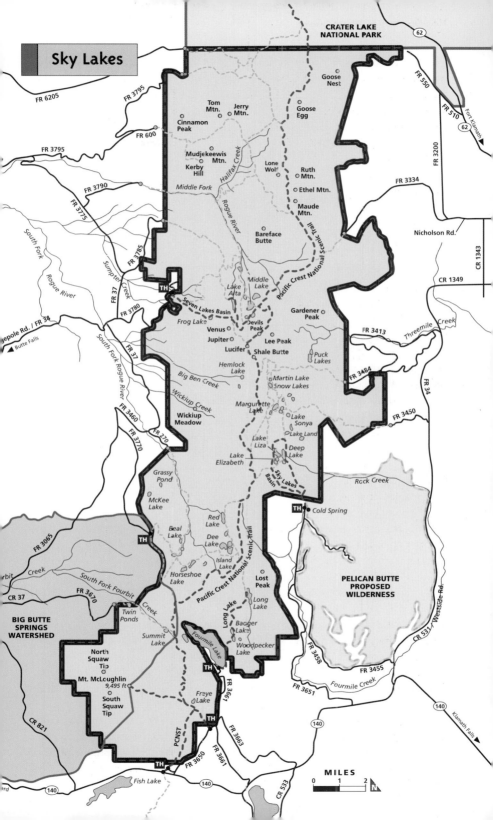

DAY HIKE: LONG LAKE
One-way Length: 3.7 miles
Elevation Range: 5,760 to 6,000 feet
Difficulty: Moderate

This nearly level trail through a lodgepole pine forest passes some nice meadows at Horse Creek. The first part of the hike circles around the shore of Fourmile Lake, offering great views of Mount McLoughlin from various lakeside vantage points. Pass tiny Woodpecker Lake and reach Badger Lake at the 1.8-mile point. Just beyond Badger Lake, you enter a bunch of flowery meadows strung along the trail for about a mile. Some 1.9 miles beyond Badger Lake, you reach Long Lake, the second largest water body in the Sky Lakes Wilderness. Retrace your steps back to the trailhead.

From Medford, get on OR 140 heading east toward Klamath Falls. Drive 36 miles to a left turn for Fourmile Lake on FR 3661. Go 5.7 miles to the campground and trailhead, on the lower end of Fourmile Lake.

LOOP HIKE: SKY LAKES BASIN
Trail Length: 6.9 miles
Elevation Range: 5,800 to 6,050 feet
Difficulty: Moderate

This level trail takes you past a dozen ponds and lakes, and through lovely old-growth lodgepole pine, mountain hemlock, and Shasta red fir forests. Some 0.6 mile from the trailhead, the trail forks. The Cold Springs Trail continues straight ahead— you'll be coming back on that path at the end of the loop. To continue the loop, take the right fork along South Rock Creek Trail, which in another 1.8 miles takes you to Heavenly Twin Lakes and the junction with the Sky Lakes Trail. To do the full tour, turn right onto the Sky Lakes Trail heading to Isherwood Lake. Go 1.2 miles to Isherwood Lake and continue another 0.6 mile past Lake Liza, Lake Elizabeth, and Lake Notasha to rejoin the Sky Lakes Trail. Go right for 0.3 mile to reconnect to the Cold Springs Trail. Follow it 2.4 miles back to the trailhead.

From Medford, take OR 140 east toward Klamath Falls. At milepost 41, turn left onto FR 3651. Follow this about 10 miles to the trailhead.

OVERNIGHT BACKPACK: SEVEN LAKES BASIN
One-way Length: 5 miles
Elevation Range: 5,250 to 6,900 feet
Difficulty: Moderate

Many enthusiasts consider the Seven Lakes Basin hike to be one of the most beautiful in southern Oregon. That may be an exaggeration, but this is certainly a delightful destination, and you should plan on spending a few days in the basin exploring the surrounding area from a base camp.

From the trailhead, follow Seven Lakes Trail #981 uphill through forests of sugar pine, white fir, lodgepole pine, and western white pine. At 2 miles from the trailhead, reach tiny Frog Lake. Some more uphill climbing, including a few switchbacks, takes you in 1.3 miles to a pass at 6,900 feet with exceptional views of the Seven Lakes Basin. A trail up Devils Peak takes off to your right from this pass. If you want to drop your pack here, it's about 1.6 miles one way to the summit of Devils Peak, where the views are superb. You can run up there before proceeding into the basin to camp.

Just below the pass, you have a choice to take a side trip to long and skinny Alta Lake. It's a half mile to the lake, and many consider it the prettiest lake in the entire Sky Lakes Wilderness. Otherwise, head straight ahead 1.7 miles into the middle of the Seven Lakes Basin, passing South Lake and Cliff Lake some 4.5 miles from the trailhead. The Seven Lakes Basin contains springs, meadows, rocky bluffs, and lakes. To reach Middle Lake, the largest in the basin, go left just beyond Cliff Lake for another 0.4 mile to the lakeshore, where you'll find plenty of camping, plus great views of Devils Peak. Retrace your steps back to the trailhead.

From Medford, drive OR 62 north to the Butte Falls Highway, turn right, and drive 15 miles to the town of Butte Falls. About a mile beyond town, turn left onto Prospect Road. After 9 miles, turn right onto Lodgepole Road (FR 34) and go 8.5 miles to FR 37. Drive 0.4 mile before veering right onto FR 3780 for the final 4 miles to the trailhead.

Whitebark pine at timberline on Mount McLoughlin, Sky Lakes Wilderness

29 Table Rock Wilderness

Forest rising above rhododendron, Table Rock Wilderness

THOUGH SMALL, THIS POCKET WILDERNESS of heavily forested basalt plateaus and cliffs is a real delight, especially in late spring when the abundant Pacific rhododendron is in bloom. The namesake 4,881-foot summit of Table Rock, the highest point in the wilderness, and many of the higher trails afford spectacular views. One of the few designated wildernesses managed by the Bureau of Land Management (BLM) in Oregon, 6,028-acre Table Rock Wilderness was designated as part of the 1984 Oregon Wilderness Act.

Table Rock and Rooster Rock are composed of rocks that were formed 17 to 10 million years ago. Younger basalt, only about 4 million years of age, forms the summit of both peaks. It is thought that these basalts may have been extruded by a High Cascades volcano.

LOCATION: 50 miles southeast of Portland

SIZE: 6,028 acres

ELEVATION RANGE: 1,300 to 4,881 feet

MAJOR FLORA: Douglas fir, western hemlock, noble fir

ADMINISTRATION: BLM Salem District, 503-375-5646

BEST SEASON: April to November

GETTING THERE: From Molalla, follow signs east to Feyrer Park, cross the Molalla, and turn right, following signs to Dickey Prairie. Continue south on Dickey Prairie Road about 4 miles past Dickey Prairie Store (your last supply stop). Bear right onto paved Molalla River Road and go south 12 miles to pavement's end at the junction of the Middle Fork and Copper Creek Roads, from where you can reach several wilderness trailheads.

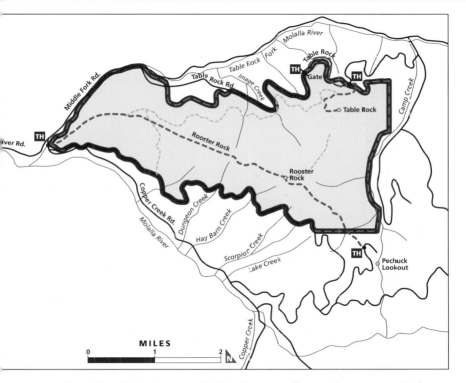

Annual precipitation exceeds 80 inches annually, mostly as snow at higher elevations and rain at the lowest parts of the wilderness in winter. As with most of the Cascades, the summers are often warm with almost no rain. Nights tend to be cool but comfortable.

Forested areas are made up of Douglas fir, western hemlock, noble fir, grand fir, and Pacific silver fir. As a result of a major fire that swept through the area in the 1880s, most of the trees here are less than 120 years old. However, scattered remnants of 400- to 600-year-old forests linger. Vine maple, rhododendron, and western chokecherry fill in the understory. Other common species here are thimbleberry, salmonberry, and beargrass.

The Table Rock Wilderness is home to elk, black-tailed deer, black bear, coyote, bobcat, marten, mountain beaver, and northern flying squirrel. Resident songbirds include Steller's jay, gray jay, chestnut-backed chickadee, and golden-crowned kinglet. Some of the perennial, spring-fed streams in the wilderness contain Pacific giant salamander, tailed frog, and cutthroat trout. Rough-skinned newts can be found traversing the forest floor on rainy or humid days.

Some 19 miles of trails provide for wonderful day-hiking opportunities, but overnight campsites are not abundant.

DAY HIKE: TABLE ROCK
One-way Length: 3.3 miles
Elevation Range: 3,750 to 4,881 feet
Difficulty: Moderate

The highest point in the wilderness, the broad and nearly flat plateau summit of Table Rock offers outstanding views of the surrounding mountains, especially Mount Jefferson. The first part of the trail follows an old road that is now blocked by a landslide. After hiking a mile, you reach the old trailhead for Table Rock and enter the Douglas fir–western hemlock forest. About 1 mile from the old trailhead, you will circle around the base of Table Rock's basalt cliffs, then cross a rockslide. Some 1.9 miles from the old trailhead you reach a junction. Go left about 0.5 mile in two long switchbacks to the 4,881-foot top of Table Rock.

If you want to take in Rooster Rock as well, go back to the trail junction, then turn left instead of right to traverse the ridge. It's about 1.5 miles to reach the base of Rooster Rock.

From the junction of the Middle Fork and Copper Creek Roads (see Getting There, p. 170), turn left onto Middle Fork Road (7-3E-14), drive 2 miles, turn right onto Table Rock Road (7-4E-7), and proceed 4 miles to the trailhead.

DAY HIKE: ROOSTER ROCK
One-way Length: 6 miles
Elevation Range: 1,250 to 4,624 feet
Difficulty: Moderate

Some 200 feet lower than Table Rock, Rooster Rock still stands high above the Table Rock plateau. Several trails meet at Rooster Rock, providing opportunities to connect to other trails in the wilderness. This 6-mile trail climbs more than 3,200 feet from the trailhead to the base of Rooster Rock, making it the most difficult hike in the wilderness. The first 2 miles are quite steep, with numerous switchbacks. The path leads up through forests of Douglas fir and western hemlock. In the months of June and July, the forest understory is resplendent with the blooms of Pacific rhododendron. Rooster Rock itself is a picturesque volcanic plug with meadows around its base. If you want to make this a one-way hike and have done a shuttle or can arrange a pick-up, continue past Rooster Rock to the Pechuck Lookout Trail, which traverses a 3-mile ridge to the east, ending at the 4,338-foot Pechuck Lookout.

The trailhead is located at the junction of the Middle Fork and Copper Creek Roads (see Getting There, p. 170).

Three Sisters Wilderness | 30

View north from Three Sisters Wilderness to Mount Washington, Three Fingered Jack, and Mount Jefferson

THE THREE SISTERS WILDERNESS is one of Oregon's largest and most popular wildlands. At the heart of Oregon's Cascades, the wilderness has just about everything you could want: magnificent, low-elevation old-growth forests; high, dramatic peaks; alpine meadows; and more than 300 lakes and ponds. Superlatives abound about the wilderness. The Three Sisters are all more than 10,000 feet high—North Sister at 10,085 feet, Middle Sister at 10,047 feet, and South Sister at 10,358 feet—and, with 9,175-foot Broken Top, make up the most concentrated and majestic collection of high peaks in the entire Cascades. South Sister

LOCATION: 15 miles west of Sisters

SIZE: 285,202 acres

ELEVATION RANGE: 1,850 to 10,358 feet

MAJOR FLORA: Old-growth Douglas fir, western hemlock, Pacific silver fir, Alaskan cedar, western red cedar, lodgepole pine, ponderosa pine, mountain hemlock, western white pine

ADMINISTRATION: Willamette NF, McKenzie RD, 541-822-3381; Deschutes NF, Sisters RD, 541-549-7700

BEST SEASON: June to October

GETTING THERE: From the Willamette Valley, take OR 126 east to OR 242; from central Oregon, take US 97 to the Cascade Lakes Highway (FR 46). Numerous trailheads, as well as Forest Roads 19, 2643, 1957, and 1993, access the wilderness.

is the third highest peak in Oregon. Teardrop Pool, near the summit of South Sister, is Oregon's highest-elevation lake. Fourteen glaciers cloak the higher peaks; Prouty Glacier, on the northeastern slope of South Sister, is Oregon's largest. Indeed, this is the most extensive glacial area south of the 45th parallel. Some 260 miles of trails cross the wilderness, including 53 miles of the Pacific Crest Trail.

Three major landscapes dominate the wilderness. The high-alpine region surrounding the Three Sisters volcanoes is the most popular. Gorgeous alpine flower meadows are abundant. Green Lakes, nestled between Broken Top and South Sister, is one of the most popular areas in the entire wilderness. This region provides abundant evidence of recent volcanic activity and glaciation. To the west lies a second landscape, the older and more highly eroded western Cascades, in which the low-elevation French Pete drainage is preserved. Steep slopes and glaciated stream valleys mantled with heavy forest cover, including old-growth Douglas fir, characterize this region. Elevations range from 1,850 feet to more than 7,000 feet. The third region lies along the Cascade Crest south of the Sisters, a plateau of rolling terrain dotted by occasional cinder cones. The highest elevations here are 6,891-foot Irish Mountain, 6,304-foot Williamson Mountain, and 6,224-foot Horse Mountain. Thick lodgepole pine forests blanket this landscape, broken by an occasional meadow. Hundreds of lakes and ponds lie here. The 180-acre Mink Lake in this region is the largest lake in the wilderness. As might be concluded by the abundance of lakes, this region makes a good destination for August or later, after the massive swarms of mosquitoes have subsided.

Two types of volcanoes exist in the Three Sisters region. The higher, better-known peaks like South Sister, Middle Sister, and Broken Top are composite volcanoes similar to Mount St. Helens in Washington. They are often explosive during eruptions.

Vine maple below old-growth Douglas fir, Three Sisters Wilderness

By contrast, North Sister is a shield volcano. Common in Hawaii, shield volcanoes are less explosive than other volcanoes and tend to create broader, dome-shaped mountains. The age of the Three Sisters volcanoes varies considerably. South Sister is the youngest; most of the mountain is older than 25,000 years in age and predates the last major Ice Age. However, some volcanic eruptions on South Sister's flank occurred as recently as 2,000 years ago.

Others, like North Sister and Broken Top, are much older and haven't erupted in more than 100,000 years. Their age is indicated by the greater amount of erosion seen on their flanks. Compared to the nearly smooth flanks of South Sister, Broken Top has been highly dissected on three sides by glaciers. Mount Bachelor, within one of the proposed additions to the Three Sisters Wilderness, was created between 11,000 and 15,000 years ago and is among the youngest volcanoes in the Cascades. Volcanic activity in the region is by no means over. Recent satellite radar interferometry has detected slight uplift and swelling up to 4 inches across a 12-mile-diameter area 3 miles west of South Sister.

During the 1930s, the Three Sisters were part of a Three Sisters National Monument proposal. Worried that it might lose administrative control of the area, the Forest Service attempted to head this move off at the pass by designating some 191,108 acres as part of the Three Sisters Primitive Area in 1937. Under the leadership of wilderness advocate Bob Marshall, who was then working for the Forest Service, 55,620 acres in the French Pete drainage were added to the primitive area in 1938. When Bob Marshall died, however, much of the momentum for wilderness protection within the Forest Service seemed to die with him.

In 1957, the Forest Service sought to reclassify Three Sisters as a Wilderness Area and wanted to reduce its size by eliminating the low-elevation, old-growth forests in the French Pete drainage. Local conservationists were appalled and rallied to save French Pete. The French Pete issue was entwined in a larger issue of wilderness protection on federal lands that eventually led to the passage of the 1964 Wilderness Act. With this Act, the Three Sisters area was given immediate protection as federally designated wilderness—but it still did not include the French Pete drainage. As activists worked to protect the French Pete area, the Three Sisters wilderness battles helped to build a strong pro-wilderness movement in Oregon. Finally in 1978, Congress enacted the Endangered American Wilderness Act. Included in this bill was formal wilderness protection for the French Pete drainage. (See Wilderness in Oregon, pp. 18–22, for more on this remarkable history.) The Three Sisters Wilderness was enlarged again in 1984, when the Oregon Wilderness Act added another 38,100 acres in the Erma Bell drainage, bringing the wilderness to its current 285,202 acres.

Precipitation ranges from more than 100 inches on western slopes to as little as 30 inches along the eastern edges of the wilderness. As with most Cascade wilderness areas, the wetter western slope is dominated by Douglas fir and western hemlock, whereas the eastern slope has substantial ponderosa pine forests. Other species found at higher elevations include Alaska cedar, Pacific silver fir, noble fir, subalpine fir, mountain hemlock, western white pine, whitebark pine, and lodgepole pine. One of the more unusual species found here is Engelmann spruce, more common in the Rockies than in the Cascades. The spruce is found along moist stream drainages where sinking cold air tends to collect. Understory shrubs include huckleberry, beargrass, Pacific rhododendron, salal, and vine maple. In dry areas, you will also find the red-barked Pacific madrone and chinquapin. Due to the overall high elevation of this wilderness, wildflower-studded subalpine and alpine meadows are abundant.

Wildlife includes elk, deer, black bear, mountain lion, pika, marmot, marten, and coyote. Wolverine and lynx may be present. Spotted owl, bald eagle, and goshawks are among the birds of prey known to reside here.

The Oregon Wild Campaign is seeking to add even more roadless lands to the Three Sisters (see Appendix C, p. 267). The 57,000-acre Maiden Peak–Charlton Butte proposed additions consist of two roadless areas along the Cascade Crest just south of the present Three Sisters border. The southern tip of the Maiden Peak unit lies just north of Willamette Pass at the headwaters of Salt Creek. Three peaks—Maiden Peak, the Twins, and Charlton Butte—rise above a heavily forested plateau. A symmetrical cinder cone rising 7,818 feet, Maiden Peak is the highest and one of the more prominent peaks of the Cascades in this region. The proposed wilderness has an abundance of water bodies; Waldo Lake Road marks the western border, the Cascades Lakes Highway the eastern border. On the western side of the proposed wilderness lies one of the largest intact mountain hemlock forests in Oregon.

A primitive dirt road separates this roadless area from the Charlton Butte Roadless Area that then connects to the Three Sisters Wilderness. Calling this rutted track a "road" is probably too generous a term. Environmentalists are calling for the closure of it and of several poor dirt roads into the area from the Cascades Lakes Highway, in order to create a unified wilderness.

East of the Cascades Lakes Highway lies the 30,000-acre Century Lakes and 14,250-acre Tumalo Mountain areas of Deschutes National Forest. The Tumalo Mountain Roadless Area lies to the east of the wilderness and encompasses much of Bend's water supply. The views from the treeless summit of Tumalo Mountain are exceptional. Century Lakes Roadless Area takes in a portion of Mount Bachelor and portions of the shoreline of several lakes. Hosmer Lake supports Oregon's only population of Atlantic salmon, an exotic fish species native to the eastern United States. Most of the area is forested with lodgepole pine, subalpine fir, and mountain hemlock. Katsuk Butte is considered a good example of an undisturbed, high-elevation, forested cinder cone. The roadless area contains about 20 miles of trail.

DAY HIKE: GREEN LAKES FROM CRATER CREEK TRAILHEAD
One-way Length: 4.8 miles
Elevation Range: 6,600 to 7,050 feet
Difficulty: Moderate

This hike makes for a full day's trip or could be a good overnight backpack trip into the heart of the Three Sisters Wilderness. The hardest part of the trip is getting to the trailhead, which requires navigating a rough, dirt road. The trail takes you past the ragged, open slopes of 9,175-foot Broken Top to the spectacular Green

Lakes below South Sister. Within a half mile, the trail crosses a nice meadow that frames the spectacular crater of Broken Top. At about 1 mile, you will cross an irrigation ditch that diverts most of the water from Crater Creek to hay irrigation near Bend. Beyond Crater Creek, the trail contours around the base of Broken Top, with views of Sparks Lake and other lakes along the Cascades Lakes Highway. The trail eventually drops into the Green Lakes Basin.

From Bend, drive west 22 miles on the Cascades Lakes Highway (FR 46) to a right turn onto FR 370 (high-clearance 4WD recommended) by a sign for Todd Lake Campground. Continue on FR 370 to FR 380 and the trailhead.

DAY HIKE: GREEN LAKES FROM FALL CREEK TRAILHEAD
One-way Length: 4.4 miles
Elevation Range: 5,400 to 6,500 feet
Difficulty: Moderate

The Green Lakes are one of the most popular destinations in the entire Three Sisters Wilderness. If you want to enjoy solitude, this is not the place to go. Nevertheless, if you make the trip to the lakes, the spectacular view of both Broken Top and South Sister rising on either side of the lake basin will make you understand the hike's popularity.

The first part of the hike follows the aptly named Fall Creek. You will pass dozens of small and large cataracts plus boulder-strewn rapids. You eventually cross the lava flow that dammed what is now Fall Creek to create the Green Lakes. At 4.2 miles from the trailhead, the trail reaches an intersection for a loop around the lakes. Go either left or right to take in the views, then head back to the trailhead.

Drive west from Bend on Cascades Lakes Highway (FR 46) for 25 miles to the trailhead, just beyond Mount Bachelor Ski Area on the north side of the highway.

DAY HIKE: TAM McARTHUR RIM
One-way Length: 2.5 miles
Elevation Range: 6,550 to 7,700 feet
Difficulty: Moderate

Tam McArthur Rim probably offers the best close-up views of the Three Sisters volcanoes reachable by trail. On a clear day, you can also see other High Cascades peaks as far north as Mount Hood. The rim is set off by 500-foot cliffs and crowned with a flower-strewn and relatively flat, plateaulike summit. From the parking area, the trail climbs rather steeply up onto the rim, then levels off. Hike at least a half mile on the plateau's summit area to reach the best views.

From Sisters, take FR 16 south 16.4 miles to the trailhead, by Three Creek Lake and opposite the Driftwood Campground.

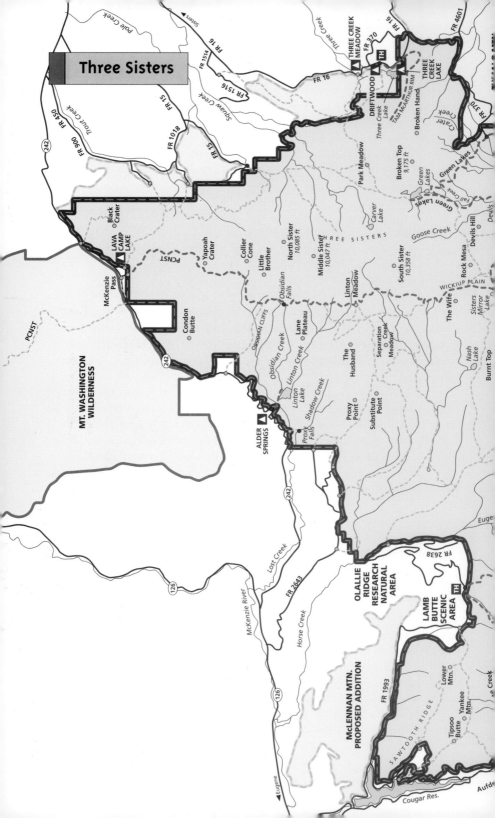

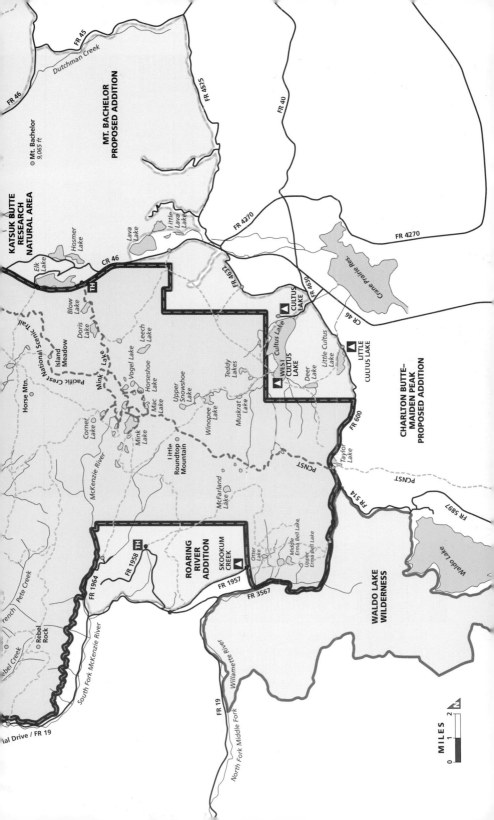

French Pete Creek, Three Sisters Wilderness

DAY HIKE: WICKIUP PLAINS
One-way Length: 2.5 miles
Elevation Range: 5,500 to 6,150 feet
Difficulty: Moderate

The Wickiup Plains were created by ash fallout from the Three Sisters volcanoes. The ash has created a "desert" of bunchgrass that provides an unobstructed and astounding close-up view of South Sister. The trail starts at Devils Lake and after a half mile reaches an old road that was bulldozed into the wilderness to access mining claims on Rock Mesa. As you hike this road, you can stew about the fact that the road, and subsequent payment by U.S. taxpayers of $2 million to a mining company, were both a consequence of the archaic Mining Law of 1872. The law allows anyone to stake claims on public lands, then acquire the property for a mere $2.50 an acre.

After 2 miles, you will reach the edge of the plains and a trail junction. For the best views of South Sister, go left toward Sisters Mirror Lake for about a half mile. You can make a nice loop backpack trip by going a mile beyond the vista toward Sisters Mirror Lake to a junction with the Pacific Crest Trail. Go south another 0.6 mile to where there are dozens of ponds and tarns for camping. To get back to the trailhead and complete the loop, go back a half mile north on the PCT to the Sisters Mirror Lake Trail, then go south 2.7 miles to the junction with the Elk–Devils Lake Trail that runs north 1.5 miles back to the Wickiup Trail. Turn right (east) on this trail for a half mile back to the parking area. As an alternative, you can continue east from the Elk–Devils Lake Trail on the Sisters Mirror Lake Trail 0.3 mile to the Cascades Lakes Highway, then hitch or walk back to the Devils Lake Trailhead parking area.

From Bend, take the Cascades Lakes Highway (FR 46) 28.7 miles west to the trailhead, by Devils Lake.

DAY HIKE: FRENCH PETE CREEK
One-way Length: 3 miles
Elevation Range: 1,850 to 2,400 feet
Difficulty: Easy

The French Pete drainage allows you to sample some of the ancient old-growth forests of the Pacific Northwest. The drainage was the center of controversy for years, with logging interests and conservationists fighting over its future. Ultimately, citizen activism prevailed, and today the French Pete drainage offers quiet solitude in the kind of lush, low-elevation, old-growth Douglas fir and western red cedar forests that have been logged throughout the rest of Oregon. The French Pete drainage was added to the Three Sisters Wilderness in 1978. Walk here and you are walking through history. Because of its low elevation, it is also one of the few trails in the Three Sisters Wilderness that can be hiked year-round.

From the trailhead, the path stays close to the bubbly creek, climbing only gradually through the forest. At 0.9 mile, you cross Yankee Creek. At 1.7 miles, you reach an old crossing where the trail once crossed to the south bank of the stream. Today a new trail continues up along the north bank. You can go as far as you like before turning around. If you can arrange a shuttle, a nice hike is to begin at the Olallie Mountain Trailhead on FR 1993 and hike downhill 9.4 miles to the French Pete Trailhead.

From Eugene, take OR 126 east about 4.5 miles east of Blue River, turn right (south) onto FR 19 (Aufderheide Memorial Drive) toward Cougar Reservoir. Go 11.5 miles to a sign for the trailhead parking.

DAY HIKE: OLALLIE MOUNTAIN
One-way Length: 3.4 miles
Elevation Range: 4,400 to 5,700 feet
   Difficulty: Moderate

Olallie Mountain is an old lookout site offering an obstructed view of the Three Sisters and the headwaters of the French Peak drainage. Wildflowers along the summit ridge can be glorious in July. From the road, the trail is nearly level until you reach a saddle at about 2.2 miles. Just beyond this point, the trail begins to climb at a moderate rate to the ridgeline leading to the summit.

From Eugene, take OR 126 east about 4.5 miles east of Blue River, then turn right (south) onto FR 19 (Aufderheide Memorial Drive) toward Cougar Reservoir. Turn left to cross the dam on the reservoir, then stay on FR 1993 for 15.4 miles to the trailhead.

LOOP OVERNIGHT BACKPACK: MINK LAKE
   Trail Length: 20 miles
Elevation Range: 4,800 to 5,760 feet
   Difficulty: Moderate

The southern part of the Three Sisters Wilderness receives far less use than the alpine region surrounding the high peaks. Two reasons for this limited use are the dense forest cover that precludes long, scenic vistas, and the hungry swarms of mosquitoes that guard the trails until August. The best time to do this hike is in September, after the first frosts. The largest lake in the Three Sisters Wilderness, Mink Lake is part of a glaciated basin dotted with dozens of water bodies, large and small. The hiking is nearly level on much of this route, which is quite easy to complete on a weekend; however, if you want to have any time to explore the lake-studded basin, plan on taking three or four days to do the loop.

From the Six Lakes Trailhead, hike west 2.4 miles, past Blow Lake, to 90-acre Doris Lake. Continue another mile to a trail junction; bear right onto Trail #3526, climbing up and over a small hill to a junction with the Pacific Crest Trail (PCT). Reach the intersection of the PCT at 5.4 miles from the trailhead. Continue west passing Vera, Goose, and Porky Lakes for another 3.4 miles to the shores of Mink Lake, where there is a shelter and numerous campsites. To complete the loop, circle around the southeastern shore of Mink Lake and hike Trail #3526 1.2 miles to S Lake and another intersection with the PCT. Turn left here and go north on the PCT past Mac and Horseshoe Lakes to Cliff Lake. From Cliff Lake, follow the PCT to the junction with Trail #3626 and back 5.3 miles on the trail past Doris and Blow Lakes to the Six Lakes Trailhead.

From Bend, drive 35 miles west on the Cascade Lakes Highway (FR 46) to the Six Lakes Trailhead by Elk Lake.

Waldo Lake Wilderness 31

Reflection at Waldo Lake beside Waldo Lake Wilderness

OREGON SUPREME COURT JUSTICE John Breckenridge Waldo (1844–1907), an early advocate for the preservation of the Cascade Range, made a horse-pack trip down the crest of the range from Mount Hood to California in 1888. This namesake wilderness protects the watershed that feeds the crystalline waters of Waldo Lake, considered one of the clearest and purest water bodies in the West. Anyone who has ever canoed or kayaked it will attest to the quality of floating on cobalt-blue air that the lake affords. More than 400 feet deep, the lake is so pure that it's possible to see more than 120 feet down into the water. The clarity is a result of its very low productivity—there are few nutrients in the lake to support

LOCATION: 60 miles west of Eugene

SIZE: 37,162 acres

ELEVATION RANGE: 2,800 to 7,144 feet

MAJOR FLORA: Old-growth Douglas fir, western hemlock, mountain hemlock, lodgepole pine, western red cedar, western white pine, Pacific silver fir

ADMINISTRATION: Willamette NF, Middle Fork RD, 541-782-2283

BEST SEASON: June to October

GETTING THERE: From Eugene, drive east 41 miles on OR 58 through Oakridge, then continue another 23 miles toward Willamette Pass. Just before the pass, turn left onto Waldo Lake Road (FR 5897). Access via Salmon Creek Road (FR 24) east from Oakridge is also possible.

microscopic plants and animals. Indeed, according to Oregon Health Department, you can drink directly from the 6,700-acre lake.

Considered to be the second purest lake in the world (after Lake Baikal in Siberia), Waldo Lake, at an elevation of 5,414 feet, was created by a combination of volcanic activity and glacial scouring. Approximately 15,000 years ago, glacial ice several miles thick covered the landscape, scraping out the Waldo Lake Basin and creating other lakes in the area. As a result of the porous, pumice-dominated soil and the consequently limited number of streams that actually feed the lake, "turnover"— the time it takes for water in the lake basin to exit via the North Fork of the Middle Fork of the Willamette River—is very long. Consequently, pollutants are not readily flushed from the lake system.

The waters of Waldo Lake are not something to take for granted. It's almost unbelievable today, but plans were drawn at one time to drain the lake to provide irrigation water to farmers in the Willamette Valley. In 1905, A. R. Black obtained a permit to construct a canal to tap into the lake's water for irrigators. He sold his interests to the Waldo Lake Irrigation and Power Company in 1908. The company constructed a tunnel in 1909 from the lake to Black Creek, which drains into the Willamette drainage. Now known as the Klovdahl Tunnel, it would have dropped the level of the lake by 25 feet. Today the headgates remain along the western shore, though divers sealed the gates in 1960.

A less obvious threat to the lake comes from current human uses. Fish stocking and motorized watercraft leaking gas and oil into the water both may be contributing to a decrease in the lake's clarity and purity. New management regulations are being considered that would ban motors from the lake. Other measures have been proposed to reduce artificial enrichment or pollution of the lake. These include relocating campgrounds away from the lakeshore (to reduce soil erosion and input from roads) and the abandonment of fish stocking.

Established in 1984, the wilderness protects two geographical regions—the High Cascades and the Western Cascades. Ironically, Waldo Lake itself is not within the wilderness boundaries. The High Cascades region here is a land of moderate relief, with numerous lakes and meadows. Besides Waldo Lake, other water bodies here include the Six Lakes, Eddeeleo Lakes, and Quinn Lakes. The Western or Old Cascades has few lakes and is characterized by steep slopes and glaciated, U-shaped stream valleys. The low point at 2,800 feet lies along the North Fork of the Middle Fork Willamette River, while the high point is atop 7,144-foot Fuji Mountain.

Like most of the Western Cascades, the area receives the bulk of its precipitation as snow in winter. Average precipitation is between 50 and 100 inches. Cloudy skies dominate in winter, but summers are usually cool and sunny. Good weather typically lasts until October; September is often a prime time to visit the wilderness. Because of the porous volcanic soils, much of the moisture soaks into the ground, and surface runoff and streams are limited.

With significant precipitation, it's not surprising that Waldo Lake Wilderness is heavily forested, with 98 percent of the land area cloaked in dense forests of Douglas fir, western hemlock, and mountain hemlock. Other associated species include Pacific silver fir, lodgepole pine, western red cedar, and western white pine. An old-growth

Douglas fir stand comprises the Constitution Grove immediately adjacent to FR 19. Much of the northern part of the wilderness was rejuvenated in 1996, when lightning strikes helped to start blazes that ultimately burned 10,400 acres. But the acreage figure only represents the outer perimeter of the blaze. Like most fires, it skipped here and there through the forest canopy, leaving many completely unburned areas that remain today as seed reservoirs, and creating stands of mixed age that can support a greater diversity of wildlife. The areas opened up by the blazes now enjoy increased wildflower blooms in summer, and the numerous snags provide an abundance of homes for cavity-dependent species, from woodpeckers to flying squirrels.

Wildlife in the wilderness consists of the usual Cascades fauna, including deer, elk, mountain lion, black bear, weasel, bobcat, coyote, mink, and otter. Waldo Lake supports brook trout and kokanee salmon—both difficult to find and harder to catch.

The main recreation activities are hiking the 84 miles of trails or fishing one of the many lakes in the basin. Canoeing and kayaking on Waldo Lake is also popular. There are several places to launch from the Forest Service campgrounds on the eastern shore of the lake. Because the lake is completely encircled by a trail, it's possible to canoe or kayak to a campsite on the opposite side of the lake and then explore adjacent lakes or mountains. Keep in mind that the lake is large, and winds can keep you shorebound for extended periods of time. In winter, some skiers access the southern end of the lake, including Mount Ray, by skiing the unplowed FR 5897 to the Mount Ray Trailhead and thence up the mountain.

A number of roadless areas, in six separate parcels totaling more than 40,000 acres, surround Waldo Lake. One of the largest is the 16,000-acre Mount Ray–Fuji Mountain Roadless Area, sandwiched between OR 58 and the current southern wilderness boundary some 18 miles east of Oakridge. High points include Mount Ray, Fuji Mountain, and Mount David Douglas, named for the botanist of Douglas fir fame. The roadless area is known for its fine forests of old-growth mountain hemlock. Many trails traverse the area, including the High Divide/Eugene–PCT Trail. Fuji Mountain Trail #3674 passes through a number of meadows and by small lakes as it climbs from FR 5897 to the summit of Fuji Mountain. Elevations range from 2,900 to 7,144 feet on Fuji Mountain. Many small, glacially carved lakes lie in the eastern portion, with 11 lakes greater than 5 acres. The wet meadow complex on Mount David Douglas has a number of uncommon plants, including two species of the carnivorous sundew.

DAY HIKE: WALDO MOUNTAIN LOOKOUT
One-way Length: 2.4 miles
Elevation Range: 4,430 to 6,357 feet
   Difficulty: Moderate

Waldo Mountain sports a lookout that provides an outstanding view of the forested plateau, 7-mile-long Waldo Lake, and views of the Three Sisters and Diamond Peak. The trail climbs at a moderate grade through beautiful Pacific silver fir and mountain hemlock forests, which in late June bloom with Pacific rhododendron, providing a lovely understory for hikers. Beargrass commonly blooms in July at higher elevations.

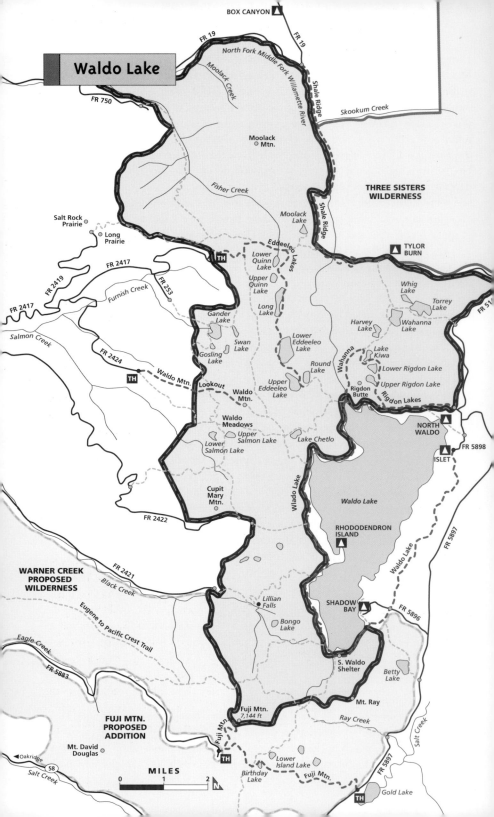

Waldo Lake

BOX CANYON

FR 19

FR 19

North Fork Middle Fork Willamette River

Moolack Creek

Shale Ridge

Skookum Creek

FR 750

Moolack Mtn.

THREE SISTERS WILDERNESS

Fisher Creek

Moolack Lake

Shale Ridge

Salt Rock Prairie

Long Prairie

Eddeeleo Lakes

TH

TYLOR BURN

Lower Quinn Lake

Whig Lake

Torrey Lake

FR 2417

FR 2419

FR 253

Upper Quinn Lake

Harvey Lake

Wahanna Lake

FR 51

FR 2417

Furnish Creek

Long Lake

Salmon Creek

FR 2424

Gander Lake

Lower Eddeeleo Lake

Lake Kiwa

Wahanna

Swan Lake

Round Lake

Lower Rigdon Lake

Waldo Mtn.

TH

Gosling Lake

Upper Eddeeleo Lake

Upper Rigdon Lake

Lookout

Waldo Mtn.

Rigdon Butte

Rigdon Lakes

NORTH WALDO

Waldo Meadows

Lake Chetlo

FR 5898

Upper Salmon Lake

ISLET

Lower Salmon Lake

Waldo Lake

Cupit Mary Mtn.

Waldo Lake

FR 2422

RHODODENDRON ISLAND

FR 5897

WARNER CREEK PROPOSED WILDERNESS

FR 2421

Black Creek

Lillian Falls

Waldo Lake

Eugene to Pacific Crest Trail

Bongo Lake

SHADOW BAY

FR 5896

Eagle Creek

FR 5883

S. Waldo Shelter

Betty Lake

FUJI MTN. PROPOSED ADDITION

Fuji Mtn. 7,144 ft

Mt. Ray

Ray Creek

Salt Creek

Mt. David Douglas

TH

Fuji Mtn.

Oakridge

58

Salt Creek

Lower Island Lake

Fuji Mtn.

FR 5897

MILES

0   1   2

N

Birthday Lake

TH

Gold Lake

From Eugene, take OR 58 to Oakridge, turn left (east) onto Salmon Creek Road (FR 24), go 11 miles, and bear left onto FR 2417. Go another 6 miles and finally turn right onto FR 2424, taking it about 4 miles to the trailhead.

OVERNIGHT HIKE: EDDEELEO LAKES
One-way Length: 4.6 miles
Elevation Range: 4,800 to 5,100 feet
Difficulty: Moderate

Unlike other trails, this one goes downhill to the glaciated lake basin that includes the Quinn Lakes, Long Lake, and the two Eddeeleo Lakes. Between all of these lakes are plenty of good shoreline campsites. The first part of the trail heads down the relatively level top of Winchester Ridge for 0.8 mile to a trail junction. Here you go left 0.3 mile to another trail junction. Turn right and drop 1.1 miles to Lower Quinn Lake, then head 2.4 miles to Lower Eddeeleo Lake. Although the trail adjoins these lakes, to get views of the lakes you must hike down short spur trails to the water. Lower Eddeeleo Lake is 160 acres and supports brook trout reported to be 10 to 14 inches long. Upper Eddeeleo Lake is 63 acres and also supports brook trout. If you tire of fishing, you can always pluck the ripe huckleberries that line the trail in August.

From Eugene, drive OR 58 to Oakridge, then turn left (east) onto Salmon Creek Road (FR 24). Follow this paved road for 11 miles to a "Y," then go left onto FR 2417, drive 10.9 miles to FR 254, and take it 0.3 mile to the trailhead.

DAY HIKE: SHALE RIDGE TRAIL #3567
One-way Length: 3.7 miles
Elevation Range: 3,000 to 4,600 feet
Difficulty: Moderate

This trail boasts outstanding old-growth forests along the beautiful upper headwaters of the Wild and Scenic North Fork of the Middle Fork Willamette River. The first 1.7 miles of the trail up to Skookum Creek is in the Waldo Lake Wilderness, but the slope across the river is outside any designated wilderness and could be logged. Conservationists propose adding this slope to the existing wilderness. Beyond Skookum Creek, you encounter even larger old-growth specimens, with some western red cedar believed to be more than 800 years old growing along the river valley. The trail continues upslope and crosses the valley, passing through more large trees with wonderful views of the river. Some 3.7 miles from the trailhead, the route leaves the river. You can turn around here for a day hike or continue as the trail switchbacks up Shale Ridge toward a high point at 5.8 miles, before making a gradual descent toward a trail junction with the Blair Lake Trail at 6.3 miles.

From Eugene, drive east on OR 58 to Westfir, then turn left (north) onto FR 19 (Aufderheide Memorial Drive) and go 30 miles to the trailhead, just before Box Canyon Campground.

DAY HIKE: FUJI MOUNTAIN
One-way Length: 1.5 miles
Elevation Range: 6,230 to 7,144 feet
Difficulty: Easy

The highest peak in the Waldo Lake Wilderness and a former lookout site, Fuji Mountain offers both a tremendous view of Waldo Lake below you, and an in-your-face view of the glacier-clad volcano Diamond Peak, opposite from you. From the trailhead, hike up a short way through a clear-cut, then go 0.3 mile to a trail junction; turn left and climb up the mountain. The lower portion of the trail climbs gradually up through mountain hemlock forest to a flower-studded rocky ridge, then on to the top of the cliff-edged mountain. A second trail up Fuji Mountain, accessible off FR 5897, requires a 5.6-mile one-way hike.

From Eugene, drive east on OR 58 past Oakridge 15.3 miles, then turn left onto Eagle Creek Road (FR 5883). It is 11.5 miles on FR 5883 to the trailhead.

LOOP OVERNIGHT HIKE: RIGDON LAKES
Trail Length: 8 miles
Elevation Range: 5,450 to 5,900 feet
Difficulty: Moderate

If you like water, this is the hike for you: four lakes lie along this loop. Much of the hike is through the 1996 Charlton Burn, so lack of shade can make it quite warm on a sunny day. Mosquitoes are thick in July; best to visit in August. From the trailhead, hike the Waldo Lake Loop Trail for 1.6 miles to a junction. Most of this way you will be near, but not right along, the lake. Pass the turn for Rigdon Lakes, which you'll use on the return route. Continue along the Waldo Lake Trail for 3 miles to the outlet of Waldo Lake, the North Fork of the Middle Fork Willamette River. Where the Waldo Lake Loop Trail crosses the river (really just a small stream at this point), watch for the trail junction with Wahanna Trail #3583. Take this trail heading north for 1.3 miles to a trail junction. Go right for another 0.3 mile to Lake Kiwa, which has several good campsites and fishing for trout. If you're still up for more hiking, head another 0.6 mile around Lake Kiwa's southern end to Lower Rigdon Lake. Upper Rigdon Lake is another 0.5 mile farther; both lakes offer campsites and fishing for trout. From Upper Rigdon Lake, it's another 0.7 mile back to the Waldo Lake Trail and then 1.7 miles back to the trailhead.

From Eugene, drive OR 58 east 24 miles past Oakridge to the Waldo Lake left turn onto FR 5897. Go about 11 miles and come to a fork. Go left on FR 5898 1.9 miles to the trailhead and parking area, by the North Waldo Lake Campground.

LOOP OVERNIGHT HIKE: WALDO LAKE TRAIL #3590
Trail Length: 22 miles
Elevation Range: 5,400 feet
Difficulty: Moderate

Circling Waldo Lake, this trail is nearly level, although a few steep pitches exist on the lake's western shore. It is just outside of the wilderness boundaries and open to mountain bikes, so beware. This gentle trail offers an easy route for families with kids, providing access to dozens of lovely, secluded campsites, with sandy beaches and quiet coves. Although most of the trail is far enough from the lake that views are limited, you can see occasional views of Waldo Mountain, Diamond Peak, Fuji Mountain, and Charlton Butte, which add to the delight of this hike. The trail passes through mountain hemlock and lodgepole forests, thick with beargrass in July. Trails from the loop trail lead to other lakes and mountains in the wilderness, offering opportunities for extended travel.

From Eugene, drive OR 58 east 24 miles past Oakridge to the Waldo Lake left turn onto FR 5897. Go about 11 miles and come to a fork. Turn left onto FR 5898, and follow it to the trailhead, at the boat launch area of North Waldo Campground.

Kayaker at Waldo Lake near Waldo Lake Wilderness

Blue Mountains

The Blue Mountains of northeastern Oregon are really a collection of mountain ranges that run roughly from the Idaho-Oregon border to Prineville. These ranges, east to west, are known respectively as the Wallowa, Elkhorn, Greenhorn, Strawberry, Aldrich, and Ochoco Mountains. Other uplands here, often plateaulike with deep canyons, have no recognized names. With its rugged, glaciated peaks, this region of Oregon most resembles the Rocky Mountains, both in appearance and in plant communities.

The mountains vary in height across this span of uplands, but a general progression from highest to lowest moves from east to west. The Wallowas are the highest, with peaks reaching to nearly 10,000 feet. The Elkhorns and Greenhorns have several peaks in the 9,000-foot range. The highest peak in the Strawberry Mountains is also slightly more than 9,000 feet. The highest summits in the Ochocos, in the western end of the Blues, reach less than 7,000 feet. Most of the highlands in this region are under the management of the Forest Service, while the valleys tend to be in private ownership.

Rivers draining this region include the Imnaha, Grande Ronde, Malheur, Power, Umatilla, and upper John Day. Many of these are National Wild and Scenic Rivers.

The Blue Mountains are the remnants of an ancient tropical island arc that fused with the westward-moving North American continent. The tops of the mountains we find today, like the Wallowas, were once on the bottom of the ocean floor. In the Wallowas you can find coral reefs now exposed as mountaintop. Hells Canyon was plumbed from the inner depths of volcanoes that erupted more than 275 million years ago—long before there was any land in what we now call Oregon. In the center of the Wallowas are granitic rocks that formed deep in the Earth as molten rock and slowly cooled. Over these rocks the Columbia River basalt flowed, covering many of the underlying rock structures. These layered rocks are evident in the deep canyons of the Umatilla, Grande Ronde, and Imnaha Rivers, among others.

Much of the central Blue Mountains, including the Elkhorn, Greenhorn, and Strawberry Mountains, are part of what is known as the Baker Terrane, which formed beneath the ocean. This jumbled rock was mixed and changed to such a degree that its early history has often been obscured.

Backpacker on the Bench Trail, Hells Canyon Wilderness

Occasional granitic outcrops pop up in the Elkhorns and Greenhorns. These rocks are similar in age to those found in the Wallowas and were formed some 165 to 145 million years ago. The westernmost part of the Blues are primarily volcanic in origin, again representing ancient islands that were attached to the growing North American continent.

The higher reaches of many of these mountains, including the Strawberry, Elkhorn, Greenhorn, and Wallowa Mountains, were covered by glacial ice that scoured out U-shaped valleys and glacial cirques. Many of the higher-elevation lakes that dot some of these mountains owe their origins to glaciers.

The climate of the region as a whole is more continental than any other part of Oregon, with greater daily and seasonal fluctuations than elsewhere in the state. The coldest spot in Oregon is located here just south of the Strawberry Mountains. Yet the Blue Mountains are also one of the state's warmest regions, with temperatures above 100 degrees along the lower elevations of the Snake River. The majority of precipitation occurs in winter, mostly coming as snow. Precipitation in some of the valleys is less than 10 inches annually, while as much as 60 inches a year may be recorded for some higher-elevation areas like the Wallowas.

Plant communities here resemble those of Idaho and western Montana. Western larch, a species common in the northern Rockies, is abundant here. Grand fir, another tree of the Inland Empire, also grows in profusion. Ponderosa pine shares lower-elevation areas with Douglas fir, and higher elevations are dominated by Engelmann spruce, lodgepole pine, subalpine fir, and whitebark pine. Open grasslands are home to bunchgrasses like Idaho fescue and bluebunch wheatgrass. Common shrubs include snowberry, ninebark, ocean spray, serviceberry, and huckleberry.

Population density is very light. La Grande, Baker, John Day, and Prineville are among the larger towns either in or on the fringes of the Blue Mountains. Less than 2 percent of the state's population resides here.

Native biodiversity is richer here than in some other ecoregions but is not as great as that in, say, the Cascades or Coast Range. Still surviving here are runs of Snake River spring Chinook salmon and steelhead, relict runs of sockeye salmon, and populations of endangered bull trout and West Slope cutthroat trout in the John Day River.

This area is well known for its populations of hawks and owls, including recorded occurrences of boreal owl. flammulated owl, and ferruginous hawk. The region supports the largest elk and mule deer populations in Oregon. Bighorn sheep are native to the region, and mountain goats were introduced into several mountain ranges. This is the only part of the state where red squirrel, Columbian ground squirrel, and southern red-backed vole are found. A subspecies of pika is recorded for the Wallowa Mountains and other parts of the Blue Mountains.

The two land uses having the greatest impacts on native biodiversity are logging and livestock grazing. Forest fragmentation, changes in forest stand composition and age, and the ill effects of logging roads, particularly on stream water quality, are all repercussions of logging activity. Livestock production, the other major impact on this region, has damaged riparian areas. Further, ranchers dewater the area's streams and rivers to grow the irrigated hay and alfalfa crops fed to cattle, negatively impacting fisheries. Finally, disease spread from domestic animals to wildlife, notably from domestic sheep to wild bighorns, has had devastating effects including die-offs of some area herds.

Strawberry Lake, Strawberry Mountain Wilderness

32 | Black Canyon Wilderness

Along the lower end of Black Canyon Creek, Black Canyon Wilderness

THE BLACK CANYON WILDERNESS features an intact stream drainage and heavily forested uplands of the Ochoco Mountains. The main drainage, Black Canyon Creek, flows off of volcanic plateaus exceeding 6,000 feet in elevation and rushes down a narrow canyon to join the waters of the South Fork of the John Day River at 2,850 feet. Because of its low elevation, the lower section of the canyon near the South Fork of the John Day is open to hiking year-round in all but the most severe snow years. However, you must wade the South Fork to gain the trailhead, and later wade bridgeless Black

LOCATION: About 57 miles east of Prineville
SIZE: 13,400 acres
ELEVATION RANGE: 2,850 to 6,483 feet
MAJOR FLORA: Ponderosa pine, fir forest
ADMINISTRATION: Ochoco National Forest, Paulina RD, 541-477-6900
BEST SEASON: May to November
GETTING THERE: From Prineville, take OR 380 east 55 miles to Paulina. Go 4 miles east on County Road 112, bear left onto CR 113, go about 7 miles, then turn right onto FR 58 to Sugar Creek Campground. Turn left (north) on FR 5810 and drive to the edge of the wilderness.

Canyon Creek numerous times. Anyone contemplating such a late-season hike would be advised to wear hip waders, while in summer sneakers or sandals will suffice for stream crossings. No lakes exist in the wilderness. In some areas, open slopes are thick with flowers in spring, and lush riparian vegetation also presents a relatively green environment for those hiking along the main canyons of the wilderness.

The Ochoco Mountains are composed of layers of volcanic materials that flowed from nearby volcanoes between 17 and 12 million years ago. These volcanic episodes completely flooded eastern Oregon and Washington with fluid basaltic lavas. Since then, the area has been uplifted, and the plateaus have been dissected by creeks and rivers, creating deep canyons. Unlike uplands farther to the east, the low-elevation Ochocos were not glaciated during the last Ice Age.

The area's weather is typical for eastern Oregon: cold, generally snowy winters with lots of sunshine, but hot, dry summer weather. Still, nights are cool, even in summer. Annual precipitation barely exceeds 20 inches except in the highest elevations.

The 13,400-acre Black Canyon Wilderness was created by the 1984 Oregon Wilderness Act. The 18 miles of trail in the wilderness weave through the rugged canyons. The canyons and slopes above them are heavily forested with western larch, fir, and pine, with juniper and mountain mahogany on the driest rocky outcrops. Dense willow, red osier dogwood, thimbleberry, wild rose, and alder crowd the stream bottoms. Some of the ponderosa pines reach immense size. The diverse vegetative conditions in the wilderness provide habitat for nearly 300 different species of wildlife, including black bear, cougar, deer, and elk.

The main canyon is the focus of the wilderness, with the Black Canyon Trail (#820) running from the headwaters on Owl Creek near Wolf Mountain to the mouth where it joins the South Fork John Day. Five feeder trails tie into this main trail system. Three trails descend to Black Canyon Creek from the north: Payton Trail (#820D), Kelsey Trail (#820C), and an unnamed trail from FR 38 that reaches the canyon bottom just a mile or so east of the confluence of Black Canyon Creek and Owl Creek. The short Owl Creek Trail (#820A), a half-mile connector, runs from Boeing Meadows Trailhead to upper Owl Creek. The South Prong Trail (#821) descends from the south rim and begins at Mud Springs Campground off FR 5840. The South Prong and Payton Trails meet near Big Ford, where there is good camping.

Black Canyon

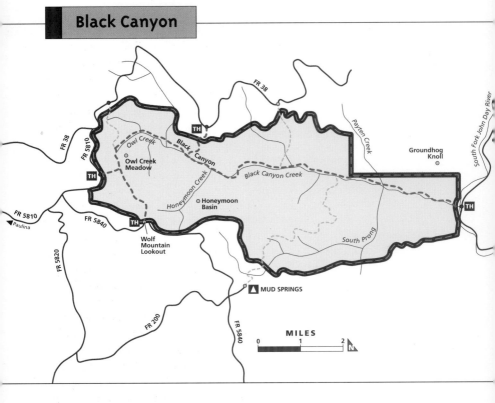

As in many wilderness areas, the boundaries for the Black Canyon were largely determined not upon biological considerations but more upon which lands were difficult for resource industries to exploit. Extending the boundaries beyond the canyon rim would add immensely to the wilderness's biological value. Opportunities to expand the wilderness exist on nearly all sides. To the north, the wilderness boundaries could be brought up to FR 38. In particular, the steep breaks running from Youngs Butte down to the South Fork of the John Day should be added to the existing wilderness. On the south, the closure of FR 5840 would allow the Tamarack Butte Battle Ridge area to be added to the wilderness, while closure of FR 5850 at Ringsmeyer Reservoir would permit addition of the west face of the John Day Canyon to be added.

DAY OR SHUTTLE HIKE: BLACK CANYON TRAIL #820
One-way Length: 14.5 miles
Elevation Range: 2,850 to 6,000 feet
Difficulty: Strenuous

This hike begins in a lovely meadow that blossoms with white mule's-ear in June but is usually skimmed by livestock of vegetation by August. There is a nice dry campsite for car camping in a grove of ponderosa pine just 100 yards down from the trailhead. The trailhead sign is set out in the meadow. The trail was recently upgraded and had new signs when I hiked it. The trail soon descends a half mile through lovely ponderosa pine, white fir, and western larch to Owl Creek. You cross the dry creek and hit the main Trail #820 that runs from Wolf Lookout down Owl Creek to Black Canyon. The trail descends gently through forest with occasional small meadows, mostly following Owl Creek, which seasonally and intermittently has water in it and can provide a nice musical backdrop for hiking. There is one level campsite big enough for a couple of tents. To find it, take a short spur trail to the left across Owl Creek.

After the campsite, you cross another spring, adorned with lush flowers of cow parsnip and larkspur. You can look across the canyon at open slopes of sage and scattered pines. These lower meadows and streams are lush, showing what the country could look like without cows trashing all the riparian zones. Compare it to the meadows seen on the drive into the trailhead.

Day hikers can turn around at the confluence of Owl Creek and Black Canyon Creek, some 2.5 miles from the trailhead. Those who wish to continue on down the canyon will find a number of other potential campsites, with a very large site where the Payten Creek and South Prong Trails meet the Black Canyon Trail. Remember, the farther downstream you go, the more stream crossings you will encounter. On a hot summer day, the stream crossings are a pleasure, but bear in mind that the lowest portion of the canyon is within a narrow gorge that has lush riparian vegetation, but also rattlesnakes. Beware of where you place your feet. The hike ends at the confluence of Black Canyon Creek and the South Fork of the John Day. The South Fork is usually knee-deep in July and August, presenting no problem for those wading it—but earlier in the year the runoff-swollen stream can be a major hazard.

From Paulina, take County Road 112 to a left onto CR 113. Proceed north to FR 58, turn right, and head toward Sugar Creek Campground. Just before the campground, turn left onto FR 5810, a good gravel road that leads through ponderosa pine forests. When you reach a junction, continue straight on FR 5810 to the Boeing Field Trailhead at 5,900 feet, or take your second right onto gravel FR 5840 to the Wolf Mountain Trailhead.

33 Bridge Creek Wilderness

Ochoco Mountains from North Point,
Bridge Creek Wilderness

LOCATION: 30 miles east of Prineville

SIZE: 5,400 acres

ELEVATION RANGE: 4,320 to 6,816 feet

MAJOR FLORA: Western larch, ponderosa pine, fir forests, meadows

ADMINISTRATION: Ochoco National Forest, Paulina RD, 541-416-6500

BEST SEASON: May to October

GETTING THERE: From Prineville, take US 26 east and north for 16 miles to Ochoco Creek Road (FR 22), and bear right. Continue past the Ochoco Ranger Station toward Walton Lake on FR 22, then turn left onto FR 2630 toward Indian Prairie. Continue the last 2 miles on a rough but passable dirt road to a parking area by Pisgah Springs. The road forms the boundary of the wilderness for 4 miles. Good car-camping spots are abundant along this valley near the spring.

DESPITE BEING one of the smallest wilderness areas in Oregon, Bridge Creek Wilderness has abundant opportunities for challenging, trailless exploration. If you want to get away from the crowds, this is a place to consider. Perhaps the best thing about the wilderness is the chance to dangle your feet over the edge of the 600-foot cliffs along its northern borders while enjoying the expansive views of the John Day drainage to the north. The wilderness's only major stream, Bridge Creek, flows through the center of the wilderness. No doubt the lack of trails, and the fact it contains no lakes, contribute to the dearth of recreational use. Water sources abound, though, for those

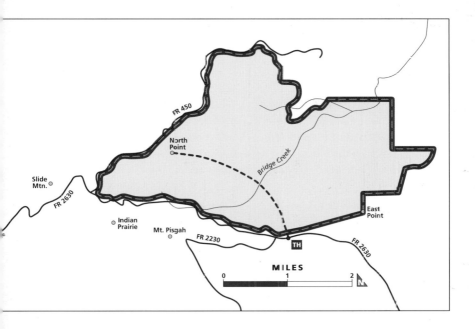

contemplating an overnight camping trip. Bridge Creek flows for approximately 4 miles through the center of the wilderness, as does a mile or so of Maxwell Creek, and there are no less than five springs here: Thompson, Pisgah, Maxwell, Nelson, and Masterson.

What I found particularly attractive about the area was the abundance of elk sign. The wilderness is riddled with more elk sign than almost any other place I've visited in Oregon. The abundance of down timber provides good hiding cover for elk against hunters, perhaps accounting for the local elk use. These logs make for tedious hiking off-trail, but numerous small and large meadows strung together allow for less troublesome hiking, not to mention gorgeous flower displays and fine views from North Point. Nearly one-fifth of the wilderness is open meadowlands; the rest is forested with ponderosa pine, white fir, western larch, lodgepole pine, and Douglas fir.

Congress created the Bridge Creek Wilderness by the 1984 Oregon Wilderness Act. Still, it's a shame that there was no Bob Marshall or Aldo Leopold to argue for protection of the Ochoco Mountains 50 or so years ago. With its ponderosa pine forests and occasional streams, this landscape would have been comparable to the Gila Wilderness in New Mexico, but in some ways better watered and with more meadows. The higher elevations of this mountain uplift are quite beautiful. The rim itself is covered with flowers, sagebrush, and grass. A few scattered, stunted ponderosa pine grow on the rim, along with subalpine fir, lodgepole pine, and other species.

Besides elk, large mammals that may be encountered include mule deer, black bear, and mountain lion. Pileated woodpeckers, goshawks, and prairie falcons are known to nest within the wilderness.

The summit of the wilderness is composed of 25 million-year-old lava flows that vented from ancient volcanoes. The 600-foot-high cliffs by North Point were created by pillar-shaped basalts.

Weather is typical for eastern Oregon: cold winters with warm-to-hot but dry summers. Precipitation averages 30 inches a year, with the majority coming as snow in winter.

The southern slope of the wilderness, accessible from the Pisgah Springs Road (FR 2630), is gentle, whereas the northern slope, accessible from FR 450 (which forms the northern boundary of the wilderness), is much steeper. Cliffs offer few opportunities for access to the summit rim. I was able to climb up to North Point from FS Road 450 by following elk trails through the forest, but it's not easy hiking. I suggest accessing the wilderness from the south. I saw references to a 3.5-mile trail in older guides, but I could find no evidence of this trail, or any trails marked on the map.

> **DAY HIKE:** NORTH POINT
> One-way Length: 1.5 miles
> Elevation Range: 6,223 to 6,607 feet
> Difficulty: Easy

Your hike takes off immediately beyond the wilderness sign. Walk north across the meadow up an old abandoned road strewn with numerous fallen trees; expect some very slow going. After a short distance in forest, the road follows the edge of a large meadow. I found it easier to strike out along the margin of the meadow to avoid the fallen trees that littered the old road. There were a lot of elk tracks in this meadow. Follow the edge of the meadow to the very northwest corner and then enter the forest. Here I intersected the old road once more and followed it a very short distance to the rim of North Point.

The rim is gorgeous, with exceptional views. One can see the Three Sisters, Mount Jefferson, Mount Hood, and Mount Adams. Closer in were views of Sutton Mountain, White Butte, and a tiny piece of the John Day River. The expansiveness of the vista is well worth the effort to reach this point. You can see a few scattered clear-cuts, and a ranch house or two off toward the John Day country, but otherwise, it's a pretty unobstructed view.

From Prineville, go northeast on US 26 to FR 22 (Ochoco Creek Road), and bear right. Follow FR 22 past Walton Lake and, at a big curve, turn left onto FR 2630. Follow this, ignoring side spurs, to a "Y" in the road, where a Bridge Creek Wilderness sign is nailed to a tree. Bear right, staying on FR 2630 past beautiful Indian Prairie. Continue past a spring development, after which the road gets worse but is still passable in a passenger car—except in early spring. Continue on this road to a parking area and another wilderness sign in a sagebrush meadow. Park here.

Eagle Cap Wilderness 34

Spring thaw at Mirror Lake below Eagle Cap Peak, Eagle Cap Wilderness

THE EAGLE CAP WILDERNESS is Oregon's answer to the Rockies. In many ways, it has more in common with Idaho wilderness areas like the Sawtooth or Frank Church River of No Return than it does with other Oregon wilderness areas. High-alpine peaks, numerous glacially carved lakes, sub-alpine meadows, and more than 500 miles of trails lie in this 385,541-acre expanse, Oregon's largest wilderness. Though the major Cascade volcanoes may be higher, the Wallowas are easily the most alpine in character of any mountain range in Oregon. Not just topography but geology and plant communities here are more closely aligned with the Rockies than the Cascades.

LOCATION: 20 miles east of La Grande

SIZE: 385,541 acres

ELEVATION RANGE: 2,700 to 9,845 feet

MAJOR FLORA: Ponderosa pine, Douglas fir, western larch, lodgepole pine, Engelmann spruce, grand fir, subalpine fir, whitebark pine, limber pine, subalpine meadows

ADMINISTRATION: Wallowa-Whitman NF, Eagle Cap RD, 541-426-4978

BEST SEASON: June to November

GETTING THERE: From La Grande, head east on OR 203 to Union, then continue east, where many Forest Service roads lead into the southwestern section of Eagle Cap. To access the northern part, drive OR 82 eastward from La Grande about 65 miles to Enterprise, south of which lie various trailheads. To reach the southeastern section, drive OR 86 eastward from Baker City to Richland and Halfway.

Most recreational use consists of backpacking and hiking in the summer, but cross-country ski trips are certainly possible. (The necessity of an often-long ski on access roads, however, keeps most day skiers from actually entering the wilderness.) You could spend months exploring the peaks and valleys in Eagle Cap; indeed, this is one of the few wilderness areas in Oregon large enough to absorb a 5- to 7-day backpack without running in circles to remain within the wilderness boundary. Large, adjacent roadless areas may even offer the opportunity to expand this wilderness in the future.

The Wallowa Mountains are an immense range more than 60 miles long by 30 miles wide. Seen from the air, the range is roughly circular, with the highest peaks in the center and most drainages radiating out from this knob of high peaks like spokes of a wheel. At 9,845 feet, Matterhorn Peak is the highest in the range, but 17 mountains here rise above 9,000 feet. What is now the Eagle Cap Wilderness experienced extensive glaciation during the Ice Age. The lower, U-shaped, glacially carved valleys are heavily forested. The core of high peaks in the Wallowas consists of a granitic batholith.

Geologically the Wallowas are part of the Wallowa Terrane, a slice of the Earth's crust that was accreted onto the North American Continent. It is composed of volcanic rocks that once were part of a large archipelago. Many similarities exist between these rocks and those of Alaska's Wrangell Mountains. The theory is that these widely separated ranges were once part of an island complex that collided with North America and melded onto the western edge of the continent. Rocks of similar origin also make up British Columbia's Vancouver and Queen Charlotte Islands.

Limestone, shale, and siltstone, indicating formation in warm, shallow seas, overlay the volcanic rocks of the Wallowa Terrane—perhaps the geological relicts of a coral atoll along the shore of a volcanic island. Some 145 to 160 million years ago, molten rock was intruded into these volcanic and sedimentary rocks. This molten rock solidified into a granitic batholith. Twelve separate granitic intrusions are known to have occurred in the Wallowa Mountains, providing some geological diversity to the rock. Some of the limestone and other sedimentary rocks surrounding the granite were metamorphosed by the heat associated with the granitic intrusions into other rock types. Sacajawea and Matterhorn Peaks are composed of limestone that was transformed into marble.

During the Pleistocene Ice Age, glaciers crowned the Wallowas; at one time, nine major and many smaller glaciers streamed down Wallowa valleys. The Lostine Glacier was 22 miles long and up to 2,500 feet thick. The Minam Glacier was 21 miles long; the Inmaha Glacier extended down its valley 20 miles. Today, these drainages display the characteristic U-shaped valleys that betoken past glaciation. The terminal moraine of the Wallowa Glacier dammed the Wallowa River to create long and narrow Wallowa Lake. The last known glacier in the Wallowa Mountains disappeared sometime after 1929.

Despite their granitic composition, the Wallowas were not a major site for gold or other mineral extraction. The exception was Cornucopia, on the southern side of the range. Gold was discovered there in 1884, and lode deposits were soon located and mined. Instead of playing out rapidly like so many other deposits, the Cornucopia mines lasted for decades. By the early 1900s, the Cornucopia Mine group employed as many as 700 men, and at one time it was the sixth largest mining operation in the United States. The mine didn't close until 1941.

The Wallowa Mountains experience a more continental climate than most of the rest of Oregon, with colder winter temperatures and generally dry summers interrupted by occasional thunderstorms. Valley locations typically receive less than 20 inches of precipitation annually, but some locations high in the Wallowa Mountains may receive as much as 60 inches, most of it as snow. Enterprise receives 15.5 inches of precipitation; Halfway on the southern side of the range gets about 21.5 inches. Pacific Northwest air masses occasionally intrude in winter, bringing milder temperatures but cloudy winter skies. High temperatures in the valleys average in the 70- to 80-degree range and in the 30s in the winter months.

Plant communities vary from low-elevation grassland and ponderosa pine forest to alpine meadows. Douglas fir, western larch, and grand fir grow in mid-elevations. At the higher basins grow lodgepole pine, Engelmann spruce, and subalpine fir, with whitebark pine clinging to some of the highest ridges. Rocky Mountain maple, ninebark, ocean spray, and Sitka alder are all common small trees or shrubs here. Grasses include bluebunch wheatgrass, Idaho fescue, green fescue, and Sandberg's bluegrass.

Most large streams, like the Wallowa and Imnaha, contain anadromous fish habitat. Many high lakes have been stocked with rainbow, eastern brook, and golden trout. Mule deer, elk, black bear, mountain lion, marten, and marmot are all recorded for the range. The pika found here is a subspecies endemic to the Wallowa and Blue Mountains. Bighorn sheep were reintroduced in the 1950s. Mountain goats, nonnative to the range, were introduced around the same time. Area wildlife species presently classified as endangered, threatened, or sensitive include the peregrine falcon, bald eagle, ferruginous hawk, Swainson's hawk, boreal owl, and the western spotted frog. The Wallowas are the only known breeding range in Oregon for both the spruce grouse and pine grosbeak. And the Wallowa rosy finch, which inhabits alpine areas in the Wallowa Mountains, is Oregon's only endemic bird.

In 1930, what was to become the Eagle Cap Wilderness was set aside by the Forest Service as a primitive area. It was subsequently redesignated a wilderness by the U.S. secretary of agriculture in 1940, but this action was merely an administrative decree that could be reversed at any time by a future agriculture secretary. In 1964, with the passage of the Wilderness Act, Congress formally designated the Eagle Cap Wilderness. Congress enacted further legislation in 1972 that enlarged Eagle Cap by an additional 72,420 acres, and in 1984 added another 66,500 acres. Further land acquisitions have brought the size to the present 358,541 acres. Eagle Cap also contains the Imnaha, Lostine, and Minam Rivers and Eagle Creek, all of which are designated Wild and Scenic Rivers.

No fewer than 47 trailheads provide access to more than 500 miles of trail here. Higher trails are not open until after the Fourth of July. Trailhead access is via several main routes; the most heavily used is OR 82 through Enterprise and Joseph to Wallowa Lake. Other main trailheads are reached from Hurricane Creek Road, Lostine River Road, and Boulder Park on the Main Eagle Road. Three trailheads—Wallowa Lake, Hurricane Creek, and Two Pan—account for 90 percent of the use. If you want solitude, avoid these trails. The southern parts of the wilderness, accessible by Eagle Creek and other drainages, offer far more solitude and are in many ways just as spectacular.

Despite previous expansions, significant unprotected roadless lands still border the Eagle Cap Wilderness. South-southwest of Eagle Cap and about 10 miles north of Halfway lie the 12,000-acre-plus Boulder Park and 8,000-acre-plus Little Eagle Meadows Roadless Areas. Bennett Peak, Two Color Lake, and headwaters of Eagle Creek lie within Boulder Park, at elevations of 4,000 to 7,000 feet. Little Eagle Meadows Roadless Area includes portions of Kettle Creek, Twin Canyon Creek, and Sullivan Creek, at elevations of 4,400 to 7,500 feet.

Twelve miles north of Halfway near Boulder Park and Little Eagle Meadows, 14,000-plus-acre Reservoir Roadless Area adjoins the mining site of Cornucopia and includes Sugarloaf and Russell Mountains. East Pine Creek, Clear Creek, and the East Fork of Pine Creek drain this area. Once part of the Eagle Cap Wilderness, a portion of this acreage was removed to make it more convenient for ranchers to tamper with water developments and irrigation storage reservoirs in the vicinity. Trails up Clear Creek and East Pine Creek and from Fish Lake all provide access to this fine roadless area.

The 32,000-acre Lake Fork Roadless Area lies along the southeast border of Eagle Cap. It is a vital link between the Eagle Cap Wilderness and Hells Canyon Wilderness. The area is recommended as wilderness in the Oregon Wild proposal (see Appendix C, p. 267). Fish Lake and the Fish Lake Campground mark its northwest corner. Elevations range from 2,600 feet, along Little Elk Creek, up to 7,000 feet. Forest, meadows, and grassy slopes characterize the area. At one time, salmon and steelhead spawned in the larger creeks in this roadless area, but runs were wiped out by the construction of Hells Canyon Dam. Nevertheless, redband trout still inhabit the drainage's streams.

The heavily timbered, 10,000-acre-plus Huckleberry Roadless Area lies on the northern flanks of Eagle Cap, 8 miles south of the town of Wallowa, and includes the drainages of Little Bear, Bear, Big, and Deer Creeks. Elevations range between 5,000 and 7,000 feet. Several trails penetrate this roadless area, including the Bear Creek Trail and Big Canyon Trail, which both start near the Bear Creek Trailhead.

The 9,000-acre Castle Ridge Roadless Area lies along the western edge of Eagle Cap, 4 miles from the community of Cove. The area includes the upper reaches of Indian, Camp, and Warm Creeks. The rolling terrain is dominated by lodgepole pine forest, although some western larch, Douglas fir, and Engelmann spruce grow at lower elevations. A rare occurrence of mountain hemlock, a species more typical of the Cascades, is protected in the Indian Creek Natural Research Area on the southwest corner of the roadless area. A number of large rock outcrops, known as monadnocks, are located here. A poor-quality dirt road that could be closed is all that separates this roadless area from the existing Eagle Cap Wilderness.

The 5,000-acre-plus Little Sheep Roadless Area near Wallowa Lake, and the 3,000-acre Little Creek Roadless Area on the western border of Eagle Cap, are among other smaller roadless areas that should be added to Eagle Cap. Addition of all of these roadless lands to the Eagle Cap Wilderness could substantially improve its ecological integrity, particularly since many of these additions include lower-elevation areas that tend to be biologically more productive.

DAY HIKE: HUCKLEBERRY MOUNTAIN
One-way Length: 2.5 miles
Elevation Range: 5,500 to 7,552 feet
Difficulty: Moderate

Huckleberry Mountain is a former lookout site on the northern edge of the Eagle Cap Wilderness. As can be imagined, the summit provides an outstanding view north across the proposed Huckleberry Mountain additions to the Eagle Cap Wilderness. From the trailhead, follow Trail #1667 along and then across a dirt road in the first 0.3 mile, before climbing at a very steep pitch all the way to the summit.

From OR 82 in Wallowa, go west, following signs for Bear Creek Road (FR 8250). Follow this road south to Bear Saddle and the trailhead.

DAY HIKE: MAXWELL LAKE
One-way Length: 3.8 miles
Elevation Range: 5,460 to 7,730 feet
Difficulty: Strenuous

Maxwell Lake rests in a beautiful glacial bowl with breathtaking views of the High Wallowa Peaks. Though only a short 7.6 miles round-trip, the trail climbs 2,400 feet, so you'll be breathing a lot. Fortunately, much of the elevation is gained by some well-graded, if not long, switchbacks. From the trailhead, the route climbs 2.8 miles up a rocky slope that offers views of the surrounding mountains most of the way. Then the trail clambers up a steeper slope for almost a mile before dropping over a ridge and down to the lake.

From La Grande, drive 50 miles east on OR 82 to Lostine. Turn right (south) on Lostine River Road and go about 18 miles to the Maxwell Lake Trailhead.

OVERNIGHT BACKPACK: CRATER LAKE
One-way Length: 5.9 miles
Elevation Range: 4,500 to 7,550 feet
Difficulty: Strenuous

The East Fork Eagle Creek was the set location for the western, *Paint Your Wagon*. Stunning Crater Lake lies in a glacially carved bowl with steep peaks rising above it, but the trail going to it is a steep one, climbing nearly 3,000 feet in slightly less than 6 miles. Like other lakes in the southern Wallowas, Crater Lake has been vandalized by irrigators who have placed a pipe in the lake to drain water to the lowlands below, where they grow hay crops for cattle fodder. The path to Crater Lake is known as Little Kettle Creek Trail. The first part of the trail passes through some sagebrush meadows, complete with flowers and aspen. It continues to climb a slope, switchbacking relentlessly. At 3.5 miles, you get a breather as the trail crosses a flat-bottomed valley before launching uphill for the final leg to the lake.

From Baker City, follow OR 86 east to Richland. Just before entering town, turn left (north) on County Road 969 toward Eagle Forks Campground. After it crosses the forest boundary, the road becomes FR 7735. Continue on this road as it joins Eagle Creek up to the East Fork and FR 7745, then turn right. Continue to the East Fork Eagle Creek Trailhead.

DAY HIKE OR OVERNIGHT BACKPACK: MINAM LAKE
One-way Length: 5.8 miles
Elevation Range: 5,600 to 7,480 feet
Difficulty: Strenuous

Just driving into the trailhead is worth the price of admission, since the road passes a long way up the highly scenic, glacially carved Lostine Wild and Scenic River valley. At 11.6 miles round-trip, this hike is long enough to be more desirable as an overnight backpack trip, but a strong hiker can make it to the lake and back in one long day hike. Remember, however, you'll have an 1,800-foot climb to get to the lake. The rewards for your efforts are a blue lake situated among wildflower-studded meadows and jagged peaks. From the trailhead, go up the East Fork of the Lostine on Trail #1670. The first part of the trail climbs through forests of Douglas fir, grand fir, and pine. At 2.8 miles, you come to a trail junction where Copper Creek joins the river and Trail #1676 goes off toward Swamp Lake. Continue straight at the junction, and head up the main river valley. It is 3 miles from this point to the lake, with the final few miles through more open terrain with an abundance of flowery meadows. The lakeshore is surrounded by trees. A look at the map shows that a nice 2- to 4-day overnight backpack and 17-mile loop are possible by continuing past Minam Lake on Trail #1661 to the East Fork of the Lostine River, then down Trail #1662 back to the trailhead.

From La Grande, drive 50 miles east OR 82 to Lostine. Turn right (south) on Lostine River Road, and go 18.3 miles to the popular Two Pan Trailhead.

OVERNIGHT HIKE: ICE LAKE
One-way Length: 7.5 miles
Elevation Range: 4,645 to 7,850 feet
Difficulty: Strenuous

Ice Lake lies in what is arguably one of Oregon's more spectacular settings. The glacially carved lake is nestled in a rocky basin between Sacajawea and Matterhorn Peaks, eastern Oregon's two highest mountains. As might be expected, such an eye-catching spot is popular with many Eagle Cap visitors. From the trailhead at Wallowa Lake, head up West Fork Wallowa River Trail #1820 for 2.8 miles to a trail junction for Ice Lake. Take Trail #1808, which switchbacks for 4.7 miles up through meadows past cascading creeks and waterfalls to the lake's outlet. Matterhorn Peak is climbable without technical gear and only requires a 1.9-mile hike up a broad ridge to the peak's 9,832-foot summit.

From La Grande, drive 70 miles east on OR 82 to Joseph, then follow signs for Wallowa Lake and the trailhead, at the south end of the lake.

OVERNIGHT BACKPACK: DOLLAR LAKE
One-way Length: 5.9 miles
Elevation Range: 6,520 to 8,470 feet
Difficulty: Strenuous

Dollar Lake sits in a stunning flower-filled alpine meadow close to timberline. Not only is the lake gorgeous, but the hike to it passes numerous flowery meadows en route. For those who want to make this a slightly longer trek, it's possible to continue on from Dollar Lake over Tenderfoot Pass, along the North Fork of the Imnaha River, and back to the Big Sheep drainage to make a 16.3-mile loop. From the trailhead, follow Big Sheep Creek upstream for 2.3 miles to a junction. Go right on Trail #1804 toward Bonny Lakes. At 3.9 miles, you reach flower-filled meadows surrounding the marshy Bonny Lakes. Day hikers can turn around here. If Dollar Lake is your goal, continue 1.7 miles to 8,420-foot Dollar Pass. From the pass it is an easy hike 0.3 mile south to Dollar Lake.

From Joseph, follow the Hells Canyon Scenic Byway (OR 350) east 8 miles to the Wallowa Mountain Loop Road (CR 4602/FR 39), then go south 13 miles to Salt Creek Summit. Continue on another 3 miles beyond the summit to FR 100. Turn right, and go up this road 3.2 miles to the Tenderfoot Trailhead.

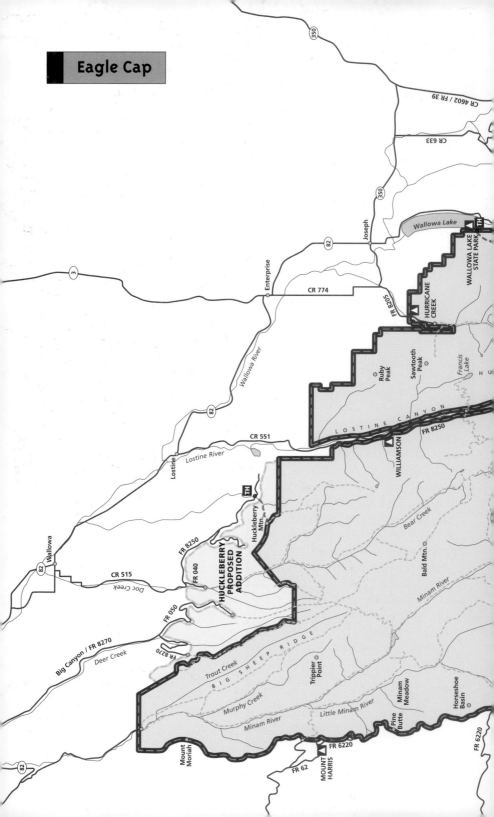

Eagle Cap

350

CR 4602 / FR 39

CR 633

350

82 Joseph

Wallowa Lake

WALLOWA LAKE
STATE PARK

3 Enterprise

CR 774

FR 8205

HURRICANE
CREEK

Wallowa River

Ruby
Peak

Sawtooth
Peak

Francis
Lake

HU

82

LOSTINE CANYON

CR 551

FR 8250

Lostine

Lostine River

WILLIAMSON

Bear Creek

Wallowa

FR 8250

Bald Mtn.

CR 515

Doc Creek

FR 040

HUCKLEBERRY
PROPOSED
ADDITION

Huckleberry
Mtn.

Minam River

FR 050

Big Canyon / FR 8270

Deer Creek

FR 8270

BIG SHEEP RIDGE

Trout Creek

Trippler
Point

Minam
Meadow

Horseshoe
Basin

Murphy Creek

Little Minam River

Pine
Butte

FR 6220

82

Minam River

FR 6220

Mount
Moriah

FR 62

MOUNT
HARRIS

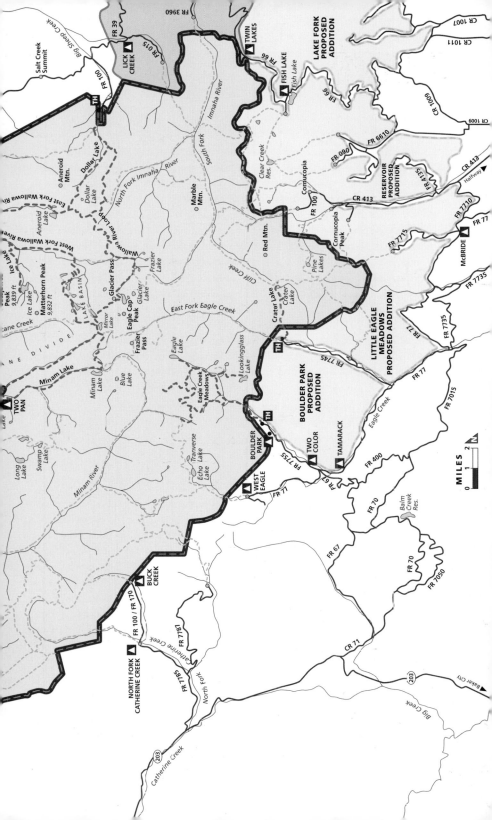

DAY HIKE: EAGLE CREEK MEADOWS
One-way Length: 4.5 miles
Elevation Range: 4,900 to 6,200 feet
Difficulty: Moderate

Eagle Creek accesses the less-traveled southern portion of Eagle Cap. This hike makes a good introduction to the area's features, notably wildflower fields below granite peaks. The main trail up Eagle Creek also provides access to more than a half dozen other cirque basins, lakes, and passes that provide various campsites and destinations including Lookingglass Lake, Bear Lake, Eagle Lake, and Arrow Lake. One could spend a week exploring this one drainage. The main trail follows an easy grade up the creek, passing at about 2.7 miles up the drainage the 60-foot Cooper Creek Falls. At 3 miles, you will pass the side trail up Bench Creek Valley and the path to reach Heart and Arrow Lakes. Continue up the main Eagle Creek Valley another 1.5 miles to Eagle Creek Meadows, a fine picnic area and turnaround point.

From Baker City, drive 25 miles north and east to Medical Springs, via I-84 and OR 203. Turn right onto County Road 71 along Big Creek, which becomes FR 67 (Big Creek Road) across the forest boundary. Continue east on winding FR 67 to Eagle Creek and FR 7755. Take FR 7755 north along the creek, following signs for Boulder Park Campground and the Eagle Creek Trailhead.

LOOP OVERNIGHT BACKPACK: WALLOWA RIVER
Trail Length: 36 miles
Elevation Range: 4,400 to 8,500 feet
Difficulty: Strenuous

This 3- to 6-day traverse provides access to some of the Eagle Cap's best scenery, lakes, meadows, and forest. These trails are also the most popular in the entire Eagle Cap Wilderness. Even so, this is a once-in-a-lifetime hike. From the trailhead, head toward Aneroid Lake on the East Fork Wallowa River Trail. Good campsites lie near this popular lake. A small parcel of private land with cabins takes up the south end of Aneroid Lake. Continue on over Tenderfoot Pass, into the valley of the North Fork of the Imnaha River, then quickly over Polaris Pass. Switchback down from Polaris Pass to the West Fork Wallowa River, then head upstream to Frazier Lake. From Frazier Lake, continue to popular and scenic Glacier Lake below 9,595-foot Eagle Cap Peak. From the lake, continue up to barren, 8,500-foot Glacier Pass and an unforgettable spectacle of glacier-carved lakes and peaks of the Lakes Basin.

Descend 1,200 feet into the aptly named Lake Basin. This is a popular destination and the focal point of most hikes in the Wallowas; expect to meet other campers. From Moccasin Lake, take Trail #1810 toward Douglas and Horseshoe Lakes, then descend to the West Fork of the Wallowa River. Follow the West Fork Wallowa Trail back to your vehicle at the trailhead.

From La Grande, drive 70 miles east on OR 82 to Joseph. Then continue 6 miles to the trailhead, at the south end of Wallowa Lake.

Hells Canyon Wilderness   35

View of Idaho's Seven Devils Mountains across Hells Canyon at Hat Point

SPANNING THE OREGON-IDAHO border along the Snake River for 70 miles, the sizable Hells Canyon Wilderness is itself part of the larger 652,488-acre Hells Canyon National Recreation Area (HCNRA), established by Congress in 1975. The Snake also divides the Hells Canyon Wilderness/HCNRA, with Oregon's portion of the total wilderness acreage at about 60 percent. More than 1,000 miles of trails crisscross Hells Canyon, a land of deep gorges, glaciated mountain peaks, bunchgrass grasslands, and beautiful old-growth ponderosa pine and Douglas

LOCATION: On the Idaho-Oregon border 80 miles east of Baker City

SIZE: 219,006 acres

ELEVATION RANGE: 930 to 7,000 feet

MAJOR FLORA: Bunchgrass grassland, ponderosa pine, Douglas fir, grand fir, Engelmann spruce, subalpine fir

ADMINISTRATION: Wallowa-Whitman NF (Oregon only), Hells Canyon National Recreation Area, 541-426-4978

BEST SEASON: Year-round

GETTING THERE: From La Grande, drive east 65 miles on OR 82 to Enterprise, then continue 5 more miles to Joseph. Veer left (east) onto Little Sheep Creek Highway (OR 350) and continue to Imnaha. The alternative access is to drive east from I-84 north of Baker City on OR 86 through Richland and Halfway to the junction with FR 39 (Wallowa Mountain Loop Road). Turn left and take FR 39 north through the Hells Canyon National Recreation Area.

fir forests—one of the most spectacular landscapes in Oregon. On the Idaho side, the Seven Devils Mountains rise up to 9,393 feet. These extensively glaciated mountains are dotted with cirque lakes and basins. The less dramatic Oregon side contains a number of plateaus that rise to nearly 7,000 feet.

The roiling waters of the Snake carry enough water to make it the sixth largest river by volume on the continent, with a gradient that drops from 1,520 feet at Hells Canyon Dam to 920 feet at Salmon Bar. Among its many superlative attributes, the Snake has cut the deepest canyon in North America—nearly 8,000 feet deep and 10 miles rim to rim. The Snake is also a designated Wild and Scenic River. The Wild section runs for 32.5 miles from Hells Canyon Dam to Upper Pittsburg Landing; the Scenic stretch runs for 34.4 miles below Pittsburg. Some 77 miles of the Imnaha River is also protected as Wild and Scenic.

Hells Canyon lies at the geographic heart of the Columbia River Basin. Situated at the western edge of the Rocky Mountains, it provides an ecological conduit to the Blue Mountains and eventually the Oregon Cascades. The canyon also links the Northern Rockies with the Great Basin of southeastern Oregon and southern Idaho. The sockeye salmon that migrate from the Pacific Ocean to Redfish Lake in central Idaho must swim up the Snake River in Hells Canyon. The wild wolf that in February 1999 migrated from central Idaho to eastern Oregon, seeking new territory, found a route through Hells Canyon. For plants and animals, Hells Canyon is not a barrier but a critical ecological stepping stone.

The canyon has been in the making for more than 300 million years. The first step in this process occurred between 300 and 130 million years ago with the eruption of a series of volcanoes along the margins of two plates. Most of the dark-colored and massive rocks exposed along the lower walls of Hells Canyon came from volcanoes that erupted on islands in the Pacific Ocean. This archipelago originated in tropical waters, as the presence of coral-derived limestone attests. Examples lie mixed among ancient volcanic flows just south of the mouth of the Grande Ronde River, and along the Oregon side of Hells Canyon Reservoir near Kinney Creek. The volcanic island arc was then covered by sediment from the erosion of surrounding areas. See this rock just south of the Oregon-Washington border and in the vicinity of Pittsburg Landing.

At the same time that sediments were accumulating on top of these ancient volcanoes, new movement of magma up through the Earth's crust penetrated the older rock. This molten magma solidified into granitic bodies known as plutons, still exposed over extensive areas in the upper elevations of the Wallowa and Seven Devils Mountains. Then the remains of this volcanic archipelago collided with North America. The rocks were again uplifted and partially eroded in the adjacent sea basin. Remnants of these eroded rocks are visible near Mitchell, Oregon. Then, between 17 and 6 million years ago, huge quantities of basalt (lava) began to flow from volcanoes in the Columbia River Basin, flooding the entire landscape. After these massive eruptions, tectonic forces again uplifted the Hells Canyon area. As the mountains rose, the Snake River cut downward, creating its deep canyon in the process.

The finishing touches on the area occurred in the past 2 million years, as Ice Age glaciers gouged out cirques and sculpted U-shaped valleys in the higher basins, particularly on the Seven Devils and Wallowa Mountains. The greater precipitation that occurred during the Ice Ages also fostered accelerated down-cutting of the canyon.

Catastrophic events also helped to shape the present landscape. Giant glacial lakes formed throughout the Great Basin during the end of the last Ice Age. Lake Bonneville, whose relict we know as Great Salt Lake, breached a natural dam and flooded the Snake River Plain some 15,000 years ago. The resulting flood had an enormous effect on the canyon as we see it today. The volume of water during this event was at least 1,000 times greater than that of average spring runoff levels today. This tremendous flow did not deepen the canyon, but it did increase its width and formed the large terraces seen near the mouth of Temperance Creek, at Johnson Bar, and at Pittsburg Landing. Though not as large as an Ice Age stream, the Snake River is still a big river. Below Hells Canyon Dam, the Snake usually carries more water than the Colorado River through the Grand Canyon.

Because of the tremendous elevation variation, it's difficult to generalize about the climate in Hells Canyon. At the bottom of the canyon, arid conditions predominate. Annual precipitation is often less than 10 inches per year, and summertime temperatures can easily exceed 100 degrees. At the same time, winters are relatively mild, with snow unusual. Spring and fall are delightful at all elevations under 4,000 feet. At higher elevations, climatic conditions are more typical of the Rocky Mountains. Annual precipitation is from 30 to 40 inches in some locations, mostly in the form of snow. Winter temperatures below freezing are common, especially at night. Summer temperatures, particularly at the higher ridgelines, usually do not exceed 80 degrees, with rapid night-time cooling. Regardless of elevation, May and June are the wettest months, with summers nearly rainless except for occasional thundershowers. September brings some of the best weather of the year, with clear, bright blue days and cool evenings.

Cottonwood and willow are the dominant tree species in riparian areas. Some of the most majestic stands of old-growth ponderosa pine, Engelmann spruce, western larch, and grand fir in the state can still be found here. But perhaps even more than forests, it is the grasslands that are special. Mostly because of ruggedness and remoteness, some of the Columbia Basin's best remnants of intact native grasslands are in the Hells Canyon ecosystem. At least 15 endemics and many more regional endemics live in the HCNRA. Wildflowers, including the localized, endangered MacFarlane's four-o'clock, are profuse, especially in the alpine regions of the Wallowa and Seven Devils Mountains. Bunchgrass communities blanket the open slopes and steep benchlands of the canyon. Unfortunately, exotic species threaten these grasslands.

In fact, many of these grasslands are no longer trampled, grazed, and compromised by domestic livestock. HCNRA contains some of the largest ungrazed (by domestic livestock) tracts of grasslands in the West. Their value to science, as a control against which other grazed lands are measured, is immense. Unfortunately, the Forest Service is currently contemplating reopening previously closed grazing allotments, negating both the scientific value of these grasslands and potentially compromising their future. Exotic weeds, particularly at lower elevations, are taking over many of these lands.

Nearly every native species of wildlife in the Pacific Northwest still inhabit the Hells Canyon ecosystem, thanks to its varied, accommodating landforms and habitats as well as its ecologically central location. Large mammalian predators, including mountain lion, black bear, bobcat, and coyote, are abundant. Wolverines, rare everywhere south of Canada, have been documented in the HCNRA. There is some speculation, although no solid confirmation, that lynx may exist here as well. Still absent are grizzly bear and perhaps wolf—although it's only a matter of time before wolves from Idaho establish themselves here, and probably no part of Oregon is better potential wolf habitat. Indeed, in the winter of 1999 a wolf from Idaho roamed across the region before being captured by the U.S. Fish and Wildlife Service and removed to Idaho.

The HCNRA supports 13 species of bats, including seven that are possible candidates for listing under the Federal Endangered Species Act. Among the sensitive species, maternity colonies of the Yuma myotis and little brown bat dwell along the Snake River corridor; big brown bats and silver-haired bats use the treed uplands.

Bird species include unique birds of prey such as bald and golden eagle, osprey, great gray owl, goshawk, and peregrine falcon. Among the rare birds in the area, the flammulated owl is known to nest in the wilderness. The boreal owl has not yet been located in the wilderness but is known from the region. Neotropical migrants such as western tanager, yellow warbler, and lazuli bunting find an accommodating spring stopover in Hells Canyon's riparian zones.

Fisheries are also an important attribute of HCNRA. Anadromous salmon fisheries were destroyed above Hells Canyon Dam, but below that point, salmon and steelhead remain. Steelhead, redband trout, and a few summer Chinook still spawn in the small streams that drain directly into the Snake River in Hells Canyon. Most of these streams are so steep and rapid that they have limited use for anadromous fish, but Temperance, Sheep, Kirkwood, and Granite Creeks enjoy the best habitat. Juvenile salmon have been reported in both Granite and Sheep Creeks, indicating some natural spawning success. Several other streams are important for native fish, including Cherry Creek, which contains pure populations of native redband trout.

The Imnaha River is perhaps the most important fishery in the HCNRA. It supports native populations of endangered bull trout, native redband trout, steelhead, and Chinook salmon. The Imnaha Chinook salmon are considered to be genetically unique. Because most of the drainage is in public hands, habitat quality overall is in good shape. Dewatering for irrigation on the private lands along the drainage, however, does reduce water flows and increases water temperatures, to the detriment of fish. The North Fork of Pine Creek also supports native redband trout. Bull trout, known to live in the Pine Creek drainage outside of the HCNRA, may also be present within it. The area also supports Columbia spotted frog, a sensitive species whose numbers have declined elsewhere.

The Hells Canyon ecosystem harbors the largest free-roaming elk herd in North America. Ironically, elk had been completely extirpated from the area by the turn of the century, but reintroductions from Yellowstone helped to reestablish the animal here. Their numbers today are between 3,000 and 4,500 animals in the HCNRA. Excellent bighorn sheep habitat also exists. Like the elk, bighorns were wiped out primarily by diseases transmitted from domestic sheep to their wild cousins. Reintroductions of the sheep first began in 1971 and have continued until the present. Today, an estimated 700 bighorn sheep inhabit the HCNRA. Despite this positive trend, recurring die-offs—often a result of diseases transmitted from domestic livestock still permitted to graze public lands—continue to threaten these populations.

The Snake River through Hells Canyon was once inhabited by the Shoshone and Nez Perce tribes. The Shoshone or "Snake" Indians were the inadvertent source of the river's name. Using a sign language, the Shoshone identified themselves to recently arrived Euro-Americans by making an undulating hand motion, meant to signify that they were the people who lived by a river full of fish. The motion, however, was mistaken

Alder frames Nelson Creek in Hells Canyon Wilderness

by the newcomers as signifying a snake, and the rest is history. Long known as Box
Canyon or Snake River Canyon, Hells Canyon acquired its current name only in the
1950s, from Hells Canyon Creek, which enters the river near Hells Canyon Dam.

In the Hells Canyon ecosystem, many reminders of these previous residents have
survived, including the ruins of pit houses and depressions in the ground, where shallow
holes were excavated and over which were built dome structures of willow branches
topped with skins or grass mats. Rock-art sites bear inscriptions either carved or painted
on the rocks. Lithic scatters, debris deposits where tools and weapons were made, are
abundant. Well over 1,000 documented archaeological sites exist within the HCNRA
alone. Some of these date back as far as 7,100 years, cultural vestiges that long predate
the Nez Perce tribal presence in the Hells Canyon ecosystem.

In 1964, Hells Canyon was thrust into the national limelight when construction
proposals were announced for what was called the Nez Perce dam site, near the confluence of the Salmon and Snake Rivers. Because the proposed dam would have blocked
salmon runs in both rivers, a new site was proposed, known as the High Mountain Sheep
site. Had it been built, the High Mountain Sheep Dam would have created a 58-mile-
long reservoir that would have flooded Hells Canyon. Environmentalists fought the
dam proposal all the way to the Supreme Court. Justice William O. Douglas ruled that
dam promoters had failed to demonstrate that the dam would be in the public interest.

Initially, environmentalists proposed protecting the canyon by the designation of the Snake as a National Wild and Scenic River—a designation that effectively prohibits dams. But then Brock Evans of the Sierra Club, Cliff Merritt of the Wilderness Society, and others decided to obtain protection for the canyon beyond the river. Together they lobbied to get wilderness protection for Hells Canyon, and in December 1975, federal legislation was passed creating HCNRA and protecting the Snake as a Wild and Scenic River.

A discussion of the designated wilderness cannot be separated from a discussion of the HCNRA as a whole. Still, among other differences, wilderness designation prohibits roads and motorized access and most resource extraction. National Recreation Area (NRA) status is less protective, permitting activities like logging, ORV use, snow-mobiling, and mining to continue. Today, controversy still swirls around what NRA status really means and whether the U.S. Forest Service is in fact protecting the area as mandated by NRA designation. When the HCNRA was established, most people thought that the new status would bring some protection for the area from traditional exploitative industries, so that impacts such as logging and livestock grazing would be prohibited, or at least very limited in extent. Instead, the Forest Service has managed the HCNRA essentially the same as other lands.

A number of major roadless areas adjoin the existing Hells Canyon Wilderness. The largest of these is the Lord Flat Roadless Area. It lies within the Hells Canyon National Recreation Area in the Wallowa-Whitman National Forest. The western edge of this area is 2 miles as the crow flies from the village of Imnaha, about 30 miles northeast of the town of Joseph. Climbing up from the depths of Hells Canyon, you can reach the west rim and gaze westward upon a forested plateau, falling at first gently, then dramatically. Composed mostly of Columbia River basalt, the Lord Flat plateau is graced with old-growth ponderosa pine and decorated with lush meadows and marshes. From the 6,500-foot plateau, the land descends northwest to the rimrock canyons of Cow, Lightning, and Horse Creeks. By the time these creeks empty into the Imnaha River at 1,000 feet above sea level, their canyons are a spectacle of knife-edged ridges.

The Lord Flat Roadless Area adjoins the Hells Canyon Wilderness at the rim, where the wilderness ends. At 110,000 acres, it is one of the largest contiguous chunks of backcountry remaining in national forestlands in Oregon. Technically, it adjoins the Imnaha Face Roadless Area, which adds another 27,000 roadless acres to the south. Lord Flat provides unparalleled habitat for the largest free-roaming elk herd in North America. Bighorn sheep, marten, peregrine falcon, and many other rare species exist in its secluded folds. Endangered spring Chinook salmon maintain a tenuous existence in its creeks.

To provide protection to the entire ecosystem, conservationists are proposing that a 1.5 million-acre Hells Canyon/Chief Joseph National Park and Preserve be designated by Congress. For more information on this proposal, contact the Hells Canyon Preservation Council in La Grande (see Appendix B, p. 266). Certainly if you take the time to visit this area, you'll understand why people want to protect and preserve it.

OVERNIGHT HIKE: WESTERN RIM NATIONAL RECREATION TRAIL—
LOOKOUT MOUNTAIN
One-way Length: 8.3 miles
Elevation Range: 6,400 to 6,792 feet
   Difficulty: Moderate

The Western Rim National Recreation Trail to Lookout Mountain winds beside
wildflower-studded meadows along Summit Ridge, providing unparalleled vistas
of the entire Hells Canyon country. The trail follows the western boundary of the
Hells Canyon Wilderness and weaves in and out of the official wilderness. Nevertheless, keep in mind that most of the route traverses a roadless area that is part of
the proposed additions to the Hells Canyon Wilderness, although a few sections
of the trail follow old jeep trails.

From the trailhead the trail descends to a junction at Freezeout Saddle, some
2 miles from the road. Along the route to the saddle, you are treated to fantastic views
of the Snake River Canyon and the Seven Devils Mountains. At the trail junction,
continue south along the open meadows of the ridge on the Western Rim Trail #1774.
You'll pass a number of other trail junctions, including a side trip on Trail #1743 to
Bear Mountain, a 2.5-mile-long (one way) ridge-top trail that offers some of the best
views of Hells Canyon anywhere, including a view of the Snake River some 5,500
feet below. Just beyond where the Bear Mountain Trail leaves the Western Rim Trail,
Squirrel Prairie makes a good potential overnight campsite. There is also reported
to be a spring at Marks Cabin, just off the main trail to the right along Trail #1763
(west) that may also offer another prospective campsite. Drop your pack here and
then day-hike either to Bear Mountain or the rest of the way to the summit of
Lookout Mountain, crowned with a radio tower. Trees obscure the view from the
summit in some directions, but you obtain a fine view of Hells Canyon. The best
views are actually en route to Lookout Mountain rather than on its summit.

From Joseph, head east 30 miles on Little Sheep Creek Highway (OR 350)
to Imnaha. Continue south and east along gravel Grizzly Ridge Road to Hat Point
Road (FR 4240). It is 17 often steep miles to the trailhead at Summit Ridge, just
before Saddle Creek Campground.

LOOP HIKE: BUCK CREEK—BENCH TRAIL
   Trail Length: 5.5 miles (with shuttle) or 6.2 miles (without shuttle)
Elevation Range: 4,000 to 6,200 feet
   Difficulty: Moderate

This loop trip makes a nice day hike and provides expansive views of Hells Canyon
and the Seven Devils Mountains. The starting and ending points are located 0.7 mile
apart on dirt FR 3965. You can either do a car shuttle prior to the hike or, better
yet, bring a mountain bike and stash it at one trailhead for the short ride back to
your vehicle at the other trailhead. Worse comes to worse, you can just walk the
road, which has little traffic and is not that different from hiking a wide trail.

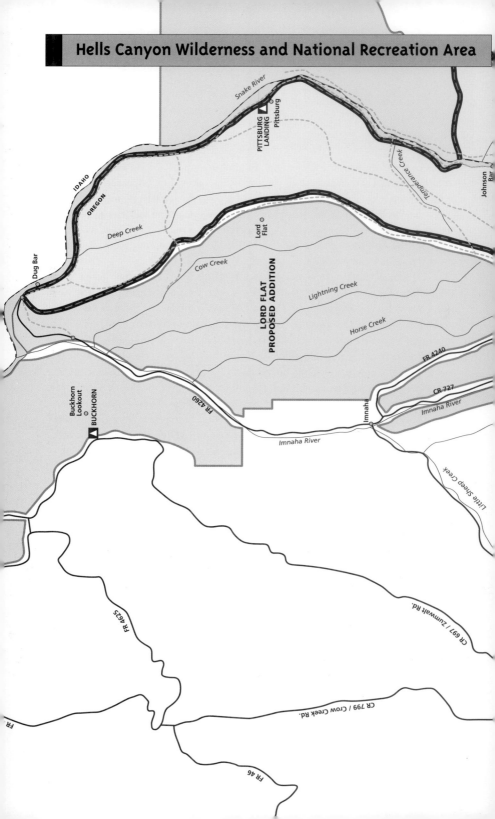

Hells Canyon Wilderness and National Recreation Area

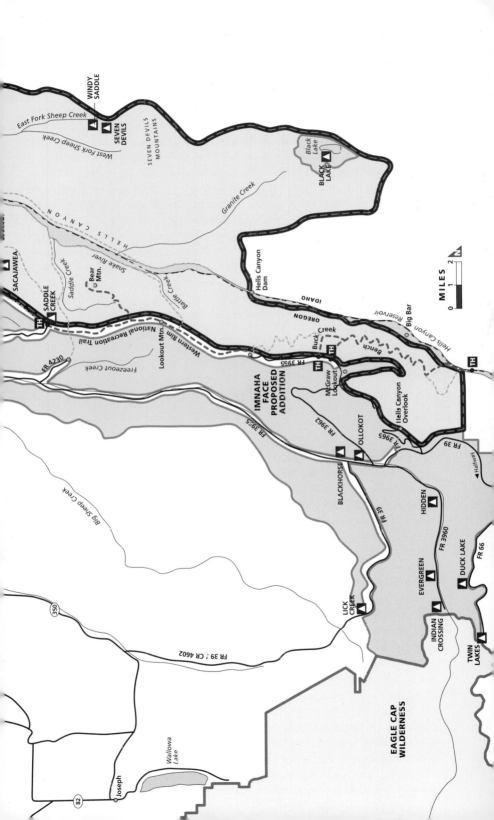

You can do the hike from either trailhead, but I recommend starting at Buck Creek. You can drop off your bike or car en route, and you won't miss the easily missed junction with 32 Point and Bench Trails.

The trail from Buck Creek descends by switchbacks through open slopes full of wildflowers in spring and early summer. Enjoy exceptional views of the entire canyon from several promontories along this trail. It eventually gains a ridge and descends by this to its junction with 32 Point Trail #1789 at 4,700 feet. From here, turn right and head south for 1.6 miles to the junction with Bench Trail #1884 at 4,000 feet. At this point, turn and follow the Bench Trail back upslope 2 steep miles to the trailhead. Most of this way, the trail passes through open terrain, alternately following ridgelines and occasionally crossing flowery, grassy slopes.

From Baker City, drive OR 86 about 54 miles east to Halfway. About 12 miles east of Halfway, take the left onto FR 39 (Wallowa Mountain Loop Road) going north. Follow this paved road to the Hells Canyon Overlook turnoff (FR 3965) on the right. Continue on this road to the Buck Creek Trailhead and campground. Less than a mile before you reach Buck Creek, note the location of the Upper Bench Trailhead on the right—your point of exit for this hike.

OVERNIGHT HIKE: BENCH TRAIL #1884
One-way Length: 11.5 miles
Elevation Range: 1,760 to 6,200 feet
Difficulty: Strenuous

This hike starts out along the Snake River but soon ascends to the mid-elevation benchlands between the highest ridges and the river below. Hiking through these meadows in April and May, when the grasslands are lush with wildflowers, is an unforgettable experience. Lovely campsites lie amid groves of ponderosa pine and Douglas fir. You'll find lots of opportunity to observe wildlife. Bighorn sheep, black bear, and elk are common along this trail.

This hike is best done as a 2- to 3-day backpack or a long one-way shuttle hike. Because of the huge amount of driving needed to do a shuttle, I don't recommend one. Still, if you can arrange to have someone drop you off at the Upper Bench Trailhead on FR 3965, the hike would be a mostly downhill run to the Hells Canyon Trailhead by Copperfield. I recommend hiking partway to the upper trailhead, pitching a base camp along one of the many fine streams that tumble down into the canyon, enjoying a day hike to the upper trailhead to see the views, then returning back to the Hells Canyon Trailhead.

The trail starts by following Hells Canyon Trail #1890. In 2.8 miles, you reach Spring Creek, where the Bench Trail swings up via switchbacks to the benchlands. You'll pass the junction with McGraw Creek Trail at 5.3 miles from the trailhead. Continue on and cross Leep Creek in 0.1 mile. From here it is 0.8 mile to Kirby Creek, then in another 0.5 mile you cross the North Fork of Kirby Creek. Continue 4.7 miles to the upper trailhead or turnaround point. You will hike at more or less the same elevation, with dips and rises as you cross creek basins including Dove, Lynch, Doyle, and Allen Creeks. Note that some of these streams are often dry in late summer, so you don't want to rely on them for water. Once you cross Squaw Creek, you reach the junction with 32 Point Trail #1789 at about 4,000 feet. Turn around or, if you want to get to the upper trailhead for some reason, bear left and go another steep 2 miles uphill through increasingly thick timber to the upper trailhead. If you have not arranged a shuttle, return as you came.

From Baker City, drive east 70 miles on OR 86 to Copperfield. Veer left (north) onto County Road 1039, and follow it 9 miles to the trailhead. To get to the upper trailhead, drive OR 86 east to Halfway. About 12 miles east of Halfway, take the left onto FR 39 (Wallowa Mountain Loop Road) going north. Follow this paved road to the Hells Canyon Overlook turnoff (FR 3965) on the right. Continue on this road to the Upper Bench Trailhead. If you reach the Buck Creek Trailhead and campground, you have gone too far.

OTHER RECREATIONAL OPPORTUNITIES

Rafting and kayaking through Hells Canyon are popular, and some people even attempt to run the Snake River in canoes. The best canoeing stretch is below Pittsburg Landing, downstream of the largest rapids. Permits to run the river are required during peak season. The float down the river takes you through designated wilderness and extraordinary scenery. Because of its low elevation, the canyon is very arid, and often hot during the summer. One major distraction is the use of jet boats on the "Wild" River in a "Wilderness." Such nonconforming uses are permitted primarily due to the political clout of a small number of commercial jet boat operations.

Most of the rapids on the Snake in Hells Canyon are Class III-IV—this is a big, powerful river and should be treated with respect. Most of the difficult rapids are at the beginning, then the pace of the trip slows considerably. The two major rapids, Wild Sheep and Granite Creek, should be scouted, especially at high flows when these rapids can easily flip the largest rafts. Those with kayaks and other small boats can portage these rapids. The remainder of the trip, if still offering some exciting rapids, is mostly serene. To avoid the slower water in the lower canyon, many boaters take out at Pittsburg Landing (mile 32); roughly half of all trips end there.

Besides the thrill of whitewater rapids and superb scenery, some are attracted to the canyon for its fishing. Species in the river include trout, bass, and catfish. Although salmon and steelhead are found in the canyon, their numbers are low because of the impacts of upstream dams on populations. Other species likely to be seen while floating the river are bighorn sheep, osprey, eagle, chukar partridge, turkey, mule deer, elk, bear, and otter.

You have several options for trip length. The run to Pittsburgh Landing is 32 miles; Heller Bar is 79 miles. Roads access both take-out points. Most camping takes place on grassy benches above the river, since sediment for creating sand beaches is trapped behind upstream dams. Sandy beaches increase below the Salmon River confluence.

Most people run the river between March and November. Flows are highest in spring and gradually decrease throughout the summer. However, dam releases upstream can affect even summertime water flows. Most people try to run the river when flows are between 5,000 and 40,000 cfs. High water, which begins around 30,000 cfs, can be a problem for all boaters except in the lower flatwater sections.

36 | Mill Creek Wilderness

Hiker along Mill Creek, Mill Creek Wilderness

LOCATION: 18 miles northeast of Prineville

SIZE: 17,400 acres

ELEVATION RANGE: 3,700 to 6,240 feet

MAJOR FLORA: Ponderosa pine, Douglas fir, lodgepole pine, aspen, bunchgrass meadows

ADMINISTRATION: Ochoco NF, Lookout Mountain RD, 541-416-6500

BEST SEASON: May to November

GETTING THERE: From Prineville, drive east on US 26 for 9 miles to Ochoco Reservoir, then turn left on FR 33 and go another 9 miles to the Mill Creek Trailhead.

CARVED WITH DEEP CANYONS and home to odd, pinnacle-like rock formations, the Mill Creek Wilderness is the largest of three designated wildernesses in the Ochoco National Forest created by the 1984 Oregon Wilderness Act. Less than an hour from Bend, the wilderness receives surprisingly little use, but don't be misled: This compact wilderness is a delight, boasting giant, old-growth ponderosa pine and a surprisingly lush riparian area along Mill Creek.

The Mill Creek Wilderness sits at the northwestern corner of the Ochoco Mountains, a volcanic range created 40 to 50 million years ago when lavas flowed across what is now eastern Oregon (on view at nearby John Day Fossil Beds National Monument). Remains of a volcano conduit, or "throat," that had probably lain more than a mile below the original volcano's surface, the Twin Pillars are a major

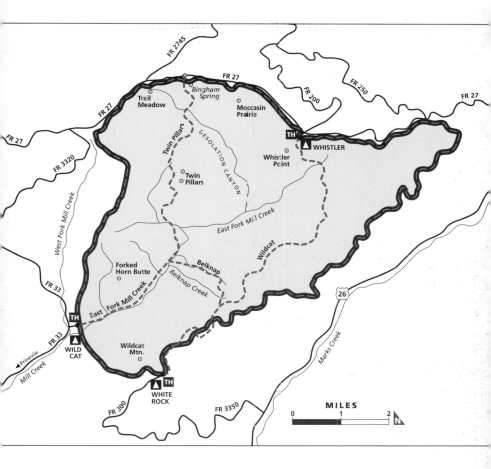

landmark in Mill Creek Wilderness. The molten rock in the volcanic duct solidified and, being harder and more resistant to erosion than the surrounding slopes of ash and lava, the ancient conduit has persisted long after the other parts of the volcano have been stripped away.

Climatic conditions are continental, with a limited amount of annual precipitation, dominated by winter snowfall and dry, sunny summer days. Winter temperatures may dip below freezing for extended periods of time, but are often broken by warm interludes. Cities like Prineville receive less than 15 inches of precipitation annually. Given the higher elevation, however, the Mill Creek Wilderness may receive between 20 and 30 inches annually.

Plant communities are mainly old-growth ponderosa pine mixed with Douglas fir and western larch. Lodgepole pine occurs in the northwestern corner. Small pocket meadows line the creeks. Shrubs include red osier dogwood, snowberry, and ocean spray.

Wildlife in the area includes elk and mule deer, plus black bear, mountain lion, coyote, marten, yellow-bellied marmot, and other smaller mammals. Wild turkey, white-headed woodpecker, goshawk, and pileated woodpecker are also reported. The perennial streams hold small rainbow trout and brook trout.

Unfortunately for the wildlife and plant communities, the area is grazed by domestic livestock, contributing to degraded water, trampled riparian areas, introduction of weeds, and loss of forage that would otherwise support native wildlife.

There are 21 miles of trail in the wilderness along three trails: the Twin Pillars, Belknap, and Wildcat.

DAY HIKE: EAST FORK MILL CREEK
One-way Length: 2.9 miles
Elevation Range: 3,700 to 4,000 feet
Difficulty: Moderate

The hike up the East Fork Mill Creek passes through small, lush, flower-studded meadows and beautiful old-growth ponderosa pine. The turnaround point is Belknap Creek, which requires fording. Early in the season this may present a challenge, but later in the summer the stream is small enough so that you can rock-hop your way across or find a log to use as a bridge. It's far easier, however, if you just bring sandals for wading the stream. The hike to Belknap Creek Trail junction is a pleasant stroll through forest and meadow. A nice campsite at the Belknap and East Fork Mill Creek Trails junction could be a good base camp if you want to explore further. If you're very motivated or making an overnight backpack trip, it's possible to continue upstream another 2.6 miles to the Twin Pillars, a geological formation, and another 2.9 miles to the Twin Pillars Trailhead.

From Prineville, drive east on US 26 for 9 miles toward Ochoco Reservoir, then turn left on FR 33 and go another 9 miles to the Wildcat Trailhead.

DAY HIKE: WILDCAT TRAIL #833
One-way Length: 8.1 miles
Elevation Range: 4,500 to 5,750 feet
Difficulty: Moderate

The Wildcat Trail runs between the White Rock Campground and Whistler Campground along the southern portion of the wilderness. The trail is very dry, so bring lots of water. You'll cross occasional meadows and traverse rolling forests of Douglas fir and occasional old-growth ponderosa pine. At 2.1 miles, you reach the Belknap Trail. The trail continues across slopes and on ridgelines until it descends to the East Fork of Mill Creek, about 7 miles from the trailhead. The final mile climbs to Whistler Campground.

From Prineville, go east on US 26 about 22 miles, turn left on FR 3350, and drive 6.5 miles on it and FR 300 to the White Rock Campground and trailhead.

OTHER RECREATIONAL OPPORTUNITIES

The road to Mill Creek Campground is usually open and plowed in winter (check locally before driving) to allow access for cross-country skiing in deep-snow seasons.

Monument Rock Wilderness 37

Monument Rock, Monument Rock Wilderness

THE 19,620-ACRE MONUMENT ROCK WILDERNESS anchors the southeastern edge of the Blue Mountains and the easternmost portion of the Strawberry Mountains. It takes in the headwaters of the Little Malheur River as well as the South Fork of the Burnt River. The mountain crests tend to be alpine and treeless, offering outstanding views. Monument Rock, Bullrun Rock, Table Rock, and other peaks here present sweeping views to the east toward the Elkhorn Mountains and south across eastern Oregon's Basin and Range country. The wilderness is for the most part heavily forested yet also contains open slopes of sage and wildflowers frequented by herds of elk.

LOCATION: 25 miles southeast of Prairie City

SIZE: 19,620 acres

ELEVATION RANGE: 5,120 to 7,873 feet

MAJOR FLORA: Ponderosa pine, lodgepole pine, western larch, white fir, aspen, subalpine fir

ADMINISTRATION: Malheur NF, Prairie City RD, 541-820-3311; Wallowa-Whitman NF, Unity RD, 541-446-3351

BEST SEASON: June to October

GETTING THERE: From Prairie City, take County Road 62 southeast 10 miles to FR 13 and turn left. Go about 12 miles, make another left onto FR 1370, and continue to the wilderness boundary.

The wilderness is named for an 8-foot cylindrical stone monument, standing at an elevation of 7,736 feet, likely erected by sheepherders. Established in 1984 by the Oregon Wilderness Act, the wilderness is managed by two national forests: the Malheur NF controls 12,620 acres, and the adjacent Wallowa-Whitman NF controls 7,030 acres. The highest elevations formerly held Ice Age glaciers that carved U-shaped valleys and glacial cirques. The area's lowest elevation is along the Little Malheur River; 7,873-foot Bullrun Rock is the highest summit in the wilderness. Table Rock, at 7,815 feet, is actually cherry-stemmed out of the wilderness by a poor dirt road that leads to the fire lookout on its summit.

Much of the area was burned and rejuvenated by fire in 1989. The abundance of snags has resulted in outstanding wildlife habitat for woodpeckers and other cavity-nesting species, while the dense thickets of lodgepole pine and other trees that now cloak the slopes have created outstanding hiding cover for elk and other species. Unlike other wilderness areas closer to Oregon's urban centers, the majority of use in the Monument Rock Wilderness occurs during hunting season. Come here in the summer, and you're likely to have the place to yourself.

Like most of eastern Oregon, the climate is continental with maritime influences. Thus winters tend to be cold, but with frequent periods of cloudy weather. Most of the annual 40 inches of precipitation occurs in the winter months. Summers tend to be dry and usually warm, but not hot. Summer nights are cool. Spring is the rainiest season. Autumns are perhaps the nicest time of year, since days tend to be clear with cool nights.

Lower-elevation forests contain ponderosa pine, with middle elevations a mix of lodgepole pine, western larch, and white fir. The abundance of lodgepole pine betokens past wildfires. Aspen often fringe the meadows. The highest elevations contain subalpine fir. In the forest understory grow elk sedge, pinegrass, and huckleberry; sagebrush and bunchgrass blanket open slopes. Wildflowers can be very plentiful in season.

Deer, elk, badger, and reportedly the rare wolverine inhabit the area. Seventy species of bird live here, including the creek-loving American dipper and the pileated woodpecker. The Little Malheur River contains redband rainbow trout.

Despite the fact that wilderness is supposed to be a place where natural processes and wildlife are given priority, this wilderness—like many in eastern Oregon—is trampled and degraded by domestic livestock. While backpackers are encouraged to practice

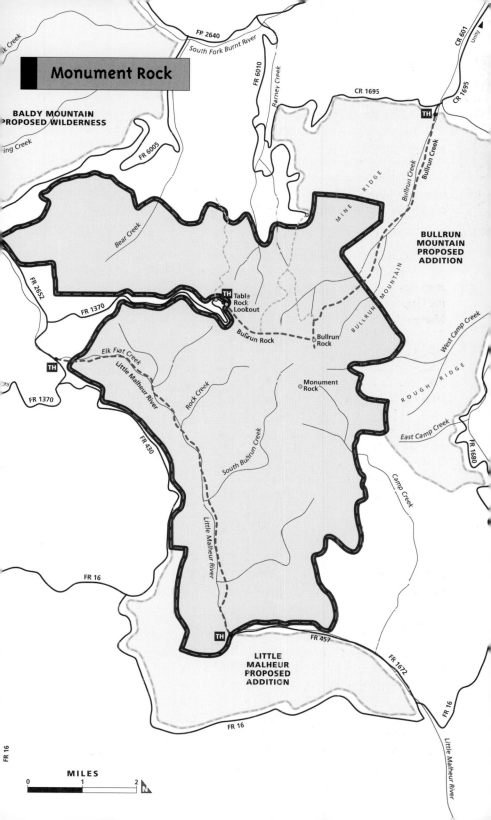

Monument Rock

BALDY MOUNTAIN PROPOSED WILDERNESS

BULLRUN MOUNTAIN PROPOSED ADDITION

LITTLE MALHEUR PROPOSED ADDITION

FP 2640
South Fork Burnt River
Elk Creek
FR 6010
Rarney Creek
CR 601
Unity
CR 1695
CR 1695
TH
Bullrun Creek
Bullrun Creek
FR 6005
ring Creek
FR 2652
Bear Creek
MINE RIDGE
BULLRUN MOUNTAIN
FR 1370
TH
Table Rock Lookout
Bullrun Rock
Bullrun Rock
West Camp Creek
ROUGH RIDGE
TH
Elk Flat Creek
Little Malheur River
Monument Rock
FR 1370
city
Rock Creek
East Camp Creek
FR 1680
FR 430
South Bullrun Creek
Camp Creek
Little Malheur River
FR 16
TH
FR 457
FR 1672
FR 16
FR 16
Little Malheur River

MILES

0   1   2

FR 16

low-impact camping techniques, cattle range across the landscape, trampling under hooves the riparian areas critically important to wildlife, and polluting the water. Forage that should be supporting native elk and other wildlife is allotted to domestic animals.

The Monument Rock Wilderness is part of a larger roadless complex. Just west of the Monument Rock Wilderness across FR 13 lies the 19,500-acre Glacier Mountain proposed wilderness. This area lies sandwiched between the Monument Rock area on the east and the Strawberry Mountain Wilderness on the west. It is a critical link in the continuous line of roadless lands in the Strawberry Mountains. Southwest of the Monument Rock Wilderness is the North Fork Malheur proposed wilderness. Giant old-growth ponderosa pine and numerous meadows characterize this area.

DAY HIKE: TABLE ROCK TO BULLRUN ROCK
One-way Length: 2 miles
Elevation Range: 7,480 to 7,873 feet
    Difficulty: Easy

Bullrun Rock and its 150-foot cliffs make a good day-hike destination. Before heading down the trail, check out the view from the fire lookout tower on Table Mountain. After taking it in, backtrack a half mile down the lookout road and take a level, 2-mile stroll along an old abandoned road, now Trail #365, to Bullrun Rock. After the first 0.6 mile, you will reach a trail junction that leads to Rock Creek Spring, where you can camp. The rest of the trail passes through open meadows of sagebrush and wildflowers early in the summer.

From Prairie City, follow paved County Road 62 southeast 10 miles, turn left onto FR 13, go 12 miles to FR 1370, turn left, and drive about 10 miles to Table Rock Lookout.

DAY HIKE: BULLRUN CREEK TO BULLRUN ROCK
One-way Length: 5.5 miles
Elevation Range: 4,800 to 7,873 feet
    Difficulty: Moderate

The Bullrun Creek Trail starts out with 2 easy miles of hiking in a steep-sided canyon, crossing the creek several times. It then takes off up a ridge, climbing 2,000 feet in 3.5 miles to Bullrun Rock, where there are terrific views. The first part of this hike is actually outside of the wilderness in an area proposed as an addition to the Monument Rock Wilderness.

From US 26 in Unity, drive a mile west on County Road 600, then turn left (south) onto gravel County Road 601 and go 4 miles. Jog to the right on FR 1695, then follow FR 210 to the trail.

SHUTTLE HIKE: LITTLE MALHEUR RIVER TRAIL #366
One-way Length: 7.2 miles
Elevation Range: 5,200 to 6,600 feet
        Difficulty: Moderate

This hike can be done as a partway, down-and-back day hike, or as suggested: a one-way shuttle hike. The Little Malheur River drains the southwestern corner of the Monument Rock Wilderness and offers fishing for wild redband rainbow trout. The best way to hike it is from the upper trailhead, although the best fishing and the largest old-growth trees lie at the lower end. The trail first follows Elk Flat Creek, one of the headwater streams of the Little Malheur River. In the first 2.1 miles along Elk Flat Creek, the trail passes through occasional meadows and descends through a forest of lodgepole pine before reaching the Little Malheur River. It then follows the Little Malheur the rest of the way to the lower trailhead. A good campsite on a riverside flat lies about 4.7 miles from the upper trailhead, near where South Bullrun Creek joins the river. South Bullrun Creek also makes a good turn-around point for those who just want to do a long day hike.

To reach the upper trailhead from Prairie City, take County Road 62 southeast 10 miles to FR 13 and turn left; drive 12 miles south, then turn left again onto FR 1370. Go about 5 miles to the trailhead, just before Elk Flat Camp. To reach the lower trailhead, follow the same directions from Prairie City, but instead of turning off of FR 13 onto FR 1370, continue straight to Short Creek Guard Station. Then turn left onto FR 16, drive to FR 1672 (which turns into FR 457), and turn left, following it along the Little Malheur River to the trailhead.

38 | North Fork John Day Wilderness

North Fork John Day River near Bear Gulch

LOCATION: 25 miles northwest of Baker City

SIZE: 121,111 acres

ELEVATION RANGE: 3,356 to 9,106 feet

MAJOR FLORA: Ponderosa pine, western larch, Douglas fir, lodgepole pine, subalpine fir

ADMINISTRATION: Umatilla NF, North Fork John Day RD, 541-427-3231; Wallowa-Whitman NF, Baker RD, 541-523-4476

BEST SEASON: June to October

GETTING THERE: Since four units make up this wilderness, the directions here are to the most accessible of these. From Baker City, drive 19 miles north on I-84 toward La Grande to North Powder (Exit 285). Drive 21 miles west, following signs for Anthony Lakes along North Powder River Lane, County Road 1146, and FR 73. Trailheads for the North Fork John Day Wilderness start along FR 73 at Anthony Lakes and continue westward.

THE ELKHORNS are easily one of the most spectacular mountain ranges in Oregon, with rugged, glaciated peaks and numerous subalpine basins. Lying west of Baker City, the North Fork of the John Day Wilderness (NFJD) encompasses portions of two 9,000-foot mountain ranges, the Elkhorns and the Greenhorns, plus other highlands. NFJD also protects the headwaters of the John Day River, Oregon's longest undammed and free-flowing salmon stream. The wilderness is famous for its large, resident elk herds and anadromous fish runs. Overall the terrain is gentle and heavily timbered. The exception is sections along the rugged Elkhorn Crest, where glaciated basins and cirque lakes abound.

Established by the Oregon Wilderness Act of 1984, the North Fork John Day comprises four units: Greenhorn, Tower Mountain, Baldy Creek, and 85,000-acre North Fork John Day, the largest unit. Six thousand acres of the Vinegar Hill–Indian Rock Scenic Area are also included. In 1988, a 39-mile segment of the North Fork John Day River was designated a Wild and Scenic River, an action in part prompted by recognition of the river's value as a salmon and steelhead fishery.

Geologically, the NFJD takes in the Wallowa Terrane, a slice of the Earth's crust that fused onto the growing western edge of the North American continent. The Elkhorn argillite formation is the predominant sedimentary rock in the upper drainage; also here are small bodies of limestone, tuff, and conglomerates. Many of these rock units have been metamorphosed, faulted, and folded, producing a variety of shapes and colors. Granitic intrusions crop out here and there in the wilderness and surrounding roadless lands.

Like most of the Blue Mountains, the climate of the NFJD is continental with maritime influences. That means winters are cold and snowy, with below-freezing temperatures the norm. Summers are warm and usually dry except for an occasional thunderstorm. Annual precipitation approaches 45 inches at the highest elevations of the Elkhorn Mountains but drops to nearly 20 inches at the lowest elevations. May and June are the wettest months. Autumns are usually dry and clear, with warm, sunny days and cool nights.

The majority of the NFJD is heavily forested with old-growth ponderosa pine, Douglas fir, Engelmann spruce, white fir, western larch, and lodgepole pine. Above 6,000 feet, lodgepole pine is by the far the most abundant species, with some subalpine fir and whitebark pine occurring at the highest forested locations. Prescribed "natural" fires here have restored vitality to the forests and drainage areas of this wilderness, itself part of the larger Elkhorn Fire Management Area.

Wildlife consists of such eastern Oregon species as elk, mule deer, coyote, mountain lion, and black bear. Mountain goats, not native to the area, have been introduced into the Elkhorn Range. Wolverine is reported for the area. Gray wolf, colonizing the area from populations in Idaho, likely already or will soon reside here. The amount of dead and dying trees as a result of insect infestations and recent fires has created very good bird habitat. The pileated woodpecker (an indicator species of old-growth habitat), goshawks, and great gray owls are known to use the area, as well as small mammals such as mink and beaver. The burned areas also provide excellent habitat for foraging deer and elk. It is probable that river otter also reside here.

But the most important natural preserve associated with the NFJD and its tributaries is its fisheries. The NFJD supports an estimated 70 percent of the total spring Chinook salmon run and 43 percent of the summer steelhead run within the John Day basin. This is the largest spawning population of wild spring Chinook and summer steelhead in the Columbia River system. The upper North Fork John Day River is also thought to have one of the few remaining, healthy bull trout populations in the state. According to fish biologists, there is a high probability that redband trout are also present in conjunction with rainbow trout in the North Fork John Day River. West Slope cutthroat trout, a species rarely found in Oregon but common in Idaho and Montana, occurs in the upper John Day drainage.

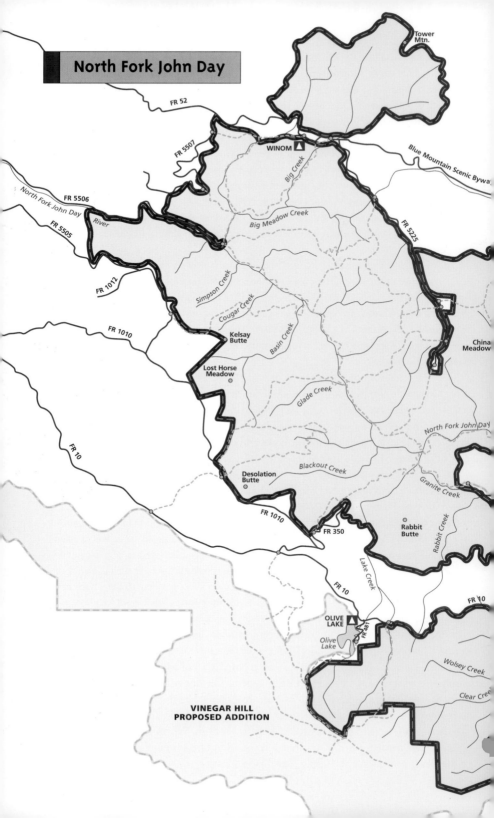

North Fork John Day

Tower Mtn.

FR 52

FR 5507

WINOM ⛺

Blue Mountain Scenic Byway

Big Creek

North Fork John Day

FR 5506

River

Big Meadow Creek

FR 5225

FR 5505

FR 1012

Simpson Creek

Cougar Creek

FR 1010

Basin Creek

Kelsay Butte

China Meadow

Lost Horse Meadow

Glade Creek

North Fork John Day

FR 10

Blackout Creek

Granite Creek

Desolation Butte

FR 1010

FR 350

Rabbit Butte

Rabbit Creek

Lake Creek

FR 10

FR 10

OLIVE LAKE ⛺

FR 481

Olive Lake

Wolsey Creek

Clear Creek

**VINEGAR HILL
PROPOSED ADDITION**

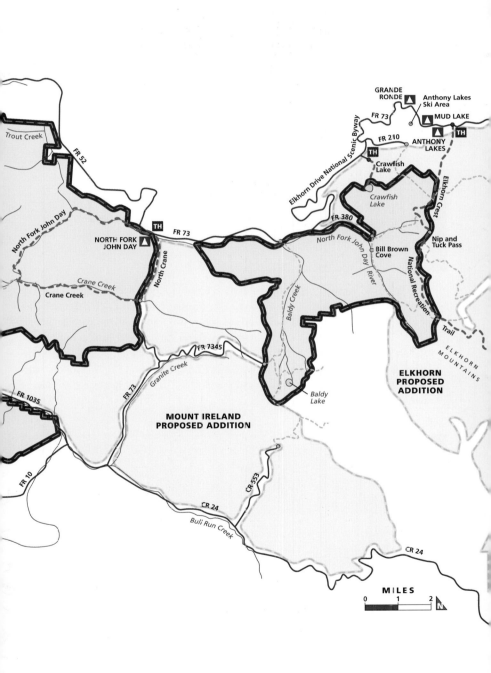

GRANDE
RONDE
Anthony Lakes
Ski Area
FR 73
MUD LAKE
TH
FR 210
ANTHONY
LAKES
TH
Crawfish
Lake
Elkhorn Drive National Scenic Byway
Elkhorn Crest
Crawfish
Lake
FR 380
Trout Creek
FR 52
North Fork John Day
North Fork John Day River
Bill Brown
Cove
Nip and
Tuck Pass
TH
FR 73
NORTH FORK
JOHN DAY
North Crane
National Recreation
Crane Creek
Crane Creek
Baldy Creek
Trail
ELKHORN
MOUNTAINS
FR 7345
ELKHORN
PROPOSED
ADDITION
FR 73
Granite Creek
FR 1035
Baldy
Lake
MOUNT IRELAND
PROPOSED
ADDITION
FR 10
CR 553
CR 24
Bull Run Creek
CR 24

MILES
0   1   2

Gold mining was the activity that first brought substantial numbers of settlers to the Blue Mountains in the 1860s, and evidence of this gold rush still exists along the river. Mining-related ruins dot the riverside: structures for habitation and use, mines, prospect holes, and the like. Other minerals such as silver, copper, lead, zinc, chromite, and manganese were produced in small quantities here.

The heaviest use of the NFJD is during the fall hunting season. Backpackers and hikers will have much of the area to themselves in other seasons, particularly if they avoid the few alpine lakes, like Crawfish and Baldy Lakes, accessible from Anthony Lakes. The Elkhorns form the scenic backdrop for the Baker Valley; many visitors come to enjoy the Elkhorn Crest National Recreation Trail, which traverses the range.

The NFJD is one of Oregon's largest wilderness areas yet could be enlarged substantially by the addition of another 160,000 roadless acres that adjoin it. These include two areas that comprise most of the Elkhorn Range: the 64,000-acre Twin Mountain Roadless Area, and the 7,100-acre Marble Point Roadless Area.

DAY HIKE: CRAWFISH LAKE
One-way Length: 1.4 miles
Elevation Range: 6,893 to 7,170 feet
Difficulty: Easy

Crawfish Lake lies just inside the wilderness boundary in a glacially carved bowl along the Elkhorn Crest. The trail to the lake climbs slightly through a sparse forest of lodgepole pine and occasional meadows before dropping down to the lakeshore.

To reach the northern trailhead from Baker City, drive 19 miles north on I-84 to North Powder (Exit 285). Drive 21 miles west, following signs for Anthony Lakes along North Powder River Lane, County Road 1146, and FR 73. Go 0.8 mile beyond the pass by Anthony Lakes, and turn left on FR 216. The trailhead is less than 0.25 mile down this road.

LOOP OVERNIGHT HIKE: NORTH FORK JOHN DAY–CRANE CREEK
Trail Length: 13.5 miles
Elevation Range: 4,500 to 5,500 feet
Difficulty: Strenuous

This loop offers a nice backpack introduction into the NFJD wilderness with potential for fishing in the river. Starting at the North Fork John Day Campground, head down the North Fork of the John Day River. Look at the depth of the river at this point, since you'll need to ford it on the return trip. Following Trail #3022 into the wilderness, proceed downstream through a mixed forest of western larch, subalpine fir, and lodgepole pine. Some 2.6 miles from the trailhead you reach Trout Creek, a tributary of the North Fork, and the Bigfoot Hilton, an old miner's cabin that is open to public use. Another 4 miles from the cabin site, you reach the confluence of the North Fork and Crane Creek. Cross the river—usually knee-deep in summer—then head 4.1 miles up Crane Creek on Trail #3011 to FR 73. Turn left and follow the North Crane Trail for 2.6 miles back to the North Fork John Day River. To get back to your vehicle and the campground, you'll need to ford the river. If the river crossing by the North Fork John Day Campground is too deep for comfort, you can always walk back to the campground from Crane Creek by following FR 73.

To reach the trailhead from Baker City, drive 19 miles north on I-84 to North Powder (Exit 285). Drive 21 miles west, following signs for Anthony Lakes along North Powder River Lane, County Road 1146, and FR 73. Continue another 17 miles on FR 73 beyond Anthony Lakes to a four-way intersection. Drive straight ahead to the North Fork John Day Campground and trailhead.

OVERNIGHT BACKPACK: ELKHORN CREST NATIONAL RECREATION TRAIL
One-way Length: 23 miles
Elevation Range: 7,160 to 8,100 feet
Difficulty: Strenuous

The Elkhorn Crest National Recreation Trail offers one of the better long-distance hikes in Oregon, with great scenic views around nearly every bend in the trail. The ideal way to experience the trail is to shuttle a vehicle between trailheads and then trek north to south. But the trail can be hiked partway from either end as well. The trail mainly follows the crest, with side trails dropping down to clear streams, meadowy basins, and glacially carved lakes. Because of limited water immediately available on the crest, it's a good idea to keep your water bottles full at every opportunity. Nice campsites exist at Dutch Flat Lake, Lost Lake, Summit Lake, and Twin Lakes. Rock Creek Butte, 9,106 feet high, is the highest peak in the range and offers an easy scramble with outstanding vistas from the summit.

From Baker City, drive 19 miles north on I-84 toward La Grande to North Powder (Exit 285). Drive 21 miles west, following signs for Anthony Lakes along North Powder River Lane, County Road 1146, and FR 73. Just before the Anthony Lakes Campground is the trailhead for the Elkhorn Crest Trail. To reach the southern trailhead, drive US 30 north of Baker City a short distance and turn left onto Pocahontas Road. Follow it for 6.5 miles, then turn left onto FR 6510. Go past the Marble Creek Picnic Area to the Marble Point Trailhead.

OTHER RECREATIONAL OPPORTUNITIES

Most of the wilderness is inaccessible in winter, on account of deep snow blocking access roads. An exception is the Mount Anthony Ski Area northwest of Baker City and immediately adjacent to the Elkhorn Mountains Unit of the NFJD. Mount Anthony provides access for cross-country skiing and snowshoeing. Ski FR 73 beyond the ski area to access trails leading to Crawfish Lake.

39 | North Fork Umatilla Wilderness

Coyote Ridge, North Fork Umatilla Wilderness

LOCATION: 30 miles east of Pendleton

SIZE: 20,144 acres

ELEVATION RANGE: 2,000 to 6,000 feet

MAJOR FLORA: Bunchgrass, ponderosa pine, western larch, grand fir, Douglas fir

ADMINISTRATION: Umatilla NF, Walla Walla RD, 509-522-6290

BEST SEASON: April to November

GETTING THERE: From Pendleton, drive OR 11 north to Weston, head east on OR 204, then take FR 3715 or FR 3719 south (right) to reach northern trailheads. To reach southern trailheads from Pendleton, take OR 11 north 13 miles to Adams, turn right onto Spring Hollow Road, go 10 miles to Thorn Hollow, and turn left onto Bingham/River Road. Continue east for about 16 miles to Umatilla Forks Campground, near where several trails start.

THIS WILDERNESS was established by the 1984 Oregon Wilderness Act to protect the high-quality waters of the North Fork of the Umatilla and its important anadromous fish runs, including steelhead. The major drainages, including the North Fork of the Umatilla, have carved deep canyons between nearly level plateaus, some 20 miles south of the Washington state line. The southern slopes of the canyons tend to be grass-covered; plateau tops and north-facing slopes are timbered.

Geologically the North Fork of the Umatilla resembles the larger Wenaha-Tucannon Wilderness to the northeast. Layer upon layer of basalt flows covered the area between 12 and

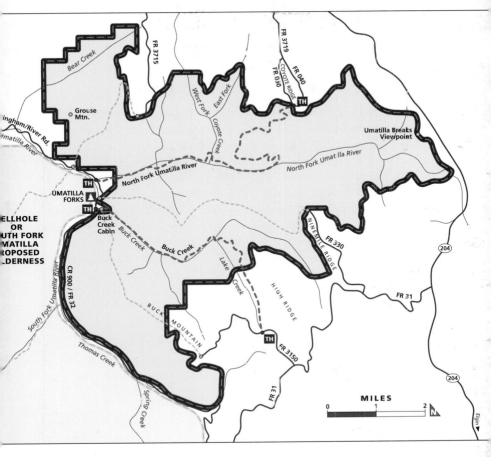

17 million years ago, creating a more or less flat surface of extensive plateaus. Since then, the North Fork of the Umatilla has carved deep canyons into the plateau basalts.

The climate is typical for eastern Oregon. Winters tend to be cold, with extensive amounts of cloudy weather and snow. Summers are warm, even hot at lower elevations, but generally dry with lots of sunshine. By far and away the best times to visit the wilderness are late spring and early fall. Spring brings wildflowers to the grassy slopes of the inner canyon, while autumn's cool nights and often dry, warm days are ideal for outdoor recreation. Precipitation varies from 20 to 40 inches annually depending on elevation.

Vegetation consists of bluebunch wheatgrass and Idaho fescue grasslands. Despite the dry, grassy slopes, riparian areas along creeks and streams are surprisingly lush. In the moister gullies, expect to find thimbleberry, cow parsnip, snowberry, red osier dogwood, ocean spray, elderberry, and serviceberry. Ponderosa pine dominates the lower, drier slopes; Douglas fir, grand fir, Engelmann spruce, western larch, and subalpine fir are common at higher elevations.

Elk and mule deer inhabit the wilderness, along with black bear, mountain lion, coyote, and smaller mammals. The chief attribute of the area, however, is the fisheries. Steelhead, bull trout, and rainbow trout are all known to reside in the river and its tributaries.

DAY HIKE: BUCK CREEK TRAIL #3073
One-way Length: 3.5 miles
Elevation Range: 2,420 to 3,180 feet
Difficulty: Moderate

The lower end of Buck Creek boasts some of the biggest old-growth ponderosa pine anywhere in the wilderness. The trail follows tiny Buck Creek upstream, crossing it a number of times before reaching the junction with Lake Creek Trail, a good place to turn around. Lake Creek Trail climbs up out of the canyon to FR 3150.

From Pendleton, take OR 11 north 13 miles to Adams, turn right onto Spring Hollow Road, go 10 miles to Thorn Hollow, and turn left onto Bingham/ River Road. Continue east for about 16 miles to Umatilla Forks Campground. Continue east on the gravel road past the campground, and take your next left onto a spur road to the trailhead. From Elgin, head west on OR 204. After 3.8 miles, turn left onto FR 3738 and drive 10.5 miles to FR 31. Turn left and go about 4 miles to Ruckel Junction. Turn right onto FR 32 and go about another 10 miles to the trailhead, just before Umatilla Forks Campground.

DAY HIKE: NORTH FORK UMATILLA RIVER TRAIL
One-way Length: 2.7 miles
Elevation Range: 2,360 to 3,400 feet
Difficulty: Easy

The North Fork Umatilla is the major drainage that cuts through this wildlands of the northern Blue Mountains. Despite the overall arid appearance of the grassy slopes above the river, the trail along the North Fork is surprisingly lush. The path takes you through forests of Douglas fir and very large grand fir. Cow parsnip, waterleaf, and snowberry create an abundant streamside riparian zone. It is 2.7 miles on this trail to Coyote Creek, where you'll find some nice campsites. At this creek confluence you might want to turn around, or continue upstream another 1.6 miles toward Coyote Ridge. At this point are a few more campsites. If you're so inclined, hike up the Coyote Ridge some 4.8 miles through open, grassy slopes, with occasional large ponderosa pine and great vistas, to a trailhead at FR 040.

See Buck Creek Trail #3073, above, for directions to the trailhead at Umatilla Forks Campground.

OTHER RECREATIONAL OPPORTUNITIES

Crossing the Blue Mountains just north of the wilderness, OR 204 provides year-round access to the plateaus surrounding the wilderness. Nordic skiers can then follow logging roads to the canyon rim. Unfortunately, in most winters, snow is not sufficiently deep to permit much elevation loss into the canyons before skiable snow disappears.

Strawberry Mountain Wilderness 40

Cirque, Strawberry Mountain Wilderness

THE VIEW OF THE STRAWBERRY MOUNTAINS from the John Day Valley near Prairie City reminds me of a canyon in the northern Rockies. The grassy John Day Valley, rising up through forested slopes to the ramparts of glaciated peaks—notably Strawberry Mountain, the highest at 9,038 feet—could be any western Montana valley scene. The preponderance of western larch, a deciduous conifer species common in western Montana, also contributes to the feeling of being outside of Oregon. Fortunately for Oregonians wanting to get a sense of the Rockies, the Strawberry Mountain Wilderness is a lot closer and just as lovely.

The wildlands value of the Strawberry Mountains was recognized early on by the Forest Service. Some 33,000 acres of the Strawberry Mountains were first given protection in 1942 as a Forest Service Wild

LOCATION: 10 miles south of Prairie City

SIZE: 68,700 acres

ELEVATION RANGE: 4,000 to 9,038 feet

MAJOR FLORA: Juniper-sage, ponderosa pine, western larch, white fir, Engelmann spruce, whitebark pine, subalpine fir

ADMINISTRATION: Malheur National Forest, Prairie City RD, 541-820-3311

BEST SEASON: June to October

GETTING THERE: From Prairie City, follow signs south to Strawberry Campground and take County Road 60 to FR 6001. Continue to the road's end and the campground.

Area. Wild Area status recognized the area's special qualities but remained an administrative designation that could be rescinded at any time. With the passage of the 1964 Wilderness Act, Congress gave the area official protection as wilderness. It was subsequently more than doubled by the 1984 Oregon Wilderness Act to its current size of 68,700 acres. One of the additions was the Canyon Creek Research Natural Area, rich in old-growth ponderosa pine. The wilderness also protects the headwaters of the Malheur River. Streams within the wilderness include Pine, Indian, Strawberry, Canyon, Bear, Lake, Wall, Roberts, and Big Creek.

The complex geological chronicle of this east-west-trending mountain range comprises very old rocks to the west that were part of an ancient volcanic-island arc, and much younger, 16-million-year-old volcanics to the east. Scenic eroded-ash deposits exist in Wildcat Basin. The Rabbit Ears is another relict of the volcanic era, representing the last vestiges of an eroded plug of a volcanic vent. More recently, Ice Age glaciers carved their classic signature—U-shaped valleys—into the mountains. The ice also hollowed out the rock beds that today hold the seven alpine lakes of the Strawberry Mountain Wilderness. The largest of these is 32-acre Strawberry Lake.

Like most of eastern Oregon, the climate is distinctly more continental than other parts of the state. Most of the 40 inches of annual precipitation falls in winter as snow. Summertime thunderstorms may occur, and typically days are warm, with comfortably cool nights. Freezing temperatures can occur at any time of the year.

Vegetation varies considerably with elevation. Sagebrush, mountain mahogany, and juniper dominate lower elevations. As you rise higher in elevation, ponderosa pine flourishes, sometimes mixed with western larch and Douglas fir. At the middle elevations grow grand fir, western white pine, Engelmann spruce, and lodgepole pine. At the highest elevations live subalpine fir and whitebark pine. Flower-studded meadows are fairly common, particularly at the subalpine level. Understory shrubs include dwarf huckleberry, elk sedge, pinegrass, Idaho fescue, and bluebunch wheatgrass. The Wildcat Fire burned through much of the Strawberry Mountain Wilderness in 1996, rejuvenating the landscape. Note the abundance of snags that now provide homes to everything from cavity-nesting birds to mammals like flying squirrel.

Wildlife that may be encountered includes elk, mule deer, black bear, mountain lion, bighorn sheep, ruffed and blue grouse, pileated woodpecker, sharp-shinned hawk, bald eagle, marten, mink, and beaver. Indeed, 378 kinds of animals and 22 fish species have been recorded here.

More than 100 miles of trail cross the wilderness. Most of the recreational use is focused on the seven lakes that dot the central part of the range. If you hike almost anyplace else in this wilderness, you'll seldom encounter other groups. The north side sees far more visitors than do destinations on the south side of the range. Most of the wilderness is too far from plowed roads to be accessible for winter ski touring.

Expansion of the Strawberry Mountain Wilderness would increase its biological value by addition of lower-elevation, forested habitat. In particular, significant roadless lands on the south part of the range include the headwaters of Corral Creek, Bear Creek, and Middle Fork Canyon Creek, and the Roberts Creek drainage in the northeast.

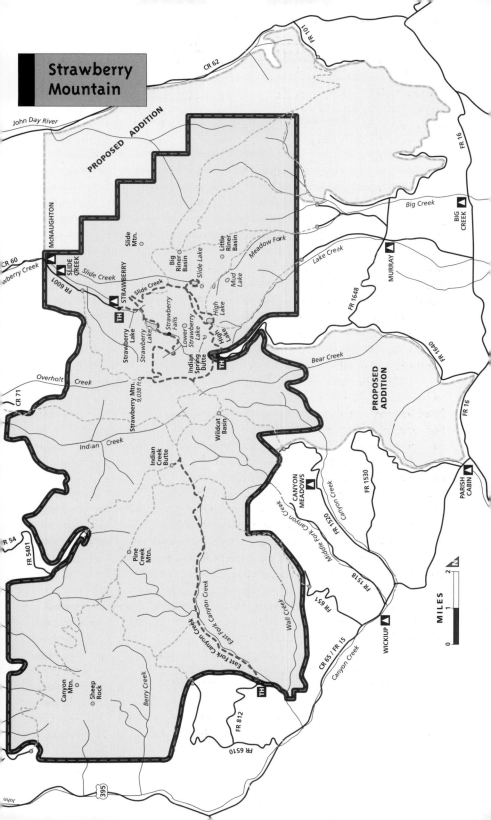

Strawberry Mountain

PROPOSED ADDITION

PROPOSED ADDITION

John Day River

CR 62

FR 101

FR 16

CR 60

McNAUGHTON

wberry Creek

SLIDE CREEK

FR 6001

STRAWBERRY

Slide Creek

Slide Creek

Strawberry Lake

Strawberry Lake

Strawberry Falls

Lower Strawberry Lake

Indian Spring Butte

Slide Mtn.

Big Riner Basin

Slide Lake

Little Riner Basin

Meadow Fork

Mud Lake

High Lake

High Lake

Big Creek

BIG CREEK

Lake Creek

MURRAY

FR 1648

FR 1640

Bear Creek

CR 71

Overholt Creek

Strawberry Mtn. 9,038 ft.

Indian Creek

Indian Creek Butte

Wildcat Basin

FR 16

PARISH CABIN

FR 1530

CANYON MEADOWS

Canyon Creek

Middle Fork Canyon Creek

FR 1520

FR 1518

FR 54

FR 5401

Pine Creek Mtn.

East Fork Canyon Creek

Wall Creek

FR 651

CR 65 / FR 15

WICKIUP

Canyon Mtn.

Sheep Rock

Berry Creek

Canyon Creek

TH

FR 812

FR 6510

395

John

MILES

0   1   2

DAY HIKE: EAST FORK CANYON CREEK
One-way Length: 2.9 miles
Elevation Range: 4,780 to 4,840 feet
    Difficulty: Easy

The East Fork of Canyon Creek provides the main access to the western side of the wilderness. Described here is a gentle hike through some magnificent ponderosa pine groves that are part of the Canyon Creek Research Natural Area. For those inclined to backpack, make this an overnight trip by continuing up the trail toward Indian Creek Butte. You can enjoy good fishing for small trout in East Fork Canyon Creek.

The trail starts downhill through some large ponderosa pine to join the East Fork Canyon Creek. At this point the trail swings northeast, following the East Fork Canyon Creek upstream. At 2.2 miles, you reach Yokum Corrals Camp, a nice flat among giant pines that would make a good campsite. Brookling Creek, some 0.7 mile beyond Yokum Corrals Camp, makes a good turnaround point for day hikers. Backpackers will pass several more potential campsites farther upstream. Indian Creek Butte is another 4.5 miles ahead and offers fine panoramic views.

From John Day, head south on US 395 for 9.7 miles, turn left onto County Road 65, go about 3 miles, and make another left onto FR 6510. Drive 1.6 miles and turn right onto FR 812. Follow it about 3 miles to the trailhead.

DAY HIKE: SLIDE LAKE
One-way Length: 4.2 miles
Elevation Range: 5,735 to 7,200 feet
    Difficulty: Moderate

Slide Lake sits in a glacial bowl on the northern slope of the Strawberry Mountains. Begin hiking from the Strawberry Campground on Trail #375. In about a mile, you come to a trail junction. Bear right to get to Strawberry Lake, the most popular destination in the wilderness. To reach the less-visited Slide Lake, bear left onto Trail #372, go a short way, and bear left again, continuing 2.5 miles to the lake.

From Prairie City, follow signs south to Strawberry Campground and take County Road 60 to FR 6001. Continue to the road's end and the campground.

DAY HIKE: STRAWBERRY LAKE
One-way Length: 1.3 miles
Elevation Range: 5,735 to 6,270 feet
Difficulty: Easy

With rugged Rabbit Ears and Indian Spring Butte rising above, Strawberry Lake lies in a dramatic bowl. Though this bowl was carved by glaciers, the lake itself is not of glacial origin, rather it was created by a landslide about 1,000 years ago. This hike is more like a stroll, barely climbing 500 feet over the course of 1.3 miles. Given how easy the hike is to the lake, you would be missing out on the best part of the trip if you didn't continue another 1.3 miles on the trail to see 60-foot Strawberry Falls. Above the falls, you can go another half mile to Little Strawberry Lake, which sits in another classic, glacially carved bowl. If you really have some energy, think about climbing up Strawberry Mountain. From the trail junction above Strawberry Falls, go right for another 3.6 miles to the 9,038-foot summit, a former lookout site.

From Prairie City, follow signs to Strawberry Campground and take County Road 60 to FR 6001. Continue to the road's end and the campground.

DAY HIKE: HIGH LAKE
One-way Length: 1.3 miles
Elevation Range: 7,450 to 8,000 feet
Difficulty: Easy

High Lake rests in a glacial cirque at the headwaters of Big Creek. The hike from the trailhead is a downhill stroll through beautiful, flower-studded meadows with patches of timber. There are fine campsites along the lake. Trails from High Lake connect to Big Creek, Slide Lake, Big Riner Basin, and other destinations. A 2- to 3-day backpacking loop of the Strawberries' highest peaks and lakes is also possible. Continue past High Lake to Slide Lake, on to Strawberry Lake, up and over Strawberry Mountain, and finally circle back around Indian Spring Butte to a trailhead only 0.3 mile from the High Lake Trailhead.

From John Day, drive south 9.7 miles on US 395 and turn left (east) onto County Road 65, which eventually becomes FR 15. Then turn left onto FR 16 near Parish Cabin Campground and continue toward Logan Valley, but after 2.5 miles turn left again onto gravel FR 1640 to the trailhead.

41 Wenaha-Tucannon Wilderness

Bluebunch wheatgrass, Wenaha River Canyon, Wenaha-Tucannon Wilderness

LOCATION: 50 miles north of La Grande

SIZE: 177,465 acres

ELEVATION RANGE: 1,800 to 6,401 feet

MAJOR FLORA: Bunchgrass meadows, Douglas fir, grand fir, ponderosa pine, lodgepole pine, subalpine fir

ADMINISTRATION: Umatilla National Forest, 541-278-3716

BEST SEASON: April to November

GETTING THERE: Of numerous trailhead access points, the easiest to reach from the Oregon side is the Wenaha River Trail, on the eastern edge of the wilderness near Troy, Oregon. From La Grande, take OR 82 east 65 miles to Enterprise, then turn left (north) onto OR 3 toward Lewiston, Idaho. After driving approximately 35 miles, turn left (west) toward the tiny town of Flora and follow the Redmond Grade Road 13 miles to Troy.

SPRAWLING EAST OF WALLA WALLA, Washington, the Wenaha-Tucannon Wilderness protects a spectacular part of the northern Blue Mountains on the Oregon-Washington border. The Wenaha River has cut a canyon of more than 2,000 feet, and the wilderness both physically and biologically resembles Hells Canyon. Unlike the nearly treeless lower elevations of Hells Canyon, however, trees shade most of the trails in the Wenaha-Tucannon Wilderness. Of the two gorges, the Wenaha is thus a far more pleasant hike in the summer, even if temperatures can still be quite warm. The majority of acres (111,048) in this fairly large wilderness actually lie in Washington. Lush bunchgrass slopes, large old-growth ponderosa pine, and lovely flowering shrubs like serviceberry and thimbleberry combine with one of the largest elk herds in Oregon to make this a particularly attractive wildland.

The Wenaha-Tucannon Wilderness was given some administrative recognition by the Forest Service as early as 1957, when 99,000 acres were designated the Wenaha-Tucannon Backcountry. This was later expanded to include 111,244 acres. But Backcountry designation was an administrative classification that offered no protection. So on the urging of environmentalists, the Wenaha-Tucannon Wilderness was designated by Congress in 1978 with the passage of the Endangered American Wilderness Act. The lowest elevations lie along the Wild and Scenic Wenaha River, the highest elevation on 6,401-foot Oregon Butte, which in fact lies in Washington. Most of the wilderness is best accessed from Walla Walla. Troy, Oregon, provides year-round access to the southern section and lower Wenaha River.

The Blue Mountains consist of a number of separate terranes melded together. Terranes are slices of the Earth's crust that originate in different locations, then fuse together as a result of subsequent plate movement. The Wenaha-Tucannon takes in the Wallowa Terrane, including parts of the Wallowa Mountains, best exposed in Hells Canyon. These ancient rocks are the crumpled and severely eroded remains of an ancient island complex that eventually fused onto the edge of the North American continent. Rocks similar to the Wallowa Terrane pop out in Alaska's Wrangell Mountains and on Chichagof Island in southeastern Alaska.

These rocks were then buried under fluid basaltic lavas that erupted between 17 and 12 million years ago from cracks and fissures in what is now southeastern Washington and adjacent parts of Idaho and northeastern Oregon. Most of the rocks exposed in the Wenaha-Tucannon Wilderness are basalts.

The climate of the wilderness is continental, with Pacific Northwest maritime influences. In general, winters are relatively cold and abundantly cloudy. Snow is common, and deep in winter at higher elevations, although most of the lower elevations remain snow-free much of the winter. It's possible to hike at least a short way along the lower Wenaha and Tucannon Rivers without encountering snow. Summers are generally quite dry, other than an occasional thunderstorm. Daytime temperatures, particularly in the lower canyons, can be quite warm—even exceeding 100 degrees—but nights are still relatively cool, making for pleasant sleeping. Spring is often the rainiest season, but it also brings green, flowery slopes to the lower elevations. Fall probably has the best weather for hiking and camping, with warm, dry days and cool nights.

Bluebunch, wheatgrass, and Idaho fescue grasslands dominate the vegetation on many lower slopes. Wildflowers like balsamroot, lupine, and paintbrush decorate these slopes in the spring and early summer. Particularly attractive in the spring are the narrow gullies along tributary creeks here, dense with red osier dogwood, serviceberry, ocean spray, and other flowering shrubs. Large old-growth ponderosa pine grow throughout the canyon, grading into Douglas fir, grand fir, western larch, lodgepole pine, and subalpine fir forests.

Wildlife here includes one of the largest elk herds in Oregon, mule deer, mountain lion, black bear, coyote, marten, and other species. A special attribute of the canyon is the herds of bighorn sheep. Both the Tucannon and Wenaha Rivers support salmon and steelhead runs, along with native populations of rainbow trout and bull trout.

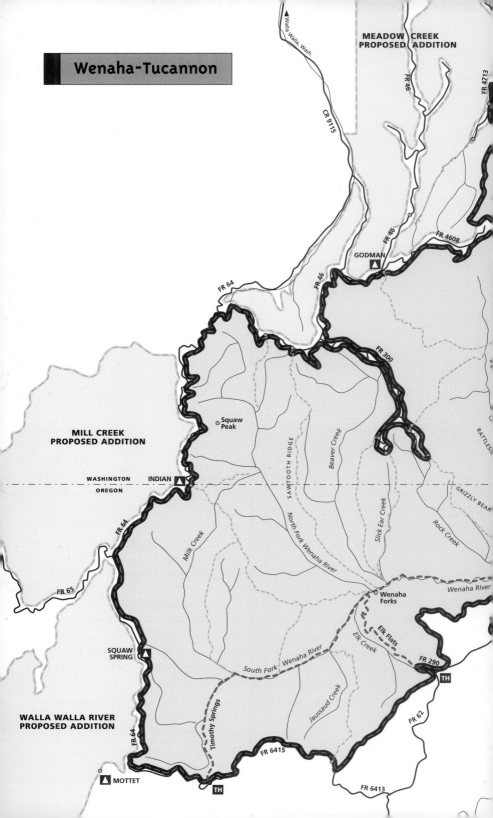

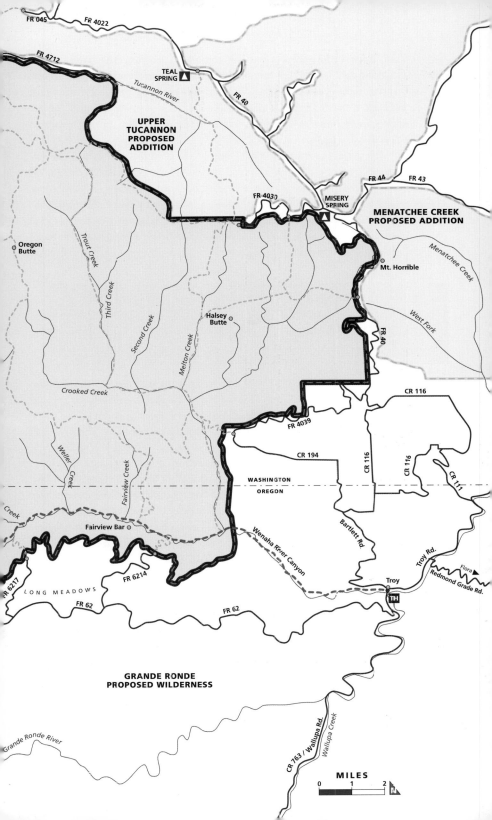

FR 045 FR 4022

FR 4712

TEAL
SPRING △

Tucannon River

FR 40

**UPPER
TUCANNON
PROPOSED
ADDITION**

FR 4030

FR 44 FR 43

MISERY
SPRING △

**MENATCHEE CREEK
PROPOSED ADDITION**

Oregon
Butte

Trout Creek

Mt. Horrible

Menatchee Creek

Third Creek

Second Creek

Melton Creek

Halsey
Butte

West Fork

FR 40

Crooked Creek

CR 116

FR 4039

CR 116

CR 116

Weller Creek

Fairview Creek

CR 194

CR 116

CR 111

WASHINGTON
OREGON

Fairview Bar

Wenaha River Canyon

Bartlett Rd.

FR 6217

LONG MEADOWS

FR 6214

Troy Rd.

Flora ►

Troy

Redmond Grade Rd.

TH

FR 62

FR 62

**GRANDE RONDE
PROPOSED WILDERNESS**

Grande Ronde River

CR 763 / Wallupa Rd.

Wallupa Creek

MILES

0   1   2

Many large roadless areas immediately adjoin the existing Wenaha-Tucannon Wilderness and should be given protection. Collectively these areas could add as much as 100,000 acres to the current wilderness. In most cases, a single dirt road separates the roadless lands from the designated wilderness. Largely located in Washington, the proposed additions—28,700-acre Upper Tucannon, 14,000-acre Willow Spring, 8,400-acre Spangler, 5,400-acre Meadow Creek, 15,500-acre Menatchee Creek, and 27,000-acre Mill Creek—are critical to expanding the wildland values of the existing wilderness.

Within Oregon, the largest proposed addition to the wilderness is the 34,000-acre Walla Walla River Roadless Area, just west of the Wenaha-Tucannon Wilderness. This proposed addition, which includes the deeply incised canyons of the South and North Forks of the Walla Walla River, is separated from the wilderness by a single road, FR 64. Much of the lower elevation in this proposed addition is important winter range for elk and deer.

DAY HIKE: WENAHA RIVER CANYON TO CROOKED CREEK
One-way Length: 6.4 miles
Elevation Range: 1,720 to 1,910 feet
      Difficulty: Moderate

The Wenaha River is a designated Wild and Scenic River, offering year-round hiking opportunities in the beautiful, view-packed lower Wenaha River Canyon. Starting at nearly 1,700 feet, the 31.5-mile Wenaha River Trail runs upstream all the way to Timothy Springs, providing superb multi-day backpacking options. The 12.8-mile round-trip hike to Crooked Creek offers a sample of the possibilities and makes for a good, long day hike. The first part of the trail drops downhill toward the river, passing through scattered stands of beautiful ponderosa pine. The trail then follows the river upstream. After crossing the National Forest boundary some 2.3 miles from the trailhead, the trail wanders along the north side of the river, sometimes above it, sometimes adjacent to it. It crosses the wilderness boundary at about 6 miles from the trailhead. The turnaround point is the footbridge over Crooked Creek.

From La Grande, drive 65 miles on OR 82 to Enterprise, then turn north onto OR 3 and go 35 miles to a left turn to the tiny town of Flora. Drive through Flora and along a steep, winding road down to the Grande Ronde River. After crossing the river, turn left and drive 2 miles toward Troy. Just before Troy, turn right on Bartlett Road, which heads to Pomeroy, Washington. Less than 0.5 mile up this road lies the trailhead.

DAY HIKE: ELK FLATS TO WENAHA RIVER
One-way Length: 4.5 miles
Elevation Range: 3,000 to 4,900 feet
    Difficulty: Moderate

The Elk Flats Trail provides access to the Upper Wenaha River, reaching the river at Wenaha Forks. The trail descends through forested slopes with occasional views. When you reach the river, you'll find plenty of campsites.

See Getting There, p. 244, for directions to Troy from La Grande. From Troy, go south 0.3 mile to a fork and take FR 62 west toward Long Meadows. After 20.2 miles, turn right onto FR 290 and drive 0.7 mile to the trailhead.

DAY HIKE: TIMOTHY SPRINGS TO UPPER WENAHA RIVER
One-way Length: 2.3 miles
Elevation Range: 3,400 to 4,660 feet
    Difficulty: Moderate

This trail begins in a mostly western larch forest. Larch needles turn golden in the fall and drop off. This route is especially beautiful in October. The trail descends, crossing several streams before reaching the South Fork of the Wenaha River. By midsummer you can easily ford the stream, but day hikers can also make this their turnaround point. If you wish, you can hike the entire 31.5 miles from Timothy Springs to Troy to make a wonderful 2- to 3-day trek; however, beware that you must ford the river in a number of places.

See Getting There, p. 244, for directions to Troy from La Grande. From Troy, drive 0.3 mile to a fork, then take FR 62 west toward Long Meadows. Go 25.1 miles to a right-hand turn onto FR 6413, drive 1.3 miles, then turn right again onto FR 6415; follow it 6.4 miles to Timothy Springs Trailhead.

Basin and Range

This Oregon ecoregion lies at the northwestern limits of the Basin and Range province, which stretches south and east to New Mexico and includes parts of Arizona, Idaho, Wyoming, Utah, Nevada, and California. Southeastern Oregon's portion of this vast area, composed of fault-block mountains (horsts) separated by broad basins (grabens), lies generally east of Lakeview and south of Burns. Average elevation is above 4,000 feet, although some of the peaks, such as Steens Mountain, can reach nearly 10,000 feet. Many of the basins receive less than 12 inches of precipitation annually; extreme daily and seasonal temperature ranges are the norm. Frosts can occur even in summer, and about the only crop that can reasonably be grown is alfalfa.

Reflecting its limited productivity, Oregon's Basin and Range is sparsely populated. The largest towns are Burns/Hines, on the fringe of the area, with a combined population of about 4,000. The next largest town, Paisley, has about 300 people. Population density here is less than one person per square mile, equal to that of Alaska. This is not the Garden of Eden.

The Basin and Range was created by stretching that broke the Earth's crust into blocks, with some rising to become mountains, and some falling to become the valleys or basins. The oldest Tertiary Age rocks are andesitic flows and breccia. The most extensive unit is a sequence of basalt and some andesite flows that originated on what is now Steens Mountain. These lava flows extend over several thousand square miles from Abert Rim to the eastern margin of the province. The flows emerged as fissure eruptions, mostly from dike swarms that were concentrated in zones of weakness along the margins of some of the future tilted fault blocks. Probably the largest concentration of feeder dikes is on the east scarp of Steens Mountain.

During the Pleistocene or Ice Age, rainfall was more abundant in the region. The additional precipitation filled many of the large structural depressions, or basins, to form pluvial lakes. Prominent shoreline features such as gravel bars, spits, wave-built terraces, and wave-cut benches remained when the drier conditions of the Holocene began. Relicts of these Ice Age lakes include Abert Lake, Summer Lake, Warner Valley wetlands, and Goose Lake. All of these drain internally and have no outlet to the sea. The colder climate at this time also produced an icecap on Steens Mountain and severe glaciation of the mountain's upper valleys.

The eastern flank of Steens Mountain rises 5,000 feet above the Alvord Desert, in foreground, Steens Mountain Wilderness.

The dominant vegetation is sagebrush steppe, including big sagebrush, silver sagebrush, low sagebrush, and two species of rabbitbrush. Patches of juniper, mountain mahogany, and aspen also exist here. A small patch of ponderosa pine at Hart Mountain, white fir at Steens Mountain, and the forested North Warner Mountains constitute the only tree communities here. Native grasses include bluebunch wheatgrass, Great Basin wild rye, Idaho fescue, Sandberg bluegrass, and bottlebrush squirreltail. All of these grasses have a low tolerance for livestock grazing pressure; in many areas, exotic species like cheatgrass and other weedy species have replaced the native ones. In the most alkaline basins, like the Alvord Desert, salt-tolerant species like greasewood, spiny hopsage, and shadscale are common. Willow, common chokecherry, red osier dogwood, and other shrubs dominate riparian areas.

Not surprisingly, most of the land area is publicly owned. The Bureau of Land Management and the Fish and Wildlife Service manage some 82 percent of Oregon's Basin and Range. It is also not an exaggeration to suggest that most of this land is managed as a feedlot for privately owned livestock. Nearly all of the BLM lands, and even large refuges such as the 185,000-acre Malheur National Wildlife Refuge, are managed primarily to produce forage for domestic livestock and only secondarily to benefit wildlife.

With so much of the landscape devoted to livestock production, it comes as no surprise that the biggest impact to the plant communities in this region comes from cows and domestic sheep. Cattle and sheep have trampled biological crusts and compacted soil, increasing runoff and erosion and decreasing fertility. Cattle and sheep consumption of native grasses and forbs leaves behind less desirable grasses or weeds to proliferate. Trampling and grazing of riparian areas has hastened stream channel down-cutting, resulting in a proportionate loss of riparian habitat. Finally, the presence of livestock has hampered natural wildfires by reducing fine fuels.

Apart from the domestic animals themselves, another impact of livestock production on public land has been the conversion of over 318,000 acres of native communities to exotic grasslands of crested wheatgrass and other species designed to increase forage production for cows. The effect of this is obvious when the number of species breeding in crested wheatgrass (16 species) is compared to those sustained by the native sagebrush/ bunchgrass communities (114 species) it replaced.

A third, less obvious effect on the regional biodiversity has been the conversion of native riparian habitat or sagebrush steppe into irrigated hay fields. These riparian zones are biologically critical to more than 75 percent of regional wildlife species, so their loss to hay meadows has had a disproportionate impact on wildlife. More than 120,000 acres here, including 50,000 acres on Malheur National Wildlife Refuge, are devoted to hay production. These irrigated hay fields are dominated by exotic grasses like alfalfa and are mowed each summer, reducing their effectiveness as hiding cover for wildlife. In addition, in many cases riparian vegetation, such as willows and other shrubs, was removed or reduced to make way for hay production. One study of southeastern Oregon found that at least 200 species of wildlife bred along the region's streams, and another 225 species used riparian habitat for feeding, making it the most biologically important habitat in the region.

Though many may view the desert as "barren" or "lifeless," the area's native wildlife is wonderfully diverse. While fish species diversity is low compared to other parts of Oregon, the many endemic species here are of great biological significance. At least 18 species of fish are endemic; of these, the majority are listed, or are candidates for listing, under the Endangered Species Act, primarily as a result of livestock-production impacts or competition from exotics favored by water-quality changes wrought by livestock production.

Two lizard species reach their northern limits in this part of Oregon, the long-nosed lizard and Mojave black-collared lizard.

Bird diversity is high in the Basin and Range, with the majority of habitat use in riparian areas and wetlands. Spring and fall are the prime seasons for migrating waterfowl. Some of the more unusual species that occur here are Franklin gull, horned grebe, and white-faced ibis. Trumpeter swans were introduced into Malheur Lake and Summer Lake, and appear to be holding their own. White pelican can also be found nesting in the region, with the Warner Valley holding the greatest number. Abert Lake supports great numbers of Wilson's and northern phalarope, avocet, and eared grebe, and as many as 750,000 waterfowl during migration.

Raptors are also well represented in this region, with more than 160 nesting pairs of golden eagles recorded for Harney County alone. Other fairly common raptors include Swainson's hawk, ferruginous hawk, red-tailed hawk, and prairie falcon. Another bird that reaches its greatest abundance in Oregon in this region is the sage grouse. Unfortunately, sage grouse populations—once so numerous that settlers could catch them with nets—are now in steep decline, primarily due to impacts on sage grouse habitat by livestock.

White-tailed antelope ground squirrel, spotted bat, kit fox, and pygmy rabbit are all recorded for this ecoregion, and many of these species reach their northern limits in southeastern Oregon. Bighorn sheep, far more abundant prior to the introduction of livestock and their diseases, still inhabit some of the higher mountain ranges, including Steens Mountain and Hart Mountain.

Of all Oregon regions, the Basin and Range has the largest, most intact roadless areas in the state. In many areas, the closure of a few dirt roads would greatly expand the acreage of potential wildland complexes. Conservationists urge that all potential roadless lands be designated. For instance, environmentalists are urging protection for 367,771 acres of the proposed Buzzard Creek Wilderness in an area north of Hart Mountain and west of Malheur National Wildlife Refuge, where the BLM found not one acre suitable for wilderness.

As a result of differences in the exact configuration of boundaries as described by various groups and agencies, different names exist for proposed wilderness areas here that cover the same general area. As a rule, the BLM has sought to minimize the size of wilderness study areas, while environmentalists have sought to increase proposed wilderness areas, often by combining several adjacent roadless areas into a single unit.

Steens Mountain Wilderness   42

Wildhorse Lake occupies a glacial cirque on Steens Mountain, Steens Mountain Wilderness.

FAULT-BLOCK STEENS MOUNTAIN rises out of the sagebrush desert of southeastern Oregon to nearly 10,000 feet and is the centerpiece of one of the most spectacular landscapes in the entire Great Basin. More like a mini-mountain range than a single peak, Steens rises steeply more than 5,000 feet above the desert, presenting for more than 40 miles a bold eastern face. Ice Age glaciers carved steep-walled, U-shaped valleys into the gently sloping western side of the mountain. To the east lies the Alvord Desert, one of the driest regions in Oregon, a place of extensive playas, sand dunes, and thermal features. To the northwest of Steens lies the Malheur National

LOCATION: 60 miles south of Burns

SIZE: 175,000 acres

ELEVATION RANGE: 4,000 to 9,773 feet

MAJOR FLORA: Sagebrush grasslands, mountain mahogany, juniper, aspen

ADMINISTRATION: BLM Burns District, 541-573-4400

BEST SEASON: June to October

GETTING THERE: From Burns, take OR 78 east (toward Winnemucca, Nevada) for 2 miles, then turn right onto OR 205 and take it south 59 paved miles to Frenchglen, a tiny store/café/hotel complex with gas and supplies in summer. (If you are coming in any other season, fill your gas tank in Burns, since gas may not be available in Frenchglen.) Just beyond this small community, a sign points to the Steens Mountain Loop Road and Page Springs Campground.

Wildlife Refuge, a spectacular birding area. One could spend a lifetime exploring the region and still not know all of its secrets.

For years, conservationists sought to protect Steens Mountain as a national park and wilderness area. They made an important step toward that goal when the Steens Mountain Cooperative Management and Protection Act of 2000 was signed into law by President Bill Clinton. One notable innovation of the bill was its creation of the first congressionally designated cow-free wilderness. Livestock grazing is now banned on 100,000 acres of the wilderness—the first ever such ban in the United States. (Normally permitted even in officially designated wilderness areas under the 1964 Wilderness Act, grazing still doesn't occur in every wilderness, especially those where none existed at the time of designation.) On the remaining 75,000 acres of official wilderness, grazing continues.

The Steens Mountain Act also prevents mining and geothermal development on 1.2 million acres. Within this larger area, the bill has established 500,000-acre Steens Mountain Cooperative Management and Protection Area. The legislation also enabled the trade of 100,000 acres of public lands for 18,000 acres of private lands. (I'll let readers decide if this was a good deal for the public). The Donner und Blitzen River was also designated a Redband Trout Reserve, while three other rivers received Wild and Scenic River protection.

The designation of 175,000 acres of wilderness, while significant, still leaves much of the mountain vulnerable to inappropriate resource extraction and development. Conservationists would like to see at least another 800,000 acres designated as wilderness, including several hundred thousand acres in the Alvord Desert east of Steens Mountain, which might make it Oregon's largest wilderness area. The greatest obstacle for designation of more wilderness is the numerous private-land inholdings that exist, particularly on Steens Mountain itself. The BLM is gradually working out land trades and buyouts to consolidate public holdings. Once these transactions are complete, designation of a large wildlands complex on Steens Mountain will be possible.

Geologically, Steens Mountain is a "layer cake" of more than 70 different lava flows that erupted some 16 million years ago from a large shield volcano in what is now southeastern Oregon. Up to 4,000 feet thick, the lava not only makes up most of the Steens Mountain complex but also extends to Sheephead Mountain, the Pueblo Mountains, and the Abert Rim near Lakeview.

Preserved in Steens Mountain's lava flows is a scientific enigma. When lava cools, tiny slivers of magnetic materials are frozen in place, aligned in the direction of Earth's magnetic field or what we know as the poles. Earth's magnetic fields have been shown to shift over time; thus what we know as the North Pole today is not necessarily where it was located millions of years ago. These changes in polarity are recorded in the Earth's lava flows. When the lavas on Steens Mountain cooled some 15.5 million years ago, a sudden switch in Earth's magnetic field was recorded from one polarity to another. Such a rapid change in polarity is highly unusual. Normally a reversal in magnetic fields is very gradual and takes thousands of years to complete. When the lavas on Steens Mountain solidified 15.5 million years ago, it appears that Earth's magnetic fields shifted almost overnight—geologically speaking. No one has yet been able to explain this phenomenon.

After the lava had solidified, faulting and uplift began. About 9 million years ago, faulting caused some of the region's crust to rise while other segments dropped, creating the characteristic Basin and Range topography. Over time, the summit of Steens Mountain was uplifted 7,000 feet—equal to the rise of the Grand Tetons in Wyoming! The presence of hot springs, steam vents, and other thermal activity near Steens Mountain indicates that the area remains active. Mickey Hot Springs includes bubbling mudpots. Borax Lake in the southern end of the Alvord Desert is an entire lake fed by hot springs and is home to the federally listed, endangered Borax Springs chub, which can tolerate temperatures of 100 degrees.

During the Pleistocene Ice Age, a lake up to 300 feet deep filled the Alvord Basin. Ancient, wave-cut terraces created by the lake can still be seen along the base of Steens Mountain. On the eastern side of the Alvord Basin, windblown sand dunes are home to several endemic plant species and nearly a thousand different species of insects. The nearly flat Catlow Valley, along the western flank of Steens Mountain, also held an Ice Age lake.

Uplift of the mountain resulted in greater precipitation, which then led to the formation of an icecap on the summit and numerous glaciers, which flowed down existing creek and river valleys. These glaciers widened, deepened, and gouged out magnificent U-shaped valleys. Some of these canyons are up to 2,000 feet deep and as much as 15 miles long. Glacially carved Wildhorse Lake, at the head of Wildhorse Canyon, is reputed to be the largest alpine lake in the Great Basin.

Steens Mountain's location in the Basin and Range assures it a relatively continental climate, with cold but generally sunny winters. Temperatures are frequently below freezing. Nevertheless, winter is also the period of greatest precipitation, most of it coming as snow. Summers are warm, with clear days and nights. Most of the surrounding valleys receive less than 10 inches of precipitation a year; the town of Andrews, east of Steens Mountain, is the state's driest location, with less than 7 inches annually. By contrast, the summit of Steens Mountain is estimated to receive 40 inches of precipitation annually, mostly between March and June.

Steens Mountain has unique and abundant flora, with more than 1,115 species documented from the mountain. Yet this is the largest mountain uplift in the Great Basin without coniferous forests. The only tree species on Steens Mountain are juniper, aspen, and two small pockets of white fir in Fir Canyon and on Moon Hill. As a result, Steens Mountain has an alpine feel to it. It reminds me more of a tundra mountain in Alaska than a range in the Oregon desert. Desert shrubs like saltbrush, shadscale, Mormon tea, iodine bush, and greasewood grow at the lowest levels in the Alvord Desert. At around 5,000 feet, you find sagebrush and juniper woodlands. As you climb to between 6,000 and 8,000 feet, sagebrush and native grasses continue to cover large areas, but patches of mountain mahogany appear on rocky sites, while huge pockets of aspen are common in the valley bottoms and in zones of deeper soils along the slopes. Between 7,000 and 8,500 feet lies the mountain's biggest sagebrush zone. This extensive region is broken by subalpine meadows full of wildflowers. Between 9,000 and 9,700 feet, you find the grasslands that look like alpine tundra. Vast, rolling landscapes adorned with alpine flowers distinguish these highest reaches. Several plants are endemic to the mountain, including the Steens Mountain paintbrush and Steens Mountain thistle.

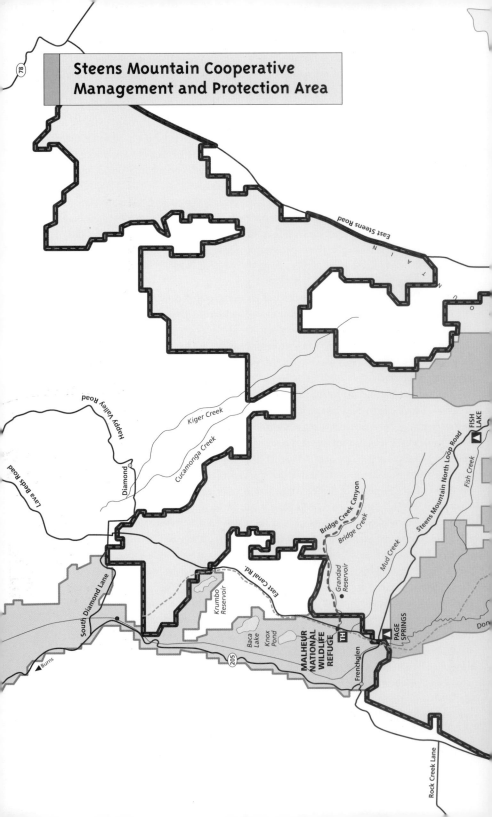

Steens Mountain Cooperative Management and Protection Area

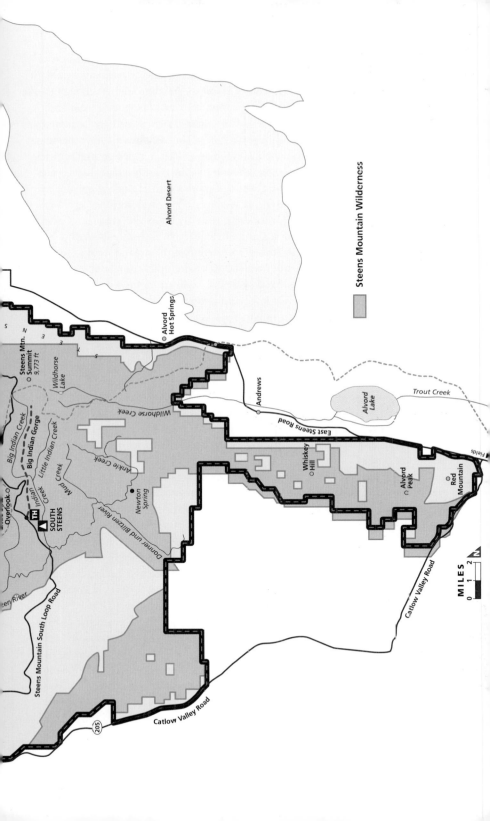

Alvord Desert

Steens Mountain Wilderness

Alvord Hot Springs

Steens Mtn.
Summit
9,773 ft

Wildhorse
Lake

Wildhorse Creek

Big Indian Creek

Big Indian Gorge

Little Indian Creek

Ankle Creek

Mud Creek

Overlook

Indian Creek

SOUTH
STEENS

Newton
Spring

Donner und Blitzen River

Andrews

Alvord
Lake

Trout Creek

East Steens Road

Fields

Whiskey
Hill

Alvord
Peak

Red
Mountain

...en River

Steens Mountain South Loop Road

Catlow Valley Road

205

Catlow Valley Road

Catlow Valley Road

MILES
0   1   2

Wildlife consists of bighorn sheep, mule deer, and a growing population of elk, estimated at more than 400 animals. Pronghorn antelope, coyote, and mountain lion inhabit lower elevations of the mountain and surrounding lands. Although they're currently absent from the mountain, Steens Mountain could potentially support at least one or more wolf packs. A wolverine was captured and released on the mountain in 1975, though there are no recent reports of these elusive animals. Other mammals on Steens Mountain include bushy-tailed woodrat, golden-mantled ground squirrel, long-tailed vole, mountain cottontail, yellow-bellied marmot, vagrant shrew, water shrew, pika, western jumping mouse, Belding's ground squirrel, and yellow pine chipmunk. Bird species include prairie falcon, long-eared owl, Swainson's hawk, red-tailed hawk, goshawk, burrowing owl, golden eagle, and rosy finch. The presence of nesting goshawk, a species normally confined to coniferous forests, is highly unusual.

The American Fisheries Society has identified the watersheds on Steens Mountain as an Aquatic Diversity Area and Key Salmonid Stronghold. Streams flowing north hold Malheur redband trout and Malheur mottled sculpin. A few streams flowing south into the Catlow Basin also hold redband trout and tui chub. Lahontan cutthroat trout, another endangered species, is found in many of the creeks that flow off of Steens' eastern face into the Alvord Basin.

Found in the Alvord Desert below Steens Mountain are several species that reach their northern limits here, such as the kit fox, white-tailed antelope ground squirrel, horned toad, western whiptail lizard, collared lizard, and leopard lizard. A species of kangaroo rat found in the basin may be a new subspecies. A pair of spotted bats, one of the rarest bat species in America, were collected near Mickey Springs. The sage grouse, once abundant here, seems to be in steep decline as a result of livestock grazing and subsequent habitat loss. Today the BLM recognizes just 15 leks on the mountain.

The most recent indigenous people associated with the Steens Mountain area were the Northern Paiute Indians. They had a hardscrabble existence in the region, but their resourcefulness allowed them to survive where many other less adaptable people would have perished. Relying upon waterfowl from the Malheur Lakes, roots, berries, jackrabbit, bighorn sheep, and whatever else they could capture, the Paiute eked out a sustenance here. Army Major Enoch Steen battled the Paiutes and named the mountain in the late 1860s, exiling Indians to reservations at Yakima and later Burns. After the Indians were removed and the land was safe for livestock, the area was invaded by the cowboy.

Peter French (for whom Frenchglen is named) launched a cattle empire here in 1872. French was killed by his neighbors in 1897, and his ranch eventually became the core property for the Malheur National Wildlife Refuge. By 1900, a second livestock scourge invaded the landscape with the arrival of domestic sheep. At one time, more than 140,000 head of sheep pounded the fragile soils and uplands on Steens Mountain, obliterating once-lush grasslands. Eventually the BLM assumed more control over the livestock usage, but livestock damage continues into the present, albeit in a reduced form and extent than at the turn of the 20th century.

With the passage of the Steens Mountain Conservation Act, the management of the area has finally turned a corner, where the long-term ecological health of the mountain will have priority over the profits of commercial interests. Despite the fact that some of Steens Mountain is now cow-free, livestock use still continues to damage and degrade much of the rest of the landscape. Efforts to eliminate livestock grazing continue. Someday, Steens Mountain will be managed as the national treasure that it is.

The 52-mile-long, gravel Steens Mountain Loop Road climbs the western slope of the mountain from Frenchglen to the alpine meadows along the crest. Four campgrounds—Page Springs, Jackman Park, Fish Lake, and South Steens—are located along the road and make good base camps for explorations. A number of trailheads are located along this loop route.

DAY HIKE: BRIDGE CREEK CANYON
One-way Length: 3.5 miles
Elevation Range: 4,200 to 5,000 feet
Difficulty: Moderate

Bridge Creek is one of the shorter canyons to traverse the lower flanks of Steens Mountain. No official trail ascends the canyon, but trails created by deer and anglers pursuing the stream's native redband trout provide passage up the creek. At about 3.5 miles up the canyon, a break in the rim allows you to scramble up it if you wish.

From Frenchglen, drive east on the Steens Mountain North Loop Road toward Page Springs Campground. Just beyond the campground entrance, cross a bridge over the Donner und Blitzen River and turn left onto East Canal Road, which leads to the Malheur National Wildlife Refuge. Drive 2.2 miles to the mouth of Bridge Creek Canyon.

OVERNIGHT BACKPACK: BIG INDIAN GORGE
One-way Length: 5.3 miles
Elevation Range: 5,400 to 6,400 feet
Difficulty: Moderate

Big Indian Gorge is one of the major glaciated canyons flowing off the western flank of Steens Mountain. A hike up the U-shaped canyon can be either a day trip or an overnight excursion. There are no bridges, so fording the creek is necessary. Begin by hiking 1.9 miles up an old road to the first creek crossing of Big Indian Creek. Continue upstream from where the old road ends, passing the confluence with Little Indian Creek. About 1 mile beyond the end of the old road, the trail reaches a point in the canyon where you can look directly upstream at the glacially carved headwall. Another 2.5 miles up the canyon through sagebrush, aspen groves, and meadows leads to a beautiful campsite among cottonwood trees next to the creek.

From Frenchglen, drive OR 205 toward Fields. Some 10 miles from Frenchglen, turn left onto the Steens Mountain South Loop Road. Go 19.5 miles to the South Steens Campground and trailhead.

OTHER RECREATIONAL OPPORTUNITIES

Steens Mountain presents some of the best backcountry skiing in Oregon. Tremendous variety in terrain, from steep headwalls to gentle, open slopes, combined with fine powder snow, makes this a potentially great ski destination. Gorgeous views are everywhere. This is a backcountry skier's heaven. It's possible to have miles of downhill skiing over essentially open slopes—slopes that are usually trackless. But given its distance from Oregon's population centers, the mountain receives few skiing visitors.

The best ski route for anyone new to the mountain is to follow the main loop road up to the high country. A locked gate blocks the road by the Page Springs Campground. In some years, you may have to walk for a couple miles on the road to reach skiable snow. The road begins at 4,300 feet. It's some 23 miles to the summit at 9,733 feet. As you climb higher, the road more or less disappears under the blanket of snow, so if you are concerned about getting to a specific destination, you should definitely have a good map and compass. If you can make it to the brink of Steens's summit vista, you will be treated to a stunning view with the eastern face of the mountain dropping thousands of feet toward the Alvord Desert below. Many consider this a good spot either to turn around or set up a base camp to explore the surrounding high terrain.

Fescues cover alpine grasslands on the summit of
Steens Mountain, Steens Mountain Wilderness.

Appendix A: Addresses

The following are useful as contacts for specific and up-to-date information on hiking trails, access, permits, and conditions.

COAST RANGE

Oregon Coastal National
Wildlife Refuge Complex
2127 SE OSU Dr.
Newport, OR 97365
541-867-4550

Siuslaw National Forest
4077 Research Way
Corvallis, OR 97333
541-750-7000

Waldport Ranger District
1094 SW Pacific Highway
Waldport, OR 97394
541-563-3211

KLAMATH MOUNTAINS

Applegate Ranger District
6941 Upper Applegate Rd.
Jacksonville, OR 97530-9314
541-899-3800

BLM Medford District
3040 Biddle Rd.
Medford, OR 97504
541-618-2200

Chetco Ranger District
555 Fifth St.
Brookings, OR 97415
541-469-2196

Gold Beach Ranger District
29279 Ellensburg Rd.
Gold Beach, OR 97444
541-247-3600

Illinois Valley Ranger District
26568 Redwood Highway
Cave Junction, OR 97523
541-592-4000

Powers Ranger District
Highway 242
Powers, OR 97466
541-439-3011

CASCADE RANGE

BLM Salem District
1717 Fabry Rd. SE
Salem, OR 97306
503-375-5646

Barlow Ranger District
780 NE Court St., P.O. Box 67
Dufur, OR 97021
541-467-2291

Butte Falls Ranger District
800 Laurel St.
Butte Falls, OR 97522-0227
541-865-2700

Chemult Ranger District
P.O. Box 150
Chemult, OR 97731
541-365-7001

Columbia River Gorge
National Scenic Area
902 Wasco Ave., Suite 200
Hood River, OR 97031
541-386-2333

Crater Lake National Park
P.O. Box 7
Crater Lake, OR 97604
541-594-3100

Crescent Ranger District
136471 Highway 97 North, P.O. Box 208
Crescent, OR 97733
541-433-3200

Detroit Ranger District
HC 73, P.O. Box 320
Mill City, OR 97360
503-854-3366

Diamond Lake Ranger District
2020 Toketee RS Rd.
Idleyld Park, OR 97447
541-498-2531

Estacada Ranger District
595 NW Industrial Way
Estacada, OR 97023
503-630-6861

Fremont National Forest
1301 South G St.
Lakeview, OR 97630
541-947-2151

Hood River Ranger District
6780 Highway 35
Parkdale, OR 97041
541-352-6002

Klamath Ranger District
1936 California Ave.
Klamath Falls, OR 97601
541-885-3400

McKenzie Ranger District
57600 McKenzie Highway
McKenzie Bridge, OR 97413
541-822-3381

Middle Fork Ranger District
46375 Highway 58
Westfir, OR 97492
541-782-2283

Mount Hood Information Center
65000 E. Highway 26
Welches, OR 97067
503-622-7674

Prospect Ranger District
47201 Highway 62
Prospect, OR 97536-9724
541-560-3400

Sisters Ranger District
Highway 20 and Pine St., P.O. Box 249
Sisters, OR 97759
541-549-7700

Sweet Home Ranger District
3225 Highway 20
Sweet Home, OR 97386
541-367-5168

Umpqua National Forest
2900 NW Stewart Pkwy., P.O. Box 1008
Roseburg, OR 97470
541-672-6601

Willamette National Forest
P.O. Box 10607
Eugene, OR 97440
541-225-6300

Zigzag Ranger District
70220 E. Highway 26
Zigzag, OR 97049
503-622-3191

BLUE MOUNTAINS
Baker Ranger District
3165 10th St.
Baker City, OR 97814
541-523-4476

Eagle Cap Ranger District
88401 Highway 82
Enterprise, OR 97828
541-426-4978

Hells Canyon National Recreation Area
88401 Highway 82
Enterprise, OR 97828
541-426-4978

Lookout Mountain Ranger District
3160 NE 3rd St.
Prineville, OR 97754
541-416-6500

North Fork John Day Ranger District
P.O. Box 158
Ukiah, OR 97880
541-427-3231

Paulina Ranger District
7803 Beaver Creek Rd.
Paulina, OR 97751
541-477-6900

Prairie City Ranger District
327 West Front St., P.O. Box 337
Prairie City, OR 97869
541-820-3311

Umatilla National Forest
2517 SW Hailey Ave.
Pendleton, OR 97801
541-278-3716

Unity Ranger District
P.O. Box 38
Unity, OR 97884
541-446-3351

Walla Walla Ranger District
1415 West Rose St.
Walla Walla, WA 99362
509-522-6290

BASIN AND RANGE
BLM Burns District
28910 Highway 20 West
Hines, OR 97738
541-573-4400

Appendix B: Conservation Organizations

AUDUBON SOCIETY OF PORTLAND
5151 NW Cornell Rd.
Portland, OR 97210
503-292-6855
www.audubonportland.org

HEADWATERS
P.O. Box 729
Ashland, OR 97520
541-482-4459
www.headwaters.org

HELLS CANYON PRESERVATION COUNCIL
P.O. Box 2768
La Grande, OR 97850
541-963-3950
www.hellscanyon.org

HCPC is promoting a million-acre-plus Hells Canyon/Chief Joseph National Park and Preserve for the Hells Canyon–Wallowa Mountains region of eastern Oregon.

OREGON CHAPTER SIERRA CLUB
3701 SE Milwaukie, Suite F
Portland, OR 97202
503-239-8478
www.oregon.sierraclub.org

OREGON NATURAL DESERT ASSOCIATION
16 NW Kansas Ave.
Bend, OR 97701
541-385-3370
www.onda.org

ONDA and other wilderness advocates have put together a nearly 6-million-acre proposal to protect Oregon's undeveloped arid lands under the Wilderness Act, known as the Oregon High Desert Protection Act (OHDPA).

OREGON NATURAL RESOURCES COUNCIL
5825 North Greeley
Portland, OR 97217-4145
503-283-6343
www.onrc.org

See Appendix C, opposite, for details on the Oregon Wild Campaign wildlands proposal (www.oregonwild.org).

OREGON TROUT
117 SW Naito Parkway
Portland, OR 97204
503-222-9091
www.ortrout.org

PACIFIC RIVERS COUNCIL
P.O. Box 10798
Eugene, OR 97440
541-345-0119
www.pacrivers.org

SISKIYOU PROJECT
P.O. Box 220
Cave Junction, OR 97523
541-592-4459
www.siskiyou.org

The Siskiyou Project has put together a proposal for a 1-million-acre Siskiyou Wild Rivers National Monument. The proposal would unite a number of wilderness areas in southwestern Oregon, including the Kalmiopsis Wilderness and Wild Rogue Wilderness, into a unified protected area.

TROUT UNLIMITED
213 SW Ash St., Suite 205
Portland, OR 97204
www.tu.org

UMPQUA WATERSHEDS
P.O. Box 101
Roseburg, OR 97470
541-672-7065
www.umpqua-watersheds.org

WATERWATCH OF OREGON
213 SW Ash St., Suite 208
Portland, OR 97204
503-295-4039
www.waterwatch.org

WILD WILDERNESS
248 NW Wilmington Ave.
Bend, OR 97701
541-385-5261
www.wildwilderness.org

Appendix C: Oregon Wild Campaign

The Oregon Natural Resources Council (ONRC) based in Portland launched its Oregon Wild Campaign in 1997. Together with the Oregon Wilderness Coalition, a statewide coalition of 15 conservation groups, they have mapped and identified 32 proposed forested wildlands across the state. Many of these wildlands surround existing wildernesses that remain as core areas. Protection of these 32 areas would go a long way toward preserving for future generations Oregon's magnificent landscapes and the clean drinking water, critical wildlife habitat, and unsurpassed recreational opportunities they provide.

NORTHWESTERN OREGON

North Umpqua Wilderness *(including Mount Bailey and Steamboat Creek)*
202,000 acres; located on portions of the Umpqua National Forest. World-famous fishing, camping, and swimming lie in the North Umpqua Wilderness proposal.

Upper Willamette Wilderness *(including Chuckney Mountain and Hardesty Mountain)*
131,000 acres; located on portions of the Willamette and Umpqua National Forests. Rare low-elevation old-growth offers key habitat for threatened fish and wildlife.

Clackamas Wilderness *(including Olallie Lakes, Roaring River, and Eagle Creek)*
112,000 acres; located on portions of the Mount Hood National Forest and Salem BLM Districts. The Clackamas Wilderness proposal has the largest trees in northwest Oregon and provides clean drinking water for 185,000 Oregonians.

Columbia Gorge Wilderness *(including Horsetail Falls and Larch Mountain)*
44,000 acres; located on portions of the Mount Hood National Forest. As one of Oregon's most scenic areas, the Columbia Gorge boasts hundreds of waterfalls that are a favorite spot for thousands of hikers every year.

Mount Hood Wilderness *(including the Bull Run Watershed and Twin Lakes)*
165,000 acres; located on portions of the Mount Hood National Forest. Protecting the Mount Hood Wilderness Additions ensures clean drinking water for Portland for future generations. Mount Hood offers 1.5 million Oregonians unparalleled urban access to wildlands recreation, including backcountry skiing, rafting, and camping.

Santiam Wilderness *(including Iron Mountain and Crabtree Valley)*
111,000 acres; located on portions of the Willamette National Forest and Salem BLM District. The biggest trees in Oregon are found in the Santiam watershed, which provides Salem with clean drinking water.

McKenzie Wilderness *(including Tamolitch Falls and Mount Hagan)*
100,000 acres; located on portions of the Willamette National Forest. The McKenzie's crystal-clear waters provide clean drinking water to over 150,000 Oregonians, and prime habitat for bull trout and Chinook salmon.

OREGON COAST

Coast Range Wilderness *(including Mount Hebo and Wasson Creek)*
144,000 acres; located on portions of the Siuslaw NF, and Coos Bay, Roseburg, and Salem BLM Districts. These last remaining pristine areas in the Coast Range are home to old-growth Douglas fir, western red cedar, and Sitka spruce, providing critical habitat for endangered species such as spotted owl, marbled murrelet, and coho salmon.

Oregon Dunes Wilderness *(including Umpqua Dunes and Takenitch Creek)*
25,000 acres; located on portions of the Siuslaw National Forest. This unique dune ecosystem provides key habitat for the endangered snowy plover.

Appendix C: continued

SOUTHWESTERN OREGON

Rogue-Umpqua Wilderness *(including Castle Rock Fork and Last Creek)*
   127,000 acres; on portions of the Umpqua and Rogue River National Forests and
   Roseburg, Medford BLM. The Rogue and Umpqua offer lush old-growth forests
   interspersed with beautiful mountain meadows.

Elk River Wilderness *(including Copper Salmon wildlands)*
   54,000 acres; located on portions of the Siskiyou National Forest. The Elk River
   watershed is arguably the most productive U.S. salmon fishery outside of Alaska.

Wild Rogue Wilderness *(including the Zane Grey and Shasta Costa Creek)*
   172,000 acres; located on portions of the Siskiyou National Forest and the Medford
   BLM District. The 20 miles of unprotected wild waters of the Rogue River are a
   haven for rafters and anglers alike.

Kalmiopsis Wilderness *(including the Illinois River and Rough and Ready Creek)*
   359,000 acres; located on the Siskiyou National Forest. This wilderness proposal
   offers unparalleled diversity of conifer species, and globally recognized plant diversity.

Klamath Basin Wilderness *(including Yamsay Mountain)*
   153,000 acres; located on portions of the Winema and Fremont National Forests
   and Lakeview BLM. Includes the pristine headwaters of Upper Klamath Marsh,
   part of the "Everglades of the West."

Siskiyou Crest Wilderness *(including Wagner Butte and the Red Buttes Additions)*
   180,000 acres; located on portions of the Rogue River and Siskiyou National Forests
   and Medford BLM. This unique convergence of several ecological zones provides
   an essential biological corridor between the Kalmiopsis and Cascade Mountains.

Soda Mountain Wilderness *(including Pilot Rock and Bruce Boccard Point)*
   18,000 acres; located on portions of the Medford BLM District. While National
   Monument designation was allotted in 2000, Wilderness designation for these
   spectacular areas is warranted and needed.

South Cascades Wilderness *(including Pelican Butte and Brown Mountain)*
   120,000 acres; located on portions of the Winema and Rogue River National Forests
   and Medford BLM. This area's high-country lakes and summits offer some of the
   most accessible and spectacular scenery in southern Oregon. Its ancient forests also
   provide habitat for numerous bald eagles and spotted owls.

Fremont Rims Wilderness *(including Coleman Rim and Deadhorse Rim)*
   230,000 acres; located on portions of the Fremont National Forest and Lakeview
   BLM District. This area contains the largest intact stands of unprotected old-growth
   ponderosa pine in Oregon.

NORTHEASTERN OREGON

Hells Canyon Wilderness *(including Lord Flat and the Imnaha River)*
   323,000 acres; located on portions of the Wallowa Whitman National Forest and
   the Vale BLM District. Hells Canyon is the deepest gorge in North America, with
   numerous old-growth-clad side canyons and hundreds of miles of trails for easy access.

South Fork John Day Wilderness *(including Utley Butte and Murderers Creek)*
   137,000 acres; located on portions of the Malheur and Ochoco National Forests
   and Prineville BLM. Old-growth ponderosa pine and conifer forests provide year-
   round habitat for Rocky Mountain elk, mule deer, and bighorn sheep.

North Fork John Day–Elkhorns Wilderness *(including the Elkhorns and Greenhorn Mountains)*
287,000 acres; located on portions of the Malheur, Umatilla, and Wallowa Whitman National Forests. It's no surprise that the North Fork John Day, the longest free-flowing river in Oregon, has the best salmon-spawning habitat in eastern Oregon.

Malheur Canyons Wilderness *(including Malheur River Canyon and Pine Creek)*
168,000 acres; located on portions of the Wallowa Whitman and Malheur National Forests. Stunning rimrock canyons lined with virgin groves of western larch and ponderosa pine, easily accessed by riverside trails.

Blue Mountains Wilderness *(including Hellhole Creek and Walla Walla River)*
267,000 acres; located on portions of Umatilla National Forests. Mixed-conifer plateaus provide prime elk habitat, coupled with old-growth in steep canyons.

Upper John Day Wilderness *(including McClellan Mountain and Baldy Mountain)*
106,000 acres; located on portions of the Malheur National Forest and the Prineville BLM District. Important John Day River headwaters provide cold water critical for salmon and steelhead spawning.

Grande Ronde Wilderness *(including the La Grande City watershed and Mount Emily)*
236,000 acres; located on portions of the Wallowa Whitman and Umatilla National Forests. The Grande Ronde River canyons offer critical seasonal habitat for big game such as mule deer and elk.

Wallowa Mountains Wilderness *(including Lake Fork and North Fork Catherine Creek)*
175,000 acres; located on portions of the Wallowa Whitman National Forest. The rocks and ice have Wilderness protection here; now the time has come to protect the surrounding fish and wildlife-inhabited forest and streams.

CENTRAL OREGON

Three Sisters Wilderness Additions *(including Waldo Lake and Tumalo Falls)*
153,000 acres; located on portions of the Deschutes and Willamette National Forests. Protection is needed to ensure the ecological integrity of ancient forest surrounding one of the purest lakes in North America.

Upper Deschutes Wilderness *(including Century Lakes/Bachelor Butte and Cowhorn Peak)*
101,000 acres; located on portions of the Deschutes National Forest. These unpro-tected High Cascade wildlands include numerous lakes and extensive old-growth mountain hemlock forests that are popular recreation areas.

Ochoco Mountains Wilderness *(including Green Mountain)*
112,000 acres; located on portions of the Ochoco National Forest and Prineville BLM District. The forests, meadows, and rivers of the Ochoco Mountains provide a critical wildlife corridor between the larger Blue Mountains and Cascade Mountains.

Paulina Wilderness *(including Newberry Crater and the Lava Cast Forest)*
108,000 acres; located on portions of the Deschutes National Forest. This volcanic wonderland boasts extensive obsidian glass flows within massive lake-filled calderas.

— Courtesy of Oregon Wild Campaign
www.oregonwild.org

Appendix D: Wilderness Facts and Figures

Key Wilderness Legislation:

1964	Wilderness Act designated	662,847 acres of wilderness in Oregon
1968	Mount Jefferson Wilderness	100,000 acres
1970	Oregon Islands Wilderness	21 acres
1972	Eagle Cap Wilderness additions	72,420 acres
1975	Hells Canyon Wilderness	131,333 acres
1978	Endangered American Wilderness Act	285,000 acres in two new areas and three additions
1978	Oregon Islands additions	464 acres
1984	Oregon Wilderness Act	828,803 acres in 23 new areas and five additions
1996	Oregon Islands additions	95 acres
1996	Opal Creek Wilderness	20,724 acres
2000	Steens Mountain Conservation and Management Act	175,000 acres

Biggest Wilderness Area: Eagle Cap Wilderness (385,541 acres), part of the Wallowa-Whitman National Forest, northeastern Oregon

Smallest Wilderness Area: Three Arch Rocks Wilderness Area (15 acres), a national wildlife refuge off the northern Oregon coast

Total acres in Oregon: 62,966,880 acres

Total Wilderness Area acres: 2,258,238 acres (about 3.6% of the state)

Total number of Wilderness Areas in Oregon: 40

Total Federal Land Acreage in Oregon:

National Park Service:	921,539 acres
U.S. Fish and Wildlife Service:	577,753 acres
U.S. Forest Service:	15,548,237 acres
Bureau of Land Management:	15,720,000 acres

Appendix E: Recommended Reading

GUIDEBOOKS

Bernstein, Art. *90 Best Day-Hikes: The Best-Selling Trail Guide to Southwest Oregon and Far Northern California.* Grants Pass, Oreg.: Magnifica Books, 1994. 3rd ed. A good source for information about hiking trails in Kalmiopsis, Red Buttes, and Sky Lakes Wilderness Areas.

Bishop, Ellen Morris, and John Eliot Allen. *Hiking Oregon's Geology.* Seattle: The Mountaineers, 1996.

Henderson, Bonnie. *120 Hikes on the Oregon Coast.* Seattle: The Mountaineers, 1999. 2nd ed. A good overview of Oregon's coastal hikes.

Ikenberry, Donna Lynn. *Hiking Oregon*. Helena, Mont.: Falcon Press, 1997. A sampling of trails from throughout the state.

Kerr, Andy. *Oregon Desert Guide: 70 Hikes*. Seattle: The Mountaineers, 2000. A comprehensive overview of Oregon's desert wildlands, written with wit.

Lorain, Douglas A. *Backpacking Oregon*. Berkeley, Calif.: Wilderness Press, 1999. A good tool for those interested in planning longer backpacking trips.

McLean, Cheryl, and Clint Brown. *Oregon's Quiet Waters: A Guide to Lakes for Canoeists and Other Paddlers*. Corvallis, Oreg.: Jackson Creek Press, 1987. A guide to canoeable lakes and small ponds generally inaccessible to motorized boat traffic.

Olson, Larry N., and John Daniel. *Oregon Rivers*. Englewood, Colo.: Westcliffe Publishers, 1997. A lovely photo book that displays Larry Olson's outstanding images of all of Oregon's Wild and Scenic Rivers.

Ostertag, Rhonda and George. *50 Hikes in Oregon's Coast Range & Siskiyous*. Seattle: The Mountaineers, 1989.

Ostertag, Rhonda and George. *100 Hikes in Oregon: Mount Hood, Crater Lake, Columbia Gorge, Eagle Cap Wilderness, Steens Mountain, Three Sisters Wilderness*. Seattle: The Mountaineers, 2000. 2nd ed. A statewide sample of hiking trails.

Sullivan, William L. *Exploring Oregon's Wild Areas: A Guide for Hikers, Backpackers, Climbers, XC Skiers & Paddlers*. Seattle: The Mountaineers, 1994. 2nd ed. A great overview of Oregon's wild places.

Willamette Kayak and Canoe Club. *Soggy Sneakers: Guide to Oregon Rivers*. Corvallis, Oreg.: The Club, 1986. 2nd ed. An excellent guide, with a whitewater rafting enthusiast's perspective.

Wood, Wendell. *A Walking Guide to Oregon's Ancient Forests*. Portland, Oreg.: Oregon Natural Resources Council, 1991. An excellent guidebook to finding Oregon's best old-growth forest stands.

Wuerthner, George. *Oregon's Best Wildflowers Hikes, Northwest Region*. Englewood, Colo.: Westcliffe Publishers, 2001. Easy hikes, botanical information, and full-color photography.

HISTORY, GEOGRAPHY, AND POLITICS

Atlas of Oregon. William G. Loy, et al., ed. Eugene, Oreg.: University of Oregon, 2001. 2nd ed. An extremely attractive statewide atlas.

Hatton, Raymond R. *High Desert of Central Oregon*. Portland, Oreg.: Binford & Mort, 1977. A good historical and geographical overview of Central Oregon.

Joslin, Les. *The Wilderness Concept and the Three Sisters Wilderness: Deschutes and Willamette National Forests, Oregon*. Bend, Oreg.: Wilderness Associates, 2000 (Bend, Oreg.: Maverick Publications). A good overview of the political definition of wilderness and the history of the Three Sisters Wilderness.

McArthur, Lewis A. *Oregon Geographic Names*. Portland: Oregon Historical Society Press, 1992. 6th ed.

Merriam, Lawrence C. *Saving Wilderness in the Oregon Cascades: The Story of the Friends of the Three Sisters*. Eugene, Oreg.: Friends of the Three Sisters Wilderness, 1999. A good overview of how citizen activism can save wildlands.

Appendix E: continued

Palmer, Tim. *Endangered Rivers and the Conservation Movement.* Berkeley, Calif.: University of California Press, 1986. Though it only deals superficially with Oregon, it does provide background on the Wild and Scenic Rivers Act.

Potter, Miles. *Oregon's Golden Years: Bonanza of the West.* Caldwell, Idaho: Caxton Printers, 1976. A history of Oregon's mining era.

Terrill, Steve. *Oregon: Then & Now.* Englewood, Colo.: Westcliffe Publishers, 2000.

NATURAL HISTORY

Bailey, Vernon. *Mammals and Life Zones of Oregon.* Washington: U.S. Government Printing Office, 1936. A historical perspective on Oregon's wildlife.

Csuti, Blair, et al. *Atlas of Oregon Wildlife: Distribution, Habitat, and Natural History.* Corvallis, Oreg.: Oregon State University Press, 1997. A guide, with maps, describing the distribution of all of Oregon's vertebrate species.

Evanich, Joseph E., Jr. *The Birder's Guide to Oregon.* Portland, Oreg.: Portland Audubon Society, 1990. If you want to know about birds, this is the book to have.

Ferguson, Denzel, and Nancy Ferguson. *Oregon's Great Basin Country.* Burns, Oreg.: Gail Graphics, 1978. A good overview of the natural and human histories of Malheur and Harney Counties.

Franklin, Jerry F., and C.T. Dyrness. *Natural Vegetation of Oregon and Washington.* Portland, Oreg.: Pacific Northwest Forest and Range Experiment Station, Forest Service, U.S. Department of Agriculture, 1973. A good overview of the natural plant communities of the region.

Harris, Stephen L. *Fire and Ice: The Cascade Volcanoes.* Seattle: The Mountaineers, 1976. A comprehensive geological and historical description.

Maser, Chris. *Mammals of the Pacific Northwest: From the Coast to the High Cascades.* Corvallis, Oreg.: Oregon State University Press, 1998. A biologist, Maser brings a lot of firsthand experience to this volume.

Neill, William, and Doug Hepburn. *The Guide to Butterflies of Oregon and Washington.* Englewood, Colo.: Westcliffe Publishers, 2001.

Orr, Elizabeth L., and William N. Orr. *Geology of Oregon.* Dubuque, Iowa: Kendall/Hunt, 1999. 5th ed. An overview of the state's foundations.

Pojar, Jim, and Andy MacKinnon, eds. *Plants of the Pacific Northwest Coast: Washington, Oregon, British Columbia & Alaska.* Redmond, Wash.; Vancouver: Lone Pine Publishing, 1994. Excellent guide to plants most likely to be encountered from the Cascades to the coast.

Puchy, Claire A., and David B. Marshall. *Oregon Wildlife Diversity Plan.* Portland, Oreg.: Oregon Department of Fish and Wildlife, 1993. A good overview of Oregon's biological treasures.

Taylor, George H., and Chris Hannan. *The Climate of Oregon: From Rain Forest to Desert.* Corvallis, Oreg.: Oregon State University Press, 1999. Provides an overview of Oregon's diverse climate.

Trimble, Stephen. *The Sagebrush Ocean: A Natural History of the Great Basin.* Reno, Nev.: University of Nevada Press, 1999 [10th anniversary ed.]. This excellent book provides an overview of the entire Great Basin region.

Wuerthner, George. *Oregon Mountain Ranges.* Helena, Mont.: American Geographic Publishing, 1987. Layperson's overview, includes geology, history, and natural history.

Index

George Wuerthner

An ecologist, writer, and photographer, George is the author of 28 books, including three previous Westcliffe publications, *California's Wilderness Areas: The Complete Guide, Vols. 1* and *2,* and *Oregon's Best Wildflower Hikes: Northwest Region.* He has traveled widely throughout the West and until recently lived in Eugene. George now lives in Vermont with his wife and two children.